The

Jazz

Crusade

Published in 1992 in the United States by
Special Request Books & Recordings Division,
Special Request Music Service
585 Pond Street
Bridgeport, Connecticut 06606

phone: 203 - 372 - 0597
fax: 203 - 371 - 4330

First Edition : Second Printing

Bissonnette, William Edward, 1937-
   The Jazz Crusade : the great New Orleans jazz revival of the
1960's / William Bissonnette
   p. cm.
  Book includes compact disc.
  Includes discography and index.
   ISBN 0-9632297-0-2
   1. Jazz music--New Orleans (La.) 2. Jazz musicians--New Orleans
(La.) I. Title. II. Title: The great New Orleans jazz revival
of the 1960's.

ML3561.Z3B5 1992   781.65
                                     QB192-1182

THE

JAZZ

CRUSADE

The inside story of the

GREAT NEW ORLEANS JAZZ REVIVAL

of the 1960's

by

Big Bill Bissonnette

DEDICATION

This book is dedicated to the memory of

SAMMY PENN

and

JIM ROBINSON

who,

between them,

never had an evil thought

or unkind word.

Acknowledgements

I thought I was going to be able to just sit down and write this book from memory. After all, the Jazz Crusade story is my story. I lived it. As soon as I began the outline, I realized that the intervening years had taken its toll on my memory. In addition, things I didn't consider important then, such as dates of recordings, which I never documented, suddenly took on significance.

On an evening in 1987, some of the principal members of the Easy Riders Jazz Band: Dick Griffith, Dick McCarthy, Bill Sinclair and I, sat down together to talk about the old days. The last time the four of us were together, Lyndon Baines Johnson was President of the United States of America. The next time will be never. In a perverse way, it was comforting to discover that their memories had faded as much as mine. But, collectively, many things came back into focus. Some did not. For example, one of the events I wanted to cover in detail was the break-up of the best known version of the Riders when Sammy Rimington was a member. Each of us had a different recollection of the event. I tried to cover it from all sides in the body of the book.

Dick Griffith made available to me his unique collection of memorabilia, some of which appear in these pages. Griff also turned up the now famous photo of the Reception Brass Band that met us at New Orleans International Airport in 1967.

Dick McCarthy made available his complete Jazz Crusade record collection for photographing album covers and contributed several interesting memories just in time for publication.

I should also like to acknowledge the assistance of Judy Faye (Bissonnette), my wife during the critical California period for her recollections. Others who furnished information were: Michael Fast, Jazz Crusade's recording engineer; Sue Griffith, Griff's wife; Nina Buck, Rimington's wife at the time; Ken Mills, Paul Boehmke, Kid Thomas Valentine, Kid Sheik Cola, James "Sing" Miller, Willie Humphrey, Louis Nelson, and finally, the late Jack Guckin, perhaps the band's best friend in the 1960's who died shortly after helping with this book.

A special thanks to the three photographers: Donald Moore, Andrew Wittenborn and Edward Lawless. These outstanding photo artists went through thousands of photographs in their personal files to come up with those special photos which best reflect the personalities of the musicians. I believe this is the finest collection of New Orleans jazz portraits ever collected.

Also, thanks to Gene and Pat Miller and to my son, Douglas, who, as non-participants to the events depicted, assisted by asking those questions only the uninitiated would think to ask.

A special thanks to Leslie Johnson, publisher of The Mississippi Rag, for breaking into her extremely busy schedule to do the final edit read of the manuscript. She picked up all the loose ends for tying together and made several suggestions for modifications to clarify certain issues and to bring me up to date on approaches to various subjects. I took her advice on every point except the one she stressed most. Sorry, Les. You were right, of course, but the old fashioned macho devil in me made me do it. I won't tell if you won't.

Thanks to the cooperation of George H. Buck Jr., this will be the first music book ever published to include the actual music within its covers. The introduction in recent years of digital compact disc technology makes this possible and I hope others will follow the lead. It is fitting that jazz is the groundbreaker in this, as it has been in so many other ways. Barry Martyn spent many hours working with me in the the GHB Jazz Foundation vaults in New Orleans getting this CD ready for production. It was the first time I had heard some of these selections in over a generation. I hope you agree with my choices. But, the chance is just as great that you will not. Jazz is like that. One man's wine is another man's poison.

ALCORN, ALVIN	FARGO, BOB
ALLEN, RED	FOSTER, CHINEE
ARCHEY, JIMMY	FOSTER, POPS
BARBARIN, PAUL	FRAZIER, CIE'
BARBER, CHRIS	FREEMAN, BUD
BARNES, MILE'	FUKUDA, TSUNETAMI
BARNES, POLO	GLASS, BOOKER T
BARRETT, SWEET EMMA	GOODWIN, HENRY
BATTISTE, MILTON	GORMAN, ISRAEL
BENNETT, CYRIL	GRIFFITH, DICK "GRIFF"
BIGARD, ALEC	GUESNON, CREOLE GEORGE
BISSONNETTE, BIG BILL	HALL, EDMOND
BOCAGE, PETER	HALL, HERB
BOEHMKE, PAUL	HAMILTON, CHARLIE
BROWN, WILLIAM	HANDY, CAPT. JOHN
BURBANK, ALBERT	HANDY, JOHN
BURKE, RAYMOND	HANDY, SYLVESTER
BUTLER, JOE	HAYES, CLANCY
CAGNOLOTTI, ERNIE	HELM, BOB
CAPRON, EARL	HENRY, CHICKEN
CASIMER, JOHNNY	HIGGINBOTHAM, J.C.
CHRISTIAN, EMILE	HOUSTON, FATS
CLUTE, PETE	HOWARD, AVERY "KID"
COLA, KID SHEIK	HUMPHREY, EARL
COLYER, KEN	HUMPHREY, PERCY
CONNELL, BILL	HUMPHREY, WILLIE
COTTRELL, LOUIS	JAFFE, ALLAN
CRAWFORD, PAUL	JAMES, JOE
CROSBY, OCTAVE	JAMES, LEWIS
CULLUM, JIM	JEFFERSON, THOMAS
CULLUM, JIM JR.	JILES, ALBERT
DEJAN, HAROLD	JOHNSON, NOONE
DePARIS, SIDNEY	JONES, CHESTER
DePARIS, WILBUR	JOSEPH, WALDREN "FROG"
ALBERT, DON	JOSEPH, PAPA JOHN
EDEGRAN, LARS	KALET, NOEL

ABOUT JAZZ MUSICIANS

KAWAI, JUNICHI
KAWAII, RYOICHI
KELLIN, ORANGE
KINDERVATER, HARVEY
LARSON, BUD
LEIGH, CAROL
LEWIS, GEORGE
LIGHTFOOT, TERRY
LOVE, CHARLIE
MARRERO, LAWRENCE
MARTYN, BARRY
MATHEWS, BILL
McCARTHY, MOULDY DICK
MILLER, PUNCH
MILLER, SING
MINOR, FRED "H.A."
MOORE, FREDDIE
MORGAN, ANDREW
MORRIS, EDDIE
MURPHY, TURK
NADIG, HANK
NELSON, LOUIS
PARENTI, TONY
PAUL, MANNY
PASSORELL, ARMI
PASSORETTI, MEADE
PAVAGEAU, SLOW DRAG
PENN, SAMMY
PIERCE, BILLIE
PIERCE, DEDE
PROBERT, GEORGE
PULVER, ART
PURNELL, ALTON
RICE , DON
REILLY, CHUCK
RIMINGTON, SAMMY

ROBINSON, BIG JIM
RUSSELL, BILL
SANTIAGO, LESTER
SAYLES, MANNY
SIMEON, OMER
SINCLAIR, BILL
SINGLETON, ZUTTY
SOMMERS, EDDIE
SPIVEY, VICTORIA
TEAGARDEN, JACK
THOMAS, BOBBY
THOMAS, SHOBOY
TILLMAN, WILBERT
TUTUNJIAN, JIM "TUT"
VALENTINE, KID THOMAS
VIGORITO, FRED
WARNER, ALBERT
WATTERS, LU
WATKINS, JOE
WILLIAMS, ALFRED
WILSON, CLIVE
ZARDIS, CHESTER

... and dedicated to the masters
who preceded them:

LOUIS ARMSTRONG
KID ORY
JOHNNY DODDS
JIMMIE NOONE
BUNK JOHNSON
SAM MORGAN
BABY DODDS
BARNEY BIGARD
JELLY ROLL MORTON
KING OLIVER

Table of Contents

Memorabilia

Photo Sections

Compact Disc Index
(Deluxe Edition only)

"The Best of the Jazz Crusade"
This exclusive, limited edition, compact disc was produced with the cooperation and authorization of the owner of the recorded material: the GHB Jazz Foundation. Our thanks to George H. Buck, Jr. and Barry Martyn for their help in its production. The complete albums of these recordings are available through the GHB Jazz Foundation, Collector's Record Club, 1206 Decatur Street, New Orleans, LA 70116 U.S.A.

Additional copies of this CD are available direct from: Special Request Music, 585 Pond Street, Bridgeport, CT 06606 U.S.A. @ $17.95 (shpg: $3.00 U.S.; $6.00 fgn).

All recordings were personally selected for inclusion by the author.

Compact Disc is located on inside back cover

XIV

Foreward

Years ago, Dick Griffith, who lives a few doors up the street, introduced me to Bill Bissonnette. They wanted me to put an article in my newspaper about their jazz band, the Easy Riders.

Because it would make a good news story, I attended a rehearsal or two, met the other musicians and wrote an article for the paper. That should have been the end of it: one more story pecked out on the old Royal. What happened was quite different.

The emotional power and transparent sincerity of New Orleans jazz struck me as a revelation. The music is direct and moving, yet subtle and complex. There is something spontaneous and genuine about it, coming from full hearts, not scheming heads. It speaks of the joys and sorrows of real people and it is entirely unsentimental.

My wife, Pat, and I began to attend more rehearsals. We followed the Easy Riders Jazz Band to saloons and recording studios. We listened to other jazz bands. . . the few that were around. Each spring we flew to New Orleans, still the fountainhead of original jazz, for the Jazz and Heritage Festival. We collected records and tapes. I wrote articles on jazz for local newspapers, the Mississippi Rag and the Second Line, the publication of the New Orleans Jazz Club.

Where had this splendid music come from and where had it been all our lives? It started, as many know, before the turn of the century among the blacks of New Orleans. Largely forgotten by the rest of the country, it has been there ever since, fading year by year as infirmity and death have silenced the musicians who learned their art in the 1920s and 1930s.

Still, the music has not been entirely lost. A few men, black and white, in New Orleans and elsewhere, have kept the original style alive in their playing. A few others have recorded the surviving black musicians so their art has been preserved for this and future generations.

Bill Bissonnette has done both.

A disciple and protege of Jim Robinson, the noted trombonist who played with Bunk Johnson and George Lewis, Bissonnette became one of the finest New Orleans slide trombonists in the country. If there is a difference between "black" playing and "white" playing (and I think there is), he is one of the few whites who play "black."

Many fine musicians learned over the years to play New Orleans style in his Easy Riders Jazz Band. His alumni are scattered over the United States and Europe.

Perhaps his most important contribution to jazz is the series of recordings he made in the 1960s of noted black musicians from New Orleans. His method was simple. He would fly small groups from the Crescent City to

Connecticut. They would perform at concerts with the Easy Riders. The money thus raised would pay for the trip and for recording sessions for Bissonnette's Jazz Crusade record label.

Some of the musicians were frequently recorded on other labels but most made few recordings other than their Jazz Crusade sessions. Their music would be almost unknown but for the efforts of Bissonnette. Through his work, a part of America's artistic heritage, which otherwise would have been lost, has been preserved for all of us to enjoy and cherish.

This book is the story, told in his own words, of Bissonnette's crusade for original, old-time New Orleans jazz. It is the story of the black musicians he met, dealt with, recorded and admired, most of whom had perfected their art long before he was born when the music and the musicians were young. Few whites knew these musicians as well as he did.

He had the true crusading spirit. Only his passionate dedication to the cause could overcome the obstacles set in his path by ignorance, indifference, hostility and paucity of resources. His greatest enemy was time itself. . . the measured tramp of time that threatened to decimate the ranks of his heroes before he could get their music on tape.

The story of jazz is full of gaps. One of these has been the question of what sparked the Great New Orleans Jazz Revival of the 1960s. Those who seek the answer to this mystery will have to rely in part on the recordings made by Bill Bissonnette and the tale which unfolds in this book.

Gene Miller

Introduction

The decade of the 1960's was a turbulent, frightening time in the United States of America. Our streets were ablaze with flame and violence. Our men were coming home from Indochina in body bags. Our leaders were being blown away with sickening regularity. Our black population was in revolt against our history. Our youth turned to drugs instead of education. Our technological upheaval propelled us out to the Moon and into the atom.

It is no wonder then that the small band of crusaders who coincidentally descended on New Orleans in a last ditch effort to preserve our jazz heritage went unnoticed save by those few who were themselves involved. What seemed so insignificant in the context of that historic decade is finally now, in the 1990's, beginning to be acknowledged for what it was: The Great New Orleans Jazz Revival. It spawned the incredible renewal of interest in New Orleans jazz now sweeping Europe and elsewhere. And it was the doing of a handful of men who, while suspecting there was history in the making, were mainly having a hell of a good time. . . at least while the music was playing.

There were so few of us that I can easily name them in half a page:

GRAYSON "KEN" MILLS - owner of Icon Records.

ALLAN JAFFE - owner of Preservation Hall; record producer and musician.

BARRY "KID" MARTYN - owner of Mono Records; tour organizer and musician.

A. GRAYSON CLARK - owner of Nobility Records and Dixieland Hall.

GEORGE H. BUCK JR. - owner of Jazzology/GHB Records.

TOM BETHELL - owner of San Jacinto Records.

LEONARD BRACKETT - owner of Center Records.

SONNY FAGGART - owner of Pearl Records.

JOE MARES - owner of Southland Records.

You will note that those I have listed have one commonalty. All were record producers. Recording was what it was all about. Nothing else matters. Nothing else counts. There is no other way to preserve a spontaneous music such as jazz. Unless you lived in New Orleans during the period, almost everything you know about the music of the Great Revival you know through the efforts of these few record producers. Counting me there were 10. We did it. Oh there were a few isolated instances of larger record companies going down to make a few recordings - most notably the superb Riverside "Living Legends" series - but they are not available today. Every time a musician died, we producers would sit in some New Orleans bar and cry on each others shoulders about the recordings we DIDN'T make. For every

George Lewis or Jim Robinson who made many recordings, there were a dozen like Albert Warner or Peter Bocage who made almost none.

But they were recorded. And making those records was the most fun any of us had in our lives.

I may not even mention some of these producers again after this tribute I just paid them. Each has their own story to tell and I urge those who can to do so. The history of the period is incomplete until they come forth.

I am not going to describe the music we made. You will not hear a word about monophony, homophony, polyphony or heterophony. Such things should be left to authorities like James Lincoln Collier or Gunther Schuller. I am not qualified to discuss them and besides they sound too damn sexual to include in a book your kid might read (I can just hear Kid Thomas now, "stay away from that guy, Bill. He's homophonic, man!"). Like Lewis, Robinson or Penn, I am a jazzman; not a musician. There is a difference. This is not a music book. It is a jazzman's book. I will describe the jazzmen to you. Who they really were. How they really acted. From that you should be able to learn all you need to know about their music for they are one and the same. Kid Thomas' explosive horn playing was the man's nature. Lewis' sensitivity on his instrument was part of his soul. Penn's raucousness was Sammy put to music. Their personalities can be described and I shall attempt to do so.

1955 - 1959

deceased

WOODEN JOE NICHOLAS, clarinet/trumpet - 1957

ALBERT GLENNY, bass - 1958

WARREN "BABY" DODDS, drums - 1959

LAWRENCE MARRERO, banjo - 1959

OMER SIMEON, clarinet - 1959

1 . Awakening

New York City, July 1955. A Sunday Afternoon.

It had taken us just over an hour to drive into the city from Bridgeport. We were now walking through the lounge of stylish Child's Paramount Restaurant heading for the main dining room. The waiters were keeping an eye on us for I wasn't old enough to stop and have a drink. . . even in New York with its 18 year old drinking requirement. Bud Larson took my arm and stopped me.

"Listen," he said, "it's the Lewis Jazzman recording coming over the P.A. system!" Sure enough, it did sound like it: the beautiful interlude between vocals on "Just A Closer Walk With Thee." You couldn't miss Lawrence Marrero's rippling single string banjo playing. And that was definitely George Lewis blowing the low-register riff under it. Bud stood there transfixed listening to his idol Avery "Kid" Howard whisper into his mute. We must have heard this recording a hundred times. There was no mistaking it.

As Bud continued to listen, I walked to the dining room entrance. I glanced inside and was frozen to the spot with what I saw. There on a huge bandstand at the far side of the room was the true source of the music we were hearing. Seated on four chairs lined up on the stand were Big Jim Robinson, Kid Howard, George Lewis and Lawrence Marrero. Arrayed around them were Alton Purnell. . . seated at a baby grand piano, Joe Watkins and Alcide "Slow Drag" Pavageau. I stared in disbelief even though I knew they were going to be there. It was to see them in person that we drove down from Connecticut. I turned and walked back to where Bud was standing, still listening.

"Bud, come with me," I said.

He replied, "Bill, wait just a minute until this one record is over."

"It's not a record, Bud."

He looked at me as I pointed to the dining room. Then he realized what I was saying. He ran across the lounge and froze at the entrance just as I had done. We were face to face with the world's hottest jazz band.

2. A Teenager Meets Jazz

By 1955 I had already been playing jazz drums for four years. All kinds of jazz. My first hearing of the famous Benny Goodman 1938 Carnegie Hall Jazz Concert had turned me away from the schmaltzy popular music of the pre-rock-and-roll era. During the 50s there was much jazz to be heard on radio. There were regularly scheduled "live" broadcasts of jazz airing from Nick's in Greenwich Village and other New York pubs. I tried to attend a few of them in person but I was turned away because I was under the drinking age.

In Connecticut there was one program, a half hour weekly, which featured traditional jazz exclusively. I listened to it frequently. I liked a lot of what I heard on the Rockin' 'N Rhythm show but I wished they'd play more of the Gene Krupa records I admired so. I was styling my drumming after Gene's. I wrote to the program's host, Rocky Clark, requesting that he do so. To my surprise, I received a telephone call from him a few days later inviting me to the studio while he did his show. I was embarrassed to have to inform him that I wasn't old enough to drive. He offered to pick me up at my home on his way to the station.

Rocky was a pleasant middle-aged man with a huge jazz record collection. . . a hard combination to beat for an impressionable teenager. He was an editor on our local newspaper, the Bridgeport Post, and wrote a weekly jazz column, The Jazz Beat. I found that I was not the only one Rocky invited along. He had a small and faithful following of young local jazz musicians who made the trek to his studio on Sunday afternoons. His broadcast booth was the size of a large bathroom. Sometimes he had a dozen fans packed into it. The hardest part was getting everybody to shut up when his mike was live. I met many musicians there who I would play with later in my career: Bob Fargo, Don Rice, Bill Connell and Bud Larson among them. Others I brought to the studio for the first time would later gain recognition in the traditional jazz field including Dick McCarthy and Bill Sinclair. For several years I went to "weekly mass" at the studios of station WICC.

Rocky Clark was not an active participant in the "Great Jazz Revival" of New Orleans jazz in the 1960s but, had he not treated us young jazzmen with such great caring, the Connecticut contingent of the Revival wouldn't have come into existence and dozens of significant recordings which helped propel it along would not have been made.

As I became more accustomed to the traditional jazz sound, I liked it more and more. Don Rice led the most popular of several high school jazz bands in the area. I was leading a Krupa style trio consisting of piano, sax and drums. Rice asked me to join his Saints of Dixieland. I quit my own trio to do so. After high school, Rice merged his band with another group from Westport led by trumpeter Bud Larson. Taking the best players from both groups we formed a two trumpet band that was the best in Connecticut. Bill Connell joined the band on clarinet. He was older than the rest of us and was widely regarded as the best traditional jazzman in the region. He continually talked about his admiration for a New Orleans clarinetist named George Lewis. I had never heard of him. Larson was on this New Orleans kick also. One night Bud brought several albums to my house to acquaint me with the New Orleans style. I worked as assistant manager in a record store but I had never heard of these strange little record labels pressed on red and blue vinyl he pulled out. Antone. Paradox. American Music.

He put on the Paradox ten-inch LP which featured the George Lewis band he and Connell raved about so often. The first track was "Bugle Boy March," a number he wanted us to play in the band. I thought it was terrible and told him so. "It sounds like a God-damned polka band!" He was not put off by my remark. To the contrary he said he was going to make me listen to it until I understood what was happening on the record. He played it again and again. The only thing I liked about it was the trombone work by a fellow named Robinson. He was hot enough to almost make you think you took up the wrong instrument

Bud left me the two Antone albums and a Jazzman session, also by the Lewis band. These had been recorded later, and much better, than the Paradox and the power of the music started to get to me. The drummer, Joe Watkins, was a hot player alright but a little too simple for my taste. The one thing I did realize was that this would not be an easy music to play. As simple as each part was it blended into a unified whole, the sum of which seemed greater than its parts. It would take a lot of work to get another band to sound like this.

Bud called excitedly one day to tell me that he had been contacted by a new record company in New Haven that wanted to record us. This was a real surprise. We had been doing a lot of playing around the area and apparently the Artist & Repertoire man for the label heard us somewhere. We recorded a 78 rpm single for them which featured "Apex Blues" on the "A" side and "Mama Don't Allow" on the flip. "Mama" even featured a drum solo on my record debut. The record actually sold several hundred copies. The Big Time!

Bud mentioned a band in New York that he frequently went to see at

Jimmy Ryan's on 52nd Street. He said it was the only New Orleans style band in New York. The band was led by trombonist Wilbur DeParis and featured Wilbur's brother Sidney on trumpet, Jelly Roll Morton's great clarinetist Omer Simeon and one of New Orleans' greatest jazz drummers, Zutty Singleton. Bud invited me to tag along on one of his trips to hear them. I told him of my problems getting into New York clubs because of my age. He told me not to worry because he was so well known there that nobody would ask me for an ID if I was with him. And so it was that I got to hear live, professional jazz for the first time. The band was spellbinding. By the time we left, I had autographed copies of the band's three available LPs. Zutty played on only one of them. The other two featured another sensational drummer: Freddie Moore. We spent many nights at Jimmy Ryan's and I got to know some of the musicians slightly.

By the summer of '55 and our trips to Child's Paramount, I had been converted to the "mouldy fig" school of New Orleans Jazz. We saw that magnificent Lewis band twice but we were so intimidated by the presence of our musical idols that we never got up the nerve to talk to them. I would never see Purnell or Marrero after that. Purnell went West and Marrero went under; six feet under. But I would become fast friends with every other one of the musicians I gaped at on those two occasions. The following month we returned to Child's to hear the Paul Barbarin band. Barbarin was another incredible New Orleans drummer who played a style I couldn't identify at the time as the "street drumming" it was. Three members of the band stood out: clarinetist Willie Humphrey, trombonist Bobby Thomas and pianist Lester Santiago. I was really getting hooked on New Orleans trombone playing. What impressed me about the trombone players were their rhythmic patterns. All the horn playing I'd heard before relied on the rhythm section to carry it along. These New Orleans trombone guys appeared to act as a bridge between the rhythm section and the front line. It was a great concept I thought; and still think.

When I went into the U.S. Army in 1959 I was offered the opportunity to serve in the Army Intelligence elite Counter Intelligence Corps (CIC). I took it and requested New Orleans as my duty station. The closest they could assign me was Ft. Sam Houston at San Antonio, Texas. I gladly took it knowing I could drive through New Orleans on the way there. As I packed my car for the trip I realized I couldn't fit both my wife, Carol, and my drumset in. I made the wrong choice and left the drums behind.

A thought struck me before I left. My friend Bob Fargo, later to be the first trumpet player with the Easy Riders Jazz Band, had a big assortment of musical instruments in his cellar and it seemed to me I remembered an old silver colored trombone there. I called him up.

"Bob, could I borrow your trombone?"

"Sure," he replied, "but I thought you were leaving for Texas in a few days."

"I am."

"Then how and when do I get the trombone back?"

"I'll hand deliver it in two years."

Silence. Then, "come and get it."

1960 - 1962

deceased

BOBBY THOMAS, trombone - 1960

STEVE ANGRUM, clarinet - 1961

ALPHONSE PICOU, clarinet - 1961

ABBEY "CHINEE" FOSTER, drums - 1962

EDDIE MORRIS, trombone - 1962

3.   New Orleans – 1960

I drove to New Orleans in March of 1960, the first of many such trips during my playing career. It was typically muggy. We stayed in a cheap motel just outside the city limits. Every day we would drive into the Vieux Carre section of town and walk around trying to get a sense of the history of the place. It was an eerie feeling to stand on the corner of Toulouse and Burgundy ("where parade bands start and end"), stroll up South Rampart Street or stare at San Jacinto Hall. Suddenly real places from my fantasy world of jazz.

We went to all of the tourist spots and heard surprisingly little interesting jazz. The Famous Door featured all white dixielanders who were no better than you could hear any night at Nick's in Greenwich Village and nowhere as good as the DeParis band at Jimmy Ryan's. I knew there must be good black jazz here somewhere but I didn't know where to find it. Being my first visit to the pre-Civil Rights Act South, I was disturbed by the segregation restrictions. Without noticing, I drank from a drinking fountain marked "colored only" in a Woolworth store and was soundly reprimanded by an elderly white woman for doing so. I started being careful of what Men's Room I entered.

I knew little about black people. I never had the occasion to socialize with any. There were only three or four blacks in my high school. I got to know one of them slightly because he was also a jazz drummer. Although he played bebop we had a mutual regard for each other's musicianship. I had met the members of the DeParis band and gone to see them often enough so that Zutty or Omer would occasionally sit at our table and talk during a break. But I had no idea what it might feel like to be a black American and, frankly, little interest at that time in finding out.

After a few nights in New Orleans, we stopped in at the Paddock Lounge which had a sign over the entrance that said in bold type: THE WORLD'S GREATEST DIXIELAND PLAYED HERE!. No doubt the sign was intended to lure people inside. In my case it had kept me out. The band was coming onstage as we sat down next to the bar. The bandstand was above the bar. Out walked six black musicians and I finally heard the sound I came to New Orleans to hear. The trumpet player was a little too flashy for my taste but I recognized the clarinet and trombone players instantly from their recordings. They were Alburt Burbank and Bill Mathews.

I asked the waiter if he would ask Burbank to join us for a drink. He looked at me in astonishment and informed me that it wasn't permitted for blacks to sit with whites. In fact blacks were prohibited from admittance to the restaurant. They could entertain the whites but they couldn't share in the entertainment. This was a strange world I had entered. Here I was in New Orleans to pay homage to my musical idols and Albert Burbank couldn't sit and have a drink with me. America 1960. It was the only country on Earth that could produce the environment suitable for the gestation and birth of jazz; which is after all not just a black music, but a black American music. When the legendary record producer Bill Russell selected a name for his record company, he didn't call it Black Music. He named it American Music. Only blacks could have invented jazz. And only in America. Only American whites could have exploited it in such a way as to bring it to the attention of the rest of the world; ultimately, though unintentionally, to the advantage of its black originators.

But, at the moment I sat in the Paddock Lounge, all I wanted to do was to meet Burbank and Mathews. I asked the waiter if there was some way I could do that and slipped him a five dollar bill. He said he would see what he could do. At the next break, he came over and asked me to follow him. He led me to a back hallway outside of the kitchen where the band took its breaks. He introduced me to Albert and left for the kitchen.

Albert seemed understandably reticent under the circumstances. I told him I had several of the records he made with the Paul Barbarin band. He was polite and cordial. He introduced me to the others in the band. Among them were Mathews, trumpeter Thomas Jefferson (imagine a black man being named after a slave-owning president!) and pianist Octave Crosby. I don't recall the others. We chatted for the rest of the break; a clandestine meeting between jazz conspirators. At break's end I returned to my table and they to their gig. A few years later it would be my pleasure to record Burbank and welcome him into my home in Connecticut as an honored guest where we could talk as long as we wished.

4.   San Antonio

From New Orleans I reported to my duty station in San Antonio, Texas. Despite the desert heat, tarantulas, scorpions, rattlesnakes and country music, I liked it there a lot. I was assigned to the 112th Counter Intelligence Corps in the Quadrangle at Fort Sam Houston and spent the next couple of years happily spying on spies.

A little checking turned up a local jazz club which had been started by a trombone playing dentist, Chuck Reilly. Within a short time of joining the club, I became editor of the club newsletter. I had my huge record collection shipped down. There was no jazz on any of the local radio stations so I approached a few hoping to get a jazz program going. The station manager of KEEZ-FM (A Texan named Roy Rogers. Would you believe it?) suggested that I produce a pilot program on tape at their facility and he would consider it. It had not been my plan to do the announcing. I wanted only to supply records. Nevertheless, here I was, auditioning for my own radio show. The tape was played for the station owner who liked it and offered me a weekly Sunday morning hour for the program. I had to clear it with both my company commander and the base commander. They readily agreed as they thought it would foster good community relations with the base.

I also started to learn the trombone in the same way I started on drums: hunt and peck. I would put on a record by my favorite trombonist, Jim Robinson, and try to play along. Within a few months I could play enough in Bb and F to sit in on the jazz club jam session finales. It was there that I met another young musician who was just starting out. He was cornetist Jim Cullum Jr. We decided to form our first band together. He was a Bix fan. I admired Bix also but my interests lay in the New Orleans idiom. We selected tunes from both styles.

One day Jim showed up at my door very excited. "Have you ever heard of Don Albert?" he asked. I had not. Albert he told me was a black New Orleans trumpet man who moved to San Antonio in the 1930's to open his own nightclub and to tour in the southwest with his big band. Both Albert and his club still existed and Jim had tracked him down. He wangled an invitation for us to meet the guy and to hear his band that evening.

Albert's chops were just fine. Jim and I hired him to play with us one night on a steady Thursday evening gig we were playing at a little dive on the outskirts of town. He was the first New Orleans musician I ever hired or played with. He would not be the last. We arranged to record four songs with him that came out very well. They were never commercially released. Later, in 1962, Albert cut an album with Chuck Reilly's Alamo City Jazz Band. He also recorded some sides for Joe Mares of Southland records.

Jim's father had been a professional jazzman in his younger years before founding the family business. Jim Jr. convinced him to start playing again. We added Harvey Kindervater on drums and Bennie Belfrey on banjo. Our first gig was a freebie for one of those businessman luncheon clubs. Jim Sr. introduced the front line of the band in this manner, "We have cornet, clarinet and Bissonnette!" After I left San Antonio this band, under the leadership of Jim Cullum Jr., went on to become one of the top traditional jazz bands in America.

Upon discharge from the service, I bade my Texas friends Happy Trails and headed for New Orleans. When I arrived at Preservation Hall from Texas, there was a telegram awaiting me. It was from Jim Jr. urging me to return immediately to San Antonio. The band had been booked for a steady gig and he wanted me to come back to stay. They had finally picked a name for the group: The Happy Jazz Band. I've often wondered how things would have turned out for everybody if I had turned around and gone back. I almost did.

THE JAZZ BEAT

New Orleans To Texas Via Connecticut

New Orleans jazz has just arrived in San Antonio, Texas. It came there by way of Connecticut and the U.S. Army.

This is the story of William E. Bissonnette, formerly of Trumbull, who became a jazz enthusiast while attending high school in Bridgeport.

Bill Bissonnette was one of a group of students whose interest in jazz was inspired by a weekly jazz program over a Bridgeport radio station.

Don Rice, another of the students, assembled the young enthusiasts into an instrumental group called the Saints of Dixieland. In 1954 they had become good enough to come to New Haven and record "Apex Blues" and "Sister Kate" for Standard Records, a subsidiary of Standard Electronics. Bissonnette, who called himself "Bill Cozy" at the time, was the drummer.

Bissonnette has been missing from the group for the last two years because of his stint in the Army.

A DISMAL STATION

As a member of the Fourth U.S. Army Operations Group, the Army sent bill to San Antonio. It might as well have been the Arizona desert, Bill thought when he arrived there. Local radio stations and juke boxes offered nothing but a choice variety of hillbilly tunes.

Then he learned that there was an organization called the San Antonio Jazz Society. Similar to the New Haven Jazz Club, it met occasionally to enable its most active enthusiasts to indulge in a jam session.

Bill joined the organization and succeeded in interesting a group of members in playing New Orleans style jazz. After a number of rehearsals, they performed at the April meeting of the SAJS which resulted in a special article in the local newspaper headed "Jazz Society Revives Music From Dixieland."

It was written by the Society editor.

Bill played trombone with the group for the first time in public.

In addition, he has become the club's historian and writes the monthly bulletin, a mimeographed pamphlet mailed to members. In one of these, he wrote, "The History Of Jazz Clubs." He also reviews jazz records.

Bill says that, "the real force behind the SAJS is Dr. Charles Reiley, the president. He is also an excellent trombonist who plays in several groups." Bill and Dr. Reiley are the only two members of the New Orleans Jazz Club in the San Antonio area.

RECORDING JAZZ GROUPS

"I am currently engaged in recording all the local jazz groups here," writes Bill, who still has about six months to serve in the Army.

"When I leave here," adds Bill, "I am going to New Orleans for a few months to try to record as many of the old-timers as I can before returning to Connecticut."

New Haven Register July 1961

PHOTO: CONNECTICUT GI Bill Bissonnette leads jazz group: Left to right are Phil Denson, banjo; Charlie Dorris, clar.; Bissonnette, trombone; Jack Taylor, drums, and Jim Cullum Jr., cornet.

THE JAZZ BEAT

Jazz-Happy Yankee
Is FM Hit In Texas

Down in San Antonio, Texas, KEEZ, which bills itself as the FM station for adults, has scored an unexpected hit with a Sunday morning Jazz Festival program.

And the program is being presented weekly by none other than William E. Bissonnette, the young Trumbull (Conn.) soldier stationed in that Texas town where he kindled new life into the San Antonio Jazz Society.

Rennicke Carey, columnist in the Santonio Light, devoted a recent column to Bissonnette whom he described as "one especially dedicated member" of SAJS. He quoted Bissonnette's description of jazz as "America's greatest contribution to the world of music" and publicized the KEEZ program which is aired at 1 pm.

Bissonnette has been editing the SAJS monthly newsletter, a copy of which got into the hands of the owner of KEEZ. Owner Balthrope, impressed, contacted station manager Roy Rogers who, in turn, invited Bissonnette to the station. Here's the story as Bissonnette tells it to THE JAZZ BEAT:

"When I arrived there, they asked me if I would be interested in doing a weekly jazz show. The problem was they didn't have a jazz library, except for three Red Nichols LPs and a few by Jack Teagarden. I decided to use my own collection on the show on the condition that I would have a free hand on musical selection and that I could use old records if I desired.

"The show's been on a few months now and the response has been better than any of us had hoped for. The station has received many cards and letters of approval, which the station manager said was very unusual for an FM station. I try to mix up the material with all traditional styles from good old mouldy New Orleans to some of the modern styles like the West Coasters play today."

TEAGARDEN INTERVIEW

When Jack Teagarden's band came to San Antonio for a jazz club appearance, Bissonnette went backstage with a tape recorder during intermission. He chatted with Teagarden, pianist Don Ewell and drummer Barrett Deems. It made a fine show for Bissonnette's program.

Teagarden told the young soldier/DJ that jazz today is not as good as it was in the Twenties, "because jazzmen no longer play with feeling or a good beat." He disclosed that Tommy Dorsey was his favorite trombonist, with Miff Mole coming in second. Mr. T said he did not care for the the oldtime New Orleans players like Jim Robinson or Kid Ory.

Teagarden mentioned that he made more than 1,000 recordings, of which he only owned about ten. When some of the jazz record collectors heard this, they taped the Teagarden records in their collections and sent them to him. Now he has all but 18 of the sides he has recorded - more than 400 hours of continuous music.

KEEZ will have to find a replacement for Bissonnette when Spring comes. He is winding up his Army service and will return to Connecticut in April.

If a Connecticut Yankee can win over a Texas audience, he certainly ought to have no trouble in building up a following on a Connecticut station. A good program of traditional jazz would be a welcome addition to radio program fare in this area.

W. Rockwell Clark

**New Haven Register
January 1962**

5.   New Orleans – 1962

The two years in Texas went by quickly. I was playing barely passable trombone but enough so that I knew it would henceforth be my principal instrument. I had a lot to learn and I knew who it was who could teach me. Upon my discharge from the Army, I headed straight for New Orleans, dragging my wife into a life she quickly grew to hate. We took a small furnished apartment for three months and I started looking for jazz. I found plenty of it this time.

In 1961 a young man named Grayson Mills had started the first kitty hall in New Orleans at 726 St. Peter Street. He called it Preservation Hall. The building was owned by real estate baron Larry Borenstein. Mills paid $400.00 a month rent to Borenstein. Mill's goal was to record as many of the oldtime jazzmen as he could. He had some financial support from his mother in California but he was doing it mostly on his own. His Icon Records had already issued several albums. As the result of a dispute with Borenstein, Mills had been forced out of Preservation Hall. Borenstein then turned the management of the hall over to Allan and Sandra Jaffe. Mills opened a second hall on St. Louis Street. He called this one Icon Hall.

On our very first night in New Orleans we stumbled across Icon Hall. We heard the music drifting out of the side street as we walked along Bourbon Street and we went down to check it out. The hall was almost empty. There wasn't even anyone sitting at the door to collect the kitty. The hall had once been a laundry. It was cavernous. The bandstand was on a balcony which was at least eight feet off the ground. You could only see the front row of musicians when you looked up. The music was superb oldtime New Orleans Jazz. I didn't recognize any of the players, all elderly blacks.

We sat down to listen. Soon a young fellow came over and introduced himself as "Ken" Mills. He apologetically asked us for $2.00. A buck apiece. We started to talk. I told him about my jazz radio program in Texas and how the station manager asked me if I would continue it on tape from Connecticut. I mentioned that I had come to New Orleans to study jazz trombone. He told me who was in the band: Kid Sheik and Charlie Love on trumpets, Albert Warner on Trombone, Alec Bigard on drums, Harrison Verrett on banjo, Papa John Joseph on bass and, to my surprise, Mile' Barnes on clarinet. I had Mile's American Music and Riverside albums. I was familiar with Warner from his Bunk Johnson and Eureka Brass Band recordings. I didn't know that Mile' was still alive. He was missing some front teeth and having a hard time playing but he still sounded beautiful. Warner's style was unique; almost tuba lines and very, very powerful.

We got to meet everyone and they were very friendly, particularly Kid Sheik who had an easy and infectious laugh. They seemed at ease with Mills and consequently with us. When I told Sheik that I was a fledgling trombone player he invited me to sit in with the band. What an offer! I didn't have my horn with me. Sheik said, "use Warner's, he won't mind." He asked Albert if it was alright. Warner handed me his axe. I played on "The Sheik of Araby" and a Bb blues. What a thrill it was. The first time playing in a true New Orleans band (on Albert Warner's trombone), and with Mile' Barnes on clarinet! Talk about being on a high. Warner had a strange horn. There was no spit valve on it. After every number, he would pull the slide all the way off and drain it. I've never seen another horn like it. I guess I didn't play very well but every one of the musicians congratulated me on my playing anyway.

We went to Preservation Hall the following night. Compared to Icon Hall, it was pretty full. Not like it would be in later years, but there were still a lot of people inside and, unlike today, they stayed set after set. I met Allan Jaffe and talked briefly. The band that was playing was Creole George Guesnon's New Orleans Stompers. I was familiar with Guesnon from his recordings with the George Lewis band. We stayed several sets and then walked over to Icon Hall until closing.

Ken gave me the address of the trombone player I was looking for and the next day I crossed North Rampart Street for the first time and entered the segregated black section of town. As I walked the streets looking for the address Ken gave me I began to feel wary about what I was doing. Ken told me he thought I would be safe in the black section. The only thing he told me to be on the lookout for was the police. Something backward about this, isn't there?

As I walked along, a frightening thing happened. I thought I heard a low rumbling sound and, suddenly, people started coming out of almost every house on the block ahead of me. They all started running toward me. I was flushed with fear and stopped dead in my tracks. They ran to me. . . and past me! It wasn't me they were interested in. I turned to see hundreds of blacks coming from all directions and converging at the corner a few blocks away. Then I heard that rumbling sound again. Boom. Boom. BOOM. It was a bass drum! I raced after the crowd and, when I turned the corner, I found myself at the end of a vast "second line" following a brass band through the black section of New Orleans. I ran to the front to get near the band and there were two of my new friends, Kid Sheik and Albert Warner, decked out in white shirts and wearing marching caps. I must have stood out in the crowd as Sheik spotted me immediately. He aimed his horn at me as he blew to let me know he'd seen me. I followed along for many blocks. There were a few white people scattered along the parade route. I spotted Allan Jaffe among them. To this day I do not know what the parade was for. I saw no hearse. They played no dirges. It was certainly not to welcome me "Back-O-Town."

As the crowd dispersed, I realized I was lost. The parade had snaked from street to street and I was now deep in the heart of the black section. I wandered around and finally found the street I had been looking for. Marais Street was just like all the others except that the house I stopped in front of was the home of one of the greatest jazz trombone players who ever lived. I walked up the steps and knocked on the door. It swung open and standing before me was the giant who so impressed me at Child's Paramount in New York in 1955.

"What you want, boy?" asked Jim Robinson.

It was the beginning of my education in more ways than one. From Jim Robinson I would learn not only the fundamentals of jazz trombone playing. I would learn also the fundamentals of what it felt like to be a black person living in the South during segregation. Most of all, Jim Robinson would teach me what it is to be a man.

Every day for months I would walk over to Jim's house. Sometimes we would play. He would blow something. I would try to duplicate it. Other times we would just sit and talk until it was time for Jim to leave for whichever kitty hall he was playing that night. We would walk to the hall together. Sometimes I would carry the master's horn for him. A real honor then as it would be today.

I asked Jim about the beautiful, soulful vibrato he often used on the blues. He didn't understand what I was talking about so I brought one of the Bunk AM's over to his house and we played it on his little record player. Jim hadn't heard the record in years and he sat there carefully listening. When one of his lead choruses came on, he would jerk his head up and his eyes would widen. He'd yell, "That's me! Jim Robinson!" Then he would laugh and slap his knee. "Pearl, come in here woman. Listen! That's me, Jim Robinson, back in '44 with George and Bunk. Listen woman! My don't that Drag play some fine bass, Bill?"

I asked again about the vibrato and Jim lifted his horn from the open case beside his chair. "You all mean like this, Bill?" He blew that marvelous wobbly, crying tone that I thought came straight from his heart. It didn't. It came straight from his stomach. "You gots to tighten up your gut, man, so them muscles get all nervous and starts to shake. Then, out it comes." I tried it over and over until I got a terrific stomachache but finally out it came. "You got it, Bill. Bill man, you got it." Jim was pleased. But then, it wasn't hard to please a friend as close as Robinson was becoming.

Jim often spoke about Louis Armstrong. He admired Louis greatly. One day I brought over a special limited edition set of "Satchmo, A Musical Autobiography" on Decca records. It was a multiple record set that Armstrong had autographed for me years before when he played in Bridgeport. Robinson went nuts over it. "I gots to get one of these. Where you get it, Bill?" I explained that it was a limited edition and was no longer available. Jim said that he had to have it and offered to buy mine. I was not about to part with it, even for Jim Robinson. I told him I would see what I could do for him. The next day I called the station manager at KEEZ-FM in San Antonio and asked if he could help me. He called someone at Decca and managed to get me another copy. He sent it to me airmail and I gave it to Jim as a farewell present when I left for Connecticut. He was overjoyed. He must have played that set of records for all of his musician friends because, over the years, I received many requests from other New Orleans jazzmen to get them copies of it. I knew how special it was to Jim so I never even tried to get another. And let me tell you something, it was the only payment I ever made to Robinson for those hours and hours of lessons. . . and he thought it was enough.

One afternoon Jim let off a burst of angst against racism that startled me. It was the only time in all the years I knew him that he did so. I don't know if something happened to him during the day to set it off. It was not directed at me but it made me feel very uncomfortable anyway.

"Bill," he said, "you know that if some little white kid say to me on the street 'Get out of my way boy' I gots to move. Quick. Me. Jim Robinson. I makes all them records and people listen to me play my horn all over the world and they writes me letters and say 'you the greatest trombone we ever heard' but that white kid call me 'boy' and I gots to move out of his way fast. I ain't no boy, Bill. No suh, I ain't no boy. I'm a man. Me, Jim Robinson, I'm a man. Don't matter what nobody calls me. I'M A MAN!"

In my wanderings I came across Bill Russell's little instrument repair shop on Chartres Street. Russell was a quiet and gentle man. I would drop in from time to time and ask him about the American Music sessions he recorded. He told me on my first visit that he no longer had any of those records to sell. After several visits, he went into the back of the shop and came back with a couple of records. They were the Baby Dodds drum instruction albums. I had mentioned to him that I was a drummer and a fan of Baby. Of course, he had seen me at Preservation Hall and knew that I had been going to Robinson's house for lessons. He said I could buy these albums if I wanted them. He asked only a couple of dollars apiece for them. He then said he had another thing I might be interested in. He went out back again and returned with a device I had never seen before. He explained that it was a drummer's ratchet; not any drummer's ratchet but the ratchet Baby Dodds used on the drum record. Baby's ratchet! Before I left the shop, it was mine. It is still mounted on my bass drum.

One morning as I passed Preservation Hall, Allan Jaffe pulled up on his motor scooter. He asked how I was enjoying my visit to New Orleans. I told him I was having a wonderful time. He invited me to join him for breakfast at a luncheonette on the corner of St. Peter and Bourbon. It was the only long talk we ever had. He said he had heard that I was taking lessons from Jim. I confirmed it and remarked that some of us younger fellows would have to carry on the tradition when guys like Jim were gone. He looked at me quizzically and asked why.

"Do you think this music should die with these men?" I asked. He responded that that was exactly what he thought.

"It's their music, isn't it?" he said.

"Not anymore," I replied. "I certainly agree that nobody else can play it like they do and maybe nobody ever will, but the music itself belongs to the world now. After all, orchestras still play Vivaldi, Wagner, Rachmaninoff and Tchaikovsky."

"They wrote their music to be played by others," he countered. "New Orleans music is too personal for that."

He raised a good point although I didn't agree that New Orleans Jazz should drop dead in its tracks the day Jim Robinson did and it surprised me to hear someone who was beginning to get involved with the music as he was making it. I don't know if he ever changed his opinion as we never discussed it again. I suspect he did as he certainly helped many young musicians by letting them play in his kitty hall as the oldtimers passed on.

There are perhaps a dozen musical highpoints that occurred over the years that stand out in my mind. One was the first night I played in Icon Hall. Another happened on the evening of Saturday, March 17, 1962. That was the first time I heard the Kid Thomas Band in person. To heighten the thrill even further, George Lewis and Creole George Guesnon were sitting in with the band. I arrived at Preservation Hall during the second set. The hall was almost full and I stood in the back until the break. It was a fascinating sight. What a rough and tumble looking band it was. I had never seen any of the Thomas band regulars before. Across the front sat Louis Nelson, trombone; Kid Thomas Valentine, trumpet; Manny Paul, tenor sax; George Lewis, clarinet and Creole George Guesnon, banjo. Behind them sat that great rhythm section: Sammy Penn, drums; Joe Butler, bass and Joe James, piano. All wore open neck white shirts except Thomas who was in a double-breasted suit and tie.

It was a powerhouse band. They charged each number as if they were the Light Brigade. After several such numbers, they went into a slow number that caught my attention. I seemed to recognize the melody but I couldn't put my finger on the title. It was different somehow from what I thought it should sound like. It was one of the most beautiful things I have ever heard. When the break came around, I approached George Lewis and told him I had seen his band in New York.

"You must be that boy Jim been talking about."

I was thrilled that Jim had mentioned me. "Yes, I've been going to his house for lessons. George, what was that slow tune you did last set? I know I know it but I just can't place it. It was great."

"That's the 'Bells of St. Mary's.' Thomas the only band that plays that one."

One of the people I wanted to meet most in New Orleans was Joe Mares, owner of Southland records. We corresponded frequently when I was in San Antonio and he sent me many Southland releases to play on my radio program. His principal income source was not records. He was very successful in the alligator skin business. I asked him in one of my letters if he could set up some interviews for me with some of the Southland artists that I could tape for broadcast. I had taped interviews in Texas with Jack Teagarden, Don Ewell, Barrett Deems and Don Albert and they were well received by my listening audience.

I phoned Joe. He told me he had arranged interviews with Paul Barbarin, Waldren "Frog" Joseph, George Lewis and white trombonist Emile Christian who had played with the Original Dixie Jass Band fifty years earlier and who was still playing in the Sixties. He also invited my wife and me to join him and his wife, Helen, for dinner at their home after the interviews.

I met him at his warehouse recording studio. Frog and Paul were already there when I arrived. I did long interviews with both of them. While I was interviewing Frog, George Lewis walked into the studio. As much as I liked Frog, I could hardly wait to get at George, who waved at me as he entered. I interviewed George at length until Emile arrived. All of the interviews were aired in Texas intermixed with their records. Where are the interview tapes today? I guess they still exist. They should have been in the boxes of master tapes I sent to George H. Buck Jr. when he purchased my Jazz Crusade label. I don't even think he knows he has them.

Joe's home was magnificent. A stately and grand dining room was the focal point of the place. China, crystal and silverware were of the highest quality. Two servants waited on the table. Joe informed us that Helen cooked the meal which featured southern specialties. The food mounded on the table in an abundance that could have served double our number. I immediately made an error of manners. After filling my plate, I asked for the salt. I didn't see a salt shaker or pepper on the table.

Mrs. Mares spoke softly, "The food is properly seasoned. No good cooking requires additional seasoning."

I apologized for my indiscretion and told her that I had always had an affinity for salt. I explained It was seldom that I ate properly prepared food (at which statement, my wife, Carol, glared at me!) and asking for salt was something I normally did without thinking. She accepted my apology. She was also right about the food. It was delicious as served. When I had eaten my fill and the table was being cleared, I expected to be served some good New Orleans chicory coffee. Instead, Joe announced, "And now for the main course!" Main course? The servants brought in platters piled high with Cajun chicken and vegetables. We started eating all over again. I don't know how I held it all in but the main course was even better than the "appetizer." Finally the coffee arrived and Joe and I adjourned to the library for some pre-Castro Havana cigars Joe had stockpiled.

Joe was a most interesting guy. He was an old line Southerner. And yet he treated black musicians with dignity and certainly did much to help spread their music. He really did believe that the white jazzmen of New Orleans were better players than the blacks and he spent much time and effort when recording blacks to make them sound white: commercial, clean and cosmetic. He was trying to give them "class" he said. His stable of black artists represented his thinking. His black star was Thomas Jefferson whom he felt he could make into a new "Looie Armstrong." I asked him if he had considered doing any recordings of the older musicians.

"I've done Punch Miller, George Lewis, Paul Barbarin. . . even one by Jim Robinson. Who else are you talking about?" he asked.

"How about Kid Thomas, Sheik, Mile' Barnes. . ."

The mention of Mile' did it. He interrupted me in mid-list. "Kid Thomas? Mile' Barnes? I'm not gonna record any of that damn nigra stuff. I'm trying to spread jazz not kill it. Putting out that crap hurts everybody. You don't play that stuff on the radio, do you?"

"Yes I do, Joe. It's my favorite music."

"Well I am surprised. I thought you would have better taste than that," he said without rancor. "Well, I'm not going to record any of it."

He did in fact record several antiseptic albums featuring Robinson, Punch, Louis Cottrell, Avery Howard and others. He never touched Mile' or Thomas. I don't pass this story along to denigrate Joe Mares or his contribution to recorded jazz. He did much that was exemplary. It was through his efforts that some of the more commercial New Orleans white musicians got their big breaks, including Al Hirt and Pete Fountain. And it was Joe who made the contacts that began the Disneyland tradition of the Young Men From New Orleans bands that played at the theme parks which, although dressed in striped coats and straw hats straight out of minstrel days, permitted many of the blacks to perform to wide new audiences. Joe just didn't like "nigra jazz."

I loved it.

The word was spreading through the Quarter that another oldtimer had been rediscovered while hanging around Congo Square and would soon be playing at Preservation Hall. Abbey "Chinee" Foster had been one of the great early drummers, having played with the legendary Buddy Petit and recording with Papa Celestine in the Twenties. He was being "dried out" and put back into playing condition for his debut.

The big event arrived and many of the black musicians turned out along with us fellow-travelers. He didn't play great that first night. It was enough for us that he played at all. His confidence and technique quickly returned and he became a favorite at the hall. Tragically it was to last only a few months. Chinee died in September of 1962. But he had his fifteen minutes of fame that Andy Warhall allowed each of us.

That segregation business was really a pain in the ass. When the halls closed at night, there would have been nothing we would have liked better than to be able to sit down in a bar and hoist a few with our idols. It was impossible to do it. Sometimes I would step into the bar next to Preservation Hall, buy a few beers and bring them out onto the sidewalk so we could stand there downing them with Sheik or Robinson or Penn. I was staying in an apartment directly over the hall and we would sometimes sneak a musician or two up and talk long into the night. By the time of my next visit in 1965 all was changed. We could come and go as we pleased as long as we didn't mind the sneers and occasional shout on the street: NIGGER LOVER!

We continued alternating nights between Icon and Preservation halls. They each used a different set of musicians with a few crossovers. At Icon I would hear and meet Israel Gorman, Eddie Morris, Johnny Casimer, Charlie Love, Alfred Williams, Albert Jiles, Sylvester Handy, Andrew Morgan, Wilbert Tillman, Homer Eugene and others. Icon Hall did not have a piano. The bands and musicians represented what I saw as an older, dance hall style of jazz. Preservation Hall featured more of a cross-section of jazz. Peter Bocage represented the dance hall variety. Noone Johnson's wonderful bazooka band was almost country jazz. Albert French's Tuxedo Band and Narvin Kimball's Dixielanders were exactly that: black dixieland. There were also the great hot bands: the Kid Thomas band, the George Lewis band, Kid Howard's La Vida Band, Kid Sheik, Percy Humphrey, Sweet Emma Barrett and the Billie and Dede Pierce band. Every night, two halls, two bands, a dozen or more of New Orleans' finest black musicians from which to choose nightly. It was pretty heady stuff.

Robinson played both halls as did Kid Thomas (although not with his own band) and Creole George. If you didn't find them at one, you would likely find them at the other. Guesnon was the most difficult of all the musicians to get to know. He didn't have many friends, even among the other musicians. He did have a few: Alec Bigard, Capt. John Handy, Louis James, Sheik and Thomas. By getting close to them, I was able eventually to get as friendly with Guesnon as any white man could. But it took a lot of time, nurturing and many cartons of cigarettes; Guesnon's own form of currency. Jim, of course, was just the opposite. If you couldn't make instant friends with Jim Robinson, you might as well move to Mars. Jim often invited me to sit in at Icon Hall and once in awhile at Preservation. A few times I did but I usually waved him off when he stuck his horn out at me and yelled, "Come on. Come on." I didn't go to New Orleans for Jim Robinson to listen to me. The only thing he could learn by doing that was how good he was! And the old codger already knew that.

The time I had allotted for my New Orleans stay was already running weeks over. We were getting ready to leave when Kid Sheik dropped by our room one night before his gig. He said, "Bill, we're playing a funeral tomorrow. You all want to play with us? Chicken can't make it." Chicken Henry was one of the two great parade-style trombonists still alive in the city who played with all of the parade bands. Albert Warner was the other.

"Do you think it would be alright Sheik? I mean there won't be any trouble with the police or anything?"

"Well, come along and bring your axe. We'll see what it looks like tomorrow."

I met them at the rendezvous point and there were no police in sight. I took out my horn and marched along in my first funeral parade. I thanked Sheik afterwards. Many of the players I met at the halls were playing the funeral and each and every one came up to me to say, "good job."

That same night we were at Icon Hall listening to Sheik's band when suddenly a half dozen uniformed police charged through the door. They told the musicians to pack up and get out. They hustled the few people in the audience out also. We told an officer we were friends of the owner and asked if we could stay. Ken Mills had three cops standing around him as he protested the closing of his hall. They arrested him. As they took him out, we went over to him and asked what we could do to help. He was really scared, as well he might be. "They're taking me to jail! Please do something!" They hauled him away. I asked the cop who was padlocking the door if he could tell me what the charge against Ken was and where they were taking him. He told me Ken had been arrested on a charge of having "improper egress" from the hall and he was being taken to the station lock-up.

"Improper egress? You put people in jail in New Orleans for improper egress?" The cop gave me a look that convinced me it had not been a good question.

"Get out of here while you still can," he said menacingly.

We walked back to Preservation Hall where we ran into Larry Borenstein. "So how are things down at Mill's place," he asked. I asked him where the police lock-up was. He asked why I wanted to know. I told him the story of what had just happened thinking he might assist us in helping Mills. Curiously, he didn't seemed surprised at the news. He was uninterested in helping. He asked me why I was going to the police station. I replied that I wanted to try to get Ken out.

"It seems to me it's none of your business," he said. Then he casually asked me when I was planning to vacate his apartment. He suddenly recalled that he had promised it to someone else starting in a few days. I got the message.

We finally found the lock-up and asked at the desk about Ken. At first the desk sergeant said he had no record of the arrest. I told him that I had been present when the arrest was made and Ken was dragged out. I insisted that he double-check. He found the warrant. About a half hour later Ken was released and we walked him back to the hall. He saw the lock on the door and shrugged. "Bourbon Street Mafia," he said without explanation. I asked if he had a place to stay. He said he was okay and we left. I didn't see him again. I understand he later reopened Icon Hall and recorded many more great sessions He is one of the unsung heroes of the 1960's jazz revival in New Orleans. He fought against unbeatable odds and ended up out of the music and back in California but he blazed the trail that I, and others, would follow. Next to Bill Russell's, his recordings were perhaps the most important New Orleans Jazz Revival recordings ever made.

A few days later I left New Orleans to return home to Connecticut. As a fitting coda to my first extended stay there, we passed Albert Warner trudging up North Rampart Street as we drove out of the city. He didn't see us. He just shuffled along carrying his trombone case. Inside it was the trombone I played my first few tunes on with a New Orleans band. Warner lived until 1966 but I never saw him again. I watched in the rearview mirror as he faded from sight. It was the view I would always carry of him in my mind.

Trudging, endlessly trudging.

Fading. fading.

PRESERVATION HALL

726 St Peter

PRESENTS

TRADITIONAL NEW ORLEANS JAZZ CONCERTS

Tuesday through Sunday

8:30 p.m. - 12:30

SCHEDULE
March 7 - 31, 1962

Wednesday 7th	Creole George Guesnon's New Orleans Stompers
Thursday 8th	Peter Bocage and His Creole Serenaders
Friday 9th	Percy Humphrey's Crescent City Joymakers with Sweet Emma
Saturday 10th	Emanuel Sayles' All-Stars with Jim Robinson, George Lewis and Kid Howard
Sunday 11th	Kid Howard's La Vida Band
Tuesday 13th	Kid Sheik and His Storyville Ramblers
Wednesday 14th	Burke - Crawford - Ferguson Band
Thursday 15th	Billie and DeDe Pierce with Louis Nelson and George Lewis
Friday 16th	Jim Robinson's New Orleans Band with Louis Cotrell
Saturday 17th	Kid Thomas and His Algier's Stompers with George Lewis
Sunday 18th	John Casimer's Young Tuxedo Band with Bill Matthews
Tuesday 20th	Creole George Guesnon's New Orleans Stompers
Wednesday 21st	Albert French's "Papa Celestine's" Original Tuxedo Band
Thursday 22nd	Punch Miller's Bunch with Paul Barnes
Friday 23rd	Narvin Kimball's Dixielanders
Saturday 24th	Percy Humphrey's Crescent City Joymakers with Sweet Emma
Sunday 25th	Paul Barbarin's Band

SUNDAY MORNING GOSPAL SINGERS - March 25, 11:00 to 1:00 - featuring
Annie Pavageau with the Morning Star Baptist Church Chorus

SUNDAY AFTERNOON PARADE - featuring Eureka Brass Band - beginning at
Hall 1:30 p.m. - concert following parade at The Royal Garden, Royal
and Ursuline Sts., until 5:30

Tuesday 27th	Noone Johnson's Bazooka Band
Wednesday 28th	Billie and DeDe Pierce with George Lewis and Paul Barnes
Thursday 29th	Jim Robinson's New Orleans Band with Louis Cotrell
Friday 30th	Emanuel Sayles' All-Stars with Jim Robinson, George Lewis and Kid Howard
Saturday 31st	Kid Thomas and His Algier's Stompers with George Lewis

Preservation Hall presents twenty-four traditional New Orleans Jazz
bands, representing the music of over one-hundred and fifty musicians.
The Hall is managed by Allan and Sandra Jaffe and is financially
supported only by contributions

Schedule featuring 19 bands
Preservation Hall
March 1962

ASSOCIATED ARTISTS STUDIO
730 ST. PETER STREET
NEW ORLEANS 16, LA.
JULY 14, 1961

THIS IS A MEMORANDUM OF AN AGREEMENT BETWEEN KEN MILLS AND LARRY BORENSTEIN, COVERING TERMS OF RENTAL OF THE PREMISES KNOWN AS 726 ST. PETER STREET GROUND FLOOR FRONT. THE PREMISES IS TO BE USED BY TENANT IN ANY WAY THAT HE WISHES IN CONNECTION WITH THE OPERATION OF A JAZZ CLUB OR JAZZ PROMOTIONAL ENDEAVOR. THERE ARE NO RESTRICTIONS GOVERNING THIS USAGE WITH THE EXCEPTION OF THOSE EXPRESSLY PROHIBITED BY LAW, BY THE VIEUX CARRE COMMISSION, OR BY ANY OTHER GOVERNMENTAL AGENCIES.

THE AREA BEING RENTED INCLUDES USE OF THE PASSAGEWAY LEADING FROM ST. PETER STREET TO THE PATIO, BUT IS LIMITED TO THESE BOUNDARIES ONLY. IT IS ALSO UNDERSTOOD THAT THIS PASSAGEWAY IS TO BE OPEN AND ACCESSIBLE TO OTHER OCCUPANTS OF THE BUILDING. IN ADDITION TENANT MAY AT HIS OPTION ENCLOSE AN AREA OF THE PATIO IMMEDIATELY BEHIND THE REAR PATIO DOOR MEASURING TEN FEET BY TEN FEET, AND IF HE ENCLOSES SUCH AN AREA THIS SPACE MAY ALSO BE USED. HOWEVER IT IS UNDERSTOOD THAT UNLESS THIS AREA IS ENCLOSED, OCCUPANCY IS LIMITED BY THE REAR DOOR.

AT THE TIME OF THIS AGREEMENT MR. MILLS HAS GIVEN MR. BORENSTEIN A CHECK FOR $900.00. THIS CHECK REPRESENTS PAYMENT FOR ONE COMPLETE PUBLIC ADDRESS SYSTEM AT $100.00, THE FIRST MONTH'S RENT OF $400.00 FOR THE ABOVE DESCRIBED PREMISES FOR THE PERIOD BEGINNING JULY 15, 1961 AND ENDING AT MIDNIGHT AUGUST 14, 1961. THE REMAINING $400.00 REPRESENTS THE LAST MONTH'S RENT AND IS NOT TO BE USED EXCEPT AS THE FINAL MONTH'S RENT AT THE TERMINATION OF THIS AGREEMENT. THIS AGREEMENT IS FOR AN INDEFINITE PERIOD OF TIME AND MAY BE EXTENDED BY MUTUAL CONSENT. AT THE TIME THE AGREEMENT IS TO BE TERMINATED KEN MILLS WILL ADVISE LARRY BORENSTEIN IN WRITING, AND AT THAT TIME THE FINAL MONTH'S RENT WILL BE USED FOR THE FINAL MONTH'S OCCUPANCY. IN OTHER WORDS ON THE FIFTEENTH DAY OF EACH MONTH MR. MILLS WILL PAY $400.00 RENT IN ADVANCE UNTIL SUCH TIME AS HE TERMINATES THE AGREEMENT IN WRITING, AT WHICH TIME THE $400.00 DEPOSIT BECOMES RENTAL FOR THE FINAL MONTH.

IN THE EVENT THAT LARRY BORENSTEIN WISHES TO TERMINATE THE AGREEMENT HE MUST GIVE MR. MILLS THIRTY DAYS WRITTEN NOTICE, AT WHICH TIME THE ABOVE MENTIONED $400.00 DEPOSIT WILL BE USED AS RENTAL FOR THAT FINAL MONTH'S OCCUPANCY.

NOTICES TO TERMINATE BY EITHER PARTY MUST OCCUR ON OR BEFORE THE FIFTEENTH OF A MONTH.

WITNESSED BY *Sylvia Shannon*   SIGN *Ken Mills*
SYLVIA SHANNON   KEN MILLS

--- SIGN
LARRY BORENSTEIN
Larry Borenstein

**Original lease agreement for Preservation Hall
between Ken Mills & Larry Borenstein
July 14, 1961**

CITY OF NEW ORLEANS
OFFICE OF THE MAYOR

August 2, 1961

VICTOR H. SCHIRO
MAYOR

Mr. Grayson Mills, President
New Orleans Society
Preservation of Traditional Jazz
726 St. Peter Street
New Orleans, Louisiana

Dear Mr. Mills:

         I was very pleased to learn
of the inception of the newly formed New
Orleans Society, Preservation of Traditional
Jazz.

         Congratulations on having been
named the Society's first president and best
wishes for success to enhance the civic and
cultural activities of the City. Kind, personal regards.

         Sincerely,

         Victor H. Schiro
         Mayor

Letter from Mayor of New Orleans to Ken Mills
Congratulating him on opening of Preservation Hall
August 2, 1961

1963

deceased

JOHNNY CASIMER, Eb clarinet

JAMES "KID" CLAYTON, trumpet

MINOR "RAM" HALL, drums

CHARLIE LOVE, trumpet

ALFRED WILLIAMS, drums

6. The Crusade Begins

I returned to a Connecticut devoid of jazz. Had I been a farmer, I could not have hoped for more virgin soil. I bought a house on Grey Rock Road in Bridgeport. I began a day gig as a draftsman in Stamford, Connecticut. I wasn't planning a crusade, but I was hopeful I could organize a band that would emulate those wonderful hot bands I heard in New Orleans.

A few weeks after my return, I was browsing through the jazz bins in a local music store. I became aware of someone across from me because he seemed to moving along bin by bin opposite me. When I changed aisles he changed too. I looked up to see Bill Sinclair staring at me. Sinclair had been a year or two behind me in high school and seemed to idolized my involvement in jazz. He used to follow me around after school and ask me questions about what records to buy, etc. Once in awhile I would invite him along to Rocky Clark's radio program. Now he was peering at me over a record bin. I still had my Army haircut and I guess he wasn't positive it was me.

"Hey, how are you doing Bill," I asked.

"I thought it was you but I wasn't sure. Where did you disappear to?" he asked.

"Army."

"Have you been doing any playing? Are you still interested in jazz? Do you want to sell your record collection?" The later was a question Bill always asked when he bumped into anyone he knew once collected jazz.

"Yes, yes and no," I replied. "How about you?"

He had been doing a little playing in a local dixie band. He said the band could use a decent drummer. I told him I was interested in starting my own band. I invited him over to my house to hear some of the hundreds of albums I had added to my collection since the last time I saw him. As he browsed, wide-eyed, through my records, I asked him if he would be interested in being co-leader of a New Orleans style band with me.

"Boy, would I!"

"You can take charge of the rhythm section and I'll lead the front line," I suggested.

"What sense does that make?" he replied. "If you're playing drums and I'm playing trombone, it should be the other way around."

I had forgotten that Sinclair played trombone. He had a very forgettable trombone style. I recalled him as a piano player. I hadn't mentioned that I had switched instruments.

"I'm planning a band that I'll play trombone in," I said.

"Trombone? Who taught you to play bone?"

"Jim Robinson."

"Jim Robinson? Come on, stop kidding me."

I told him about my months in New Orleans with Jim and the new kitty halls.

"You know Jim Robinson?" he gasped.

I told him the whole story. When I finished, he said,"I can't believe it. You played with Mile' Barnes. You met Kid Thomas and George Lewis? It's incredible."

As the thought of lessons with Robinson sank in, he agreed that I should be the trombone player without hearing me play a note. Sinclair is essentially a frustrated brass band trombone player of the Chicken Henry school so I suggested that we also have a brass band contingent within the band in which he could blow his horn now and then. He was satisfied with that. He said he had a friend named Noel Kalet who played in the dixie band with him. I said I was hoping to get Bill Connell on clarinet. He remembered how good Connell was but Kalet was his one and only friend.

"Kid Rena recorded with two clarinets," he reminded me.

"Okay let's try it with both. Connell is not very dependable because he has so many other interests. Might be a good idea to have a back-up."

Bob Fargo was an area businessman who had a deep love for New Orleans music. He was the one person I knew who had seen Bunk Johnson at the Stuyvesant Casino in New York. Fargo played trumpet. I approached him about joining the band. He said he would like to do it for fun but he didn't have the confidence to play in public. Fargo recommended Earl Capron for the banjo chair. I didn't know him personally but agreed. We tried out several bass players and drummers with singular lack of success.

Dick McCarthy, an old friend of mine who used to show up now and then at the Rocky Clark show, dropped in to listen to the band one night during a rehearsal. He was a New Orleans jazz fan but his musicianship was limited to fooling around a little with an old albert system clarinet. As we discussed the bass player problem, Fargo mentioned that he owned a string bass. It wasn't a difficult instrument to learn he said. Maybe we could teach someone to play it. All eyes turned towards McCarthy.

"I'll try anything once," he said as he was passed a complimentary beer.

Not knowing what else to do, I started running a classified want ad in the Bridgeport Post. I received a call from an insurance man named Art Pulver who wanted to try out for the drum chair. He liked the music when we played him some recordings. We warned him, and everybody else, that there was no big money potential in the band. It was not a wedding band. Nobody seemed to mind at the time.

Now that we had a band, we needed an audience. I thought Connecticut might be ripe for a jazz club similar to the one in San Antonio. There was one man who could help in this more than anyone else. I phoned Rocky Clark and asked if he would assist us in organizing a club. In addition to his radio program, Rocky was then an editor on the New Haven Register newspaper. If anyone could spread the word and get us maximum free publicity, he was the guy. He liked the idea and agreed to be a member of the governing board. He suggested a few others who might help. He contacted them to fill out the board.

We all got together and quickly discovered that our interests in jazz were wildly divergent. But, what did it matter? The umbrella of the traditional jazz genre could cover us all. Several names for the club were proposed. I suggested the Connecticut Traditional Jazz Club. It was rejected. The New Haven contingent of the board which Rocky had brought aboard thought nobody would understand the term "Traditional Jazz." Some of them didn't. The only way we could sell this club to the public, we were told, was if the word "Dixieland" was in the title. We swallowed hard and agreed to the "Dixieland Society of Southern Connecticut." By adopting this silly name we managed, in a single stroke, to put limits on our club in both geographic area and musical ideology. The club's fate was sealed before the first note had sounded.

I had two other names to invent that would prove to be more important. I decided to record an album of our band. I needed a name for the band and one for my fledgling record company.

We kicked several names around for the band. None seemed right. I started going through my file of song titles hoping for a lead and found it. The old blues "See See Rider" had originally been named the "Easy Rider Blues." It was changed to legitimize it just as "Muscat Ramble," which had been named for the staggering walk one acquired after drinking too much muscat wine, had been changed to the "Muskrat Ramble," which is meaningless. The term "easy rider" derived from the Storyville days in New Orleans. The street whores used the expression to identify their favorite pimps. Gee, that sounds like us I thought. We became the Easy Riders Jazz Band. Little did we know at the time that, within a few years a movie would come out that used the same term corrupted to a totally different meaning. When I selected it, it still had all of the dignity and class that a bunch of top pimps deserved.

I don't even remember the circumstances involved with picking the Jazz Crusade name for my record company. I guess I just picked it. In retrospect, it was certainly appropriate.

Several things became apparent as we proceeded with rehearsals for the album. The most pleasant one was that Dick McCarthy was a natural on the string bass. He had studied piano in his youth; enough so that he could "read" Sinclair's left hand on the keyboard and tell what chord he was playing. Once he learned the fingering positions on the bass, and I had tipped him off to Slow Drag's trick of taping his fingers with adhesive tape so he could "whip" the strings, he was a bass player.

The bad news was that two of our members simply didn't like or understand what we were trying to do musically. Kalet and Capron came to us from strict dixieland backgrounds and the few differences they could detect between dixieland and New Orleans jazz they didn't like. Fair enough. What they liked or didn't like was none of my business. How they played in the Easy Riders Jazz Band was. To their credit both tried, to the best of their ability, to give me the sound I wanted and to a limited degree succeeded in doing so. It was an arrangement that couldn't last and we all knew it. They knew I was looking around and I knew they were.

Pulver liked what he was doing and was making a good effort to learn the music. Fargo, Connell, Sinclair, McCarthy and I certainly had no ideological problems. We loved New Orleans jazz from all periods. We spent many evenings together listening to Johnny Dodds, Bunk, Lewis, Sam Morgan and our other heroes. Elmer "Coo Coo" Talbert was my favorite trumpet player; followed by Kid Thomas, Papa Mutt Carey, Kid Shots Madison and Bunk. I never could make a final choice between Dodds and Lewis on clarinet. I loved them both.

Of all of us, McCarthy was the "mouldiest." The term derived from a caustic review written about a New Orleans jazz record by a critic whose name I have conveniently forgotten. He called the players and fans of the old style "mouldy fyges." Every time anyone in the band suggested playing a tune that hadn't been recorded by Bunk, McCarthy would demand to know why we were "going modern." The favored response to him became, "You are one mouldy bastard, Dick." In the interests of good taste, we dropped the "bastard" in public and he became "Mouldy Dick." Has an almost Herman Melville feel to it don't you think?

We cut the album tape in the unheated cellar of my house in the middle of winter using a recording engineer I plucked out of the Yellow Pages. The sound he got was a disaster but we actually received a few favorable reviews including one in Downbeat magazine.

The Dixieland Society was getting off to a shaky start. The infighting began at once. It was the New Haven Dixielanders vs. the Bridgeport Mouldies. The first few concerts featured white New York dixie guys. We managed to get the Riders on as warm-up band once in awhile. I tried to get the DeParis band to play for us. When I told Wilbur DeParis how much we could afford to pay him, he laughed in my face. Then he got serious and just said no.

I heard from my New Orleans grapevine that the George Lewis band was going to Boston. I called Allan Jaffe. He said he could arrange a stopover for the band in Hamden to do a concert for us at a reasonable price. I brought the proposal to the governing board and the battle raged.

"Look," I said, "this is the whole Lewis band. Lewis, Robinson, Kid Howard, Drag, Joe Watkins, Emanuel Sayles and Charlie Hamilton. There has been nothing like it around here before."

One of the New Haven guys chimed in, "Listen, you start fooling around with these old black guys and you're asking for trouble. Believe me I know. I've played with their kind in New York. You're not going to get people to come out for this kind of thing."

The South might have its problems, I thought, but I never heard this kind of bigotry down there. I replied, "I spent time in New Orleans and this music is beginning to go crazy down there. I think our members will love this band. And maybe we'll start getting some new members."

Fargo started pushing for the concert also. He said, "We were the ones who started this club and we're the ones doing all the work getting out the newsletter. Now I think it's time we did something that we want or I'm getting out."

They caved in. Better to have to sit through a night of black jazz then to have to start pulling their share of the work. The Lewis band came to Hamden, Connecticut. The Riders met their train with our brass band blaring away. They got a kick out of it. Allan and Sandy Jaffe were with them. Once the decision had been made to hire them, Rocky pitched in and did a magnificent PR job for the concert. The restaurant was packed. The concert had a strange, funny beginning. Lewis kicked off with "Chinatown My Chinatown" as the first number. The band sounded horribly out of tune. Suddenly we realized what had happened. Half the band was in one key and half in another. They plugged along, each man trying to figure out what key the others were in. By the end of the first chorus, every one of them knew exactly what to do. And they did it. Going into the second chorus, they ALL changed key! They were right back where they started from and struggled through another chorus in two keys before they finally hit the solos and straightened things out. A third of the audience didn't even notice. Another third smiled an I-told-you-so smile at us. Our third smiled limply back. From then on the band was brilliant for the rest of the evening. Everybody, with the exception of a few disgruntled dixielanders went home very happy indeed.

I invited the band back to my home after the concert. When we arrived I put on a new tape the Riders had just cut for a second album. Each member of the Lewis band listened intently and congratulated his counterpart in the Riders on their performance. They seemed genuinely impressed with the tape. Robinson asked me to send him a copy of the album when released,"and make sure you sign it for me." Were they just being polite? I don't know. And I didn't care, then or now. If you were a young jazz trombonist, and Jim Robinson had just shaken your hand and asked for an autographed copy of your new album, you wouldn't care either.

The liner notes on that album, when released, were written by the Rev. A. L. Kershaw. He was a minister who had just become nationally famous for his appearances on a TV show called The $64,000 Question. It was a quizz show and his topic was jazz. He ran his winnings up to $32,000 and then failed to identify the players in Louis Armstrong's Hot Five. The show suffered an infamous scandal when it was learned that some participants were coached in their answers. Kershaw was never implicated in the scandal in any way.

The Dixieland Society was also able to bring in several British bands. Chris Barber's band gave an outstanding performance one evening after slogging their way through a Connecticut "Nor'Easter" snow storm to arrive an hour late for their concert. Most of the audience was late too for the same reason. We played a hastily thrown together warm-up set as we awaited their arrival.

We also played an intermission set when we had the Terry Lightfoot band from England play for the club. They were proponents of British dixieland. As our set ended and they came back on the bandstand, Lightfoot came over to where Bob Fargo and I were standing. Fargo was a fan of the great English Ken Colyer band. He asked Lightfoot what he thought of the Colyer group.

"We have a hundred bands in England that sound like that," Lightfoot sniffed.

"Really?" Fargo replied. "Why didn't they send us one of them?"

Commendable!-N.Y.Times

An Inspired Group!-N.H.Register

Fine Walloping Ensemble!-Downbeat

Enthusiastic Ensemble Jazz!-High Fidelity Mag.

A Very Fine Band-George Lewis

"JAZZ CRUSADE"

presents the

EASY RIDERS JAZZ BAND

JC-1002 HIGH FIDELITY $4.95pp

A tremendous follow-up to their first JAZZ CRUSADE release

liner notes by The Rev. A. L. Kershaw

WALK THROUGH THE STREETS OF THE CITY

MAKE ME A PALLET ON THE FLOOR

MY LIFE WILL BE SWEETER SOMEDAY

THE BUCKET'S GOT A HOLE IN IT

PRECIOUS LORD, LEAD ME ON

WHEN YOU WORE A TULIP

DON'T GO 'WAY NOBODY

JAZZ CRUSADE

135 Grey Rock Road

Bridgeport, Connecticut, U.S.A.

OVER IN THE GLORYLAND

THE BELLS OF ST. MARY'S

JAZZIN' BABIES BLUES

Advertisement for JAZZ CRUSADE JC-1002
"My Life Will Be Sweeter Someday"
The Easy Riders Jazz Band

1964

deceased

JOE JAMES, piano

ALBERT JILES, drums

BILL MATHEWS, trombone

7.   Tom & Manny In Connecticut

We had all been fans of Ken Colyer since his first London records release in the U.S. I wrote to him asking about obtaining some of his earlier Crane River Jazz Band albums. He graciously sent me an album from that period and suggested Dobell's Record Shoppe as a source for others. We corresponded several times. I sent him our first album and he made some helpful criticisms. Unfortunately these letters were destroyed, along with hundreds of Jazz Crusade albums and other important jazz related papers, in a flooded basement in the 1970's. Therefore, I cannot quote them directly. His comments on the band were forthright, honest and encouraging. That he bothered to respond at all showed the quality of the man to be equal to that of his great band. I tried repeatedly to get Colyer to come to America for a tour with the Riders but he wouldn't leave his band. On one of the albums I received was a new clarinet player who we all went crazy over. His name was Sammy Rimington.

I also began to correspond with another Englishman named Barry Martyn. Mutual friends in New Orleans put me into contact with him. His MONO records were starting to make an impact here in the States. I desperately wanted some New Orleans musicians on my Jazz Crusade label. I wrote Barry asking permission to put out a sampler album featuring some of his unissued material. He agreed and I released the first in my Jazz Renaissance series. In one of his letters he mentioned that he was planning to bring Kid Thomas and Manny Paul to England for their first tour there. I had been thinking about doing an album with a few of the New Orleans musicians who lived in New York joined by members of the Riders. Now I saw an opportunity to do a session with Tom and Manny instead. I wrote Barry and offered to pay their plane fare to New York and book them for a concert and recording session. He readily agreed as it helped defray some of his transportation costs for them and gave Tom and Manny some extra work. He contacted Thomas and got his permission. I called Tom also to refresh his memory of meeting me in New Orleans.

In the meantime, I released the second ERJB album. By the time we taped it, Bill Connell had gone back to his other top interest of playing tennis and Capron had been replaced by a new banjo player, Dave Duquette, who would last an even shorter time than Earl had. Other than that, the personnel stayed as it had been on the first album.

Soon there were other personnel changes. Bob Fargo, for all his love of the music was unable to overcome the stress he felt playing in public. There was just something about it that got to him and he would freeze every time he made a public appearance. Terminal stage fright. He decided he could not continue with the band. We would sorely miss him.

Sinclair was having the time of his life playing New Orleans jazz and looking forward to meeting and playing with some of his idols. Then he received a job offer he just couldn't refuse: he was drafted. Not only that but he was to report for duty before Tom and Manny arrived. If you think he took it hard, you should have seen Mouldy Dick.

"What the hell am I gonna do without your left hand to read?" he demanded.

Even though Sinclair's loss would be temporary, if you can call two years in the life of a band temporary, it raised more immediate problems than did Fargo's leaving. We needed a piano player for the Thomas/Paul concert and recording. I asked my old friend and former bandleader Bud Larson if he would help us out. Bud had turned away from New Orleans jazz and was fronting a modern jazz group on valve trombone. The idea of playing piano with Kid Thomas did not appeal to him. He reminded me that he was not a trained pianist. He had learned just enough on the instrument to help him with his arranging.

"That's alright," I said, "All I need is your left hand." He consented.

I still needed a permanent trumpet player so I put another classified ad in the Bridgeport Post. It amazes me that this always worked. You put an ad in the Help Wanted section that says something like: WANTED; TRUMPET PLAYER FOR NEW ORLEANS STYLE JAZZ BAND. WE WILL TRAIN YOU IN THE STYLE. LITTLE OR NO MONEY. LOTS OF FUN. PHONE...... and your phone rings off the hook for a month with applicants. It has worked every time I tried it. This time I got more than I bargained for. The first call I received wasn't even from a trumpet player.

"Hello my name's Dick Griffith, 'Griff' for short. I'm calling about the ad you have in the paper. The one about the trumpet player."

"How long have you been playing trumpet, Griff?"

"I don't."

"Don't what?"

"Play trumpet."

My eyes started to glaze over. "If you don't play trumpet, why are you answering my ad. Do you answer ads as a hobby or something?"

"No. No. Listen. I play banjo. I have a band here in Huntington. The Jada Jazz Band. I thought you guys might like to drop over and jam with us."

I thought I knew every traditional jazz band in Connecticut but this was a new one on me. He seemed friendly enough. Besides, maybe I could steal his trumpet player while we were there. Both of our bands rehearsed on the same evening so I told him we would be over.

The next call held more promise. It was from a young trumpeter named Fred Vigorito.

"Are you a jazz fan?" I asked.

"I haven't really heard much jazz," he replied.

"What made you call?"

"My mother made me call," he said.

Oh great. What next? First a banjo player I never heard of and now a kid whose mother wants him to be the next Louis Armstrong. I needed a trumpet man really badly. I made arrangements for him to try out for the band. He became our next trumpet player.

I took the whole band, including Fargo, who was staying on until we found his replacement, over to Griffith's house. His band was about what I expected it to be. But he wasn't. He was a big guy about Robinson's size. Older than the rest of us. And one hell of a banjo player. He had never heard any New Orleans jazz before and we bowled him over. Before the night was over, he and I stepped into the kitchen to talk things over. I wanted him in the Riders from the minute I heard him play but we still had our other banjo player to contend with.

"Look, Griff," I said, "I just can't fire this guy no matter how badly I want you. You have to understand that. But I'll add you to the rhythm section right now if you don't mind playing for awhile with two banjo players."

"How's that going to go down with your other guy.? I don't think he's going to be too happy with me sitting beside him."

"I hope and trust your right."

By the time Kid Thomas arrived, Griff was our sole banjo player. Our other man gave us a lesson we would never forget and quit. With the addition of Griff and Fred, the band's personnel stabilized for the next year and a half.

We had one final hurdle to clear regarding the Thomas/Paul dates. We had to sell them to the Dixieland Society. To help do that I brought a few of their recordings to the board meeting. It was a mistake. The New Haven gang savaged them both upon hearing the records.

"What are you people trying to put over on us?," one of them screamed. "These guys don't play dixieland or anything like it! They're worse than that Lewis mob!"

"Well they're coming!" I shouted back, "and you damn well better book them!"

The club finally did take them but we knew it was the end of the line for our involvement with the club. In little more than a year the club collapsed.

The Dixieland Society concert was held at Frankie's Villa Pompeii restaurant in Orange. As before, Rocky Clark, while siding with the New Haven gang at the board meeting, did a masterful job of promotion. It takes a gentleman to put aside your feelings and dig in and work for something you oppose. Rocky is such a gentleman.

Nevertheless, the concert was not a financial success because others who were not as gentlemanly did not join in to help and, instead, urged members to stay away. There was a big and enthusiastic crowd but not enough to turn a profit. None of this prevented those who came from having a great time.

Jack Guckin was a television producer at WTIC-TV in Hartford. He was also a New Orleans jazz fan and a personal friend. He had televised two specials with the Easy Riders on his station. He offered to engineer the Thomas/Paul recording session at the television sound studio after hours. Thus we would have access to the latest state-of-the-art audio for our first important recording. I only had the money to record five tracks at musician union scale. I decided to fill out the album using Vigorito on trumpet on a few additional tracks.

We arrived at the studio ready to cut the first album ever to feature Kid Thomas or Manny Paul with a white band. We began with the old marching tune "Joe Avery's Piece," which Kid Thomas called "Victory Walk." Manny said he would like to bring it in with a tenor solo. We did two takes to have a safety but we used the first of the two on the album. We then did several takes each on "Eh! La Bas," "I Can't Escape From You" and "Just A Closer Walk With Thee." On "Closer Walk," we discussed whether to do it fast or slow. When we couldn't decide, McCarthy with his usual wit said, "Why not do it the way we do everything else. . . half-fast." We did it at the same tempo as the famous George Lewis Climax session version.

We bogged down on our final number with Tom and Manny. "In the Mood" was the tune I wanted most because Tom's unusual slow tempo arrangement of it had never been recorded. There is a triple ending on it similar to the Glenn Miller one where the drummer brings the band back in after a false ending. Pulver just couldn't get the timing right. We did it four times only to have it all fall apart at the ending. Tom was getting visibly angry. It was the first time I ever saw his lower jaw jut out. I was to learn that that was Tom's unconscious way of voicing displeasure. I was to see it many times again over the years. We tried doing just the ending a few more times hoping that we might be able to splice together a usable track at the editing stage. It was futile. We scrapped the tune.

We cut the additional tracks with Fred while Tom and Manny watched and listened. Tom congratulated Fred on his first recording. We used Bud Larson on the album as we had on the concert gig. He did a credible job. At the editing stage we discovered we did not have a good complete take of "Eh! La Bas." Guckin suggested we splice the best parts of two takes together for a final mix. As a rule I do not like to fiddle with a jazz band's taped product but, in this case, it was "cut it or shut it." We cut it.

Jazz Crusade had its fourth album in the can and it was an important recording; even an historic one. Stop and think for a moment. One of the rarest of events in recorded jazz history up to and including this recording is that event where a noted black jazzman recorded with a group of young white musicians. Ferd "Jelly Roll" Morton did it first in the early 1920s with the New Orleans Rhythm Kings. I don't believe it happened again until Bunk Johnson cut those sides with Lu Watters' Yerba Buena Jazz Band in 1944. Then Sidney Bechet made some recordings with Bob Wilbur's Bobcats. And in the 1950s George Lewis made some excellent sides with Dick Oxtot and Conrad Janis did some with Freddie Moore at the beginning of his career. That's all I can think of in America until this Kid Thomas session with the Easy Riders. We are talking about the entire recorded history of jazz from day one. But the Thomas recording with us opened a floodgate of such recordings all around the world. Within a year or two the New Orleans musicians were recording with every good, and sometimes bad, band that sent for them. Our band in America and Barry Martyn's in England started this trend which added a new element to jazz recording.

ONE NIGHT ONLY!!
DIRECT FROM NEW ORLEANS

✦✦

KID THOMAS &
MANUEL PAUL

Featured With

The
EASY RIDERS JAZZ BAND

Tuesday, May 19,1964 at Frankie's•Villa Pompeii

551 Post Road, Orange, Ct. Exit 39 (east) Conn. Tnpke.

8:00 P.M. - MIDNIGHT

presented by the
DIXIELAND SOCIETY OF SOUTHERN CONNECTICUT

a **JAZZ CRUSADE** booking   **Donation $2.00**

Autographed Poster
First Kid Thomas/Manny Paul tour of Connecticut.
May, 1964

Thomas, Paul To Play
For Dixieland Society

By ROCKY CLARK

Two of the most colorful jazz pioneers from New Orleans will perform at the season's final session of the Dixieland Society of Southern Connecticut on Tuesday night, May 19, at Frankie's Villa Pompeii in Orange. Trumpeter "Kid" Thomas and saxist Emanuel Paul will play for the DSSC on the eve of their first world tour.

The Easy Riders Jazz Band, a group of DSSC members who specialize in oldtime New Orleans style jazz, will accompany the New Orleans veterans who, following the concert, will leave for England where they will tour the British "trad" groups. After that, they will cross the European continent, appearing at various jazz concerts, and continue on to Japan for further appearances.

Kid Thomas — his real name is Thomas Valentine — was born in 1896 in a New Orleans suburb, Reserve, La. His father played trumpet in the Picquit Brass Band, and young Thomas delighted in raiding the band's storage room with his friends and trying out the various instruments.

Through the years Thomas became leader of the hardest-driving New Orleans jazz band since Bunk Johnson. His band is featured on two of the historic Riverside "Living Legends" albums of New Orleans jazz.

With Eureka Band

Emanuel Paul has been the featured saxophonist with the famed Eureka Brass Band, last of the famous bands that perform in the traditional Negro funeral processions in New Orleans. Their story is well known —how they march slowly to the graveyard playing dirges; then, after the burial, the band returns exultantly with booming bass drum and oocompahing tuba as a long line of enthusiasts fall in behind, swining in rhythm beneath brightly colored parasols.

Some of America's finest jazz has been born in these bands returning from a graveyard . . . tunes like "Oh Didn't He Ramble," "Joe Avery's Blues," "Just a Little While to Stay Here," and so on.

In a recent Associated Press feature on the Eureka band, Emanuvel Paul expressed his views on the origin of the funeral bands. He thinks they were started by undertakers who thought that if a band was marching in front of the cortege, the horses hauling the hearse couldn't trot and thus wouldn't wear out as fast.

Paul's sax work can be heard to good advantage in the recent LP by the Eureka band in Atlantic's "Jazz at Preservation Hall" series. Paul and Kid Thomas have both been featured at Preservation Hall in New Orleans' French Quarter where the old-style traditional jazz is performed nightly by surviving pioneers of this gay brand of music.

* * *

The Photo Artistry of

Don Moore

Don Moore has been involved with photography for over 40 years. He was a member of the production staff at WTIC-TV in Hartford, Ct., where he would photograph special moments with guests during live productions. During the Sixties, his love of New Orleans jazz, combined with the station's policy of featuring many jazz programs, enabled him to take the memorable photos featured in this section.

In 1972, Don and his family moved to the coast of Maine where he has directed and photographed several award winning documentary & wildlife films for television and the home video market. Someday, he plans to weave his stills with live footage into an intimate look at New Orleans jazz of the Sixties.

Victoria Spivey

Willie Humphrey

Kid Thomas Valentine

Kid Thomas Valentine

Booker T Glass

Manny Paul

Billie Pierce

DeDe Pierce

Peter Bocage

Percy Humphrey

George Lewis

Big Jim Robinson

Sammy Rimington

Big Bill Bissonnette, Kid Thomas, Sammy Rimington

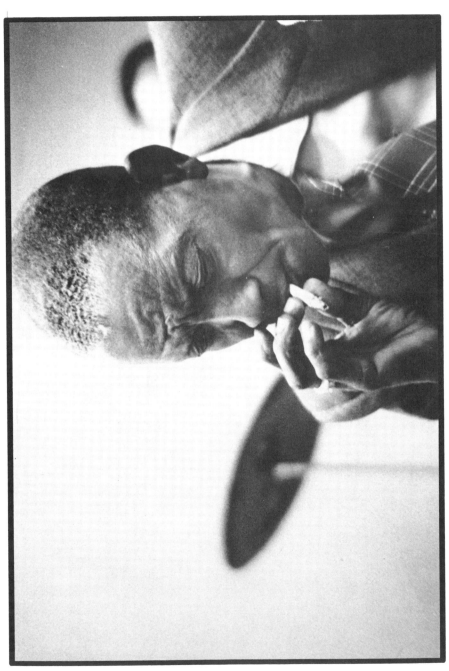

Kid Thomas Valentine

8.   The International Jazz Band

The Dixieland Society dissolved into two clubs. Those of us who loved New Orleans jazz started the Connecticut Traditional Jazz Club. Now we could concentrate on promoting our music. And a good opportunity to do so was at hand.

As part of the deal Martyn and I made to get Thomas and Paul to Connecticut, I also agreed to sponsor an exchange bringing Barry and Ken Colyer's young clarinetist Sammy Rimington to the States for a tour. Rimington's reputation preceded him in the form of several albums he made with Colyer and in a session I was releasing on Jazz Crusade which featured him, along with Martyn's rhythm section, playing a collection of George Lewis standards.

Still, the Brits were not sufficiently known here to carry the kind of tour that would be necessary to cover the costs of bringing them over. As the Thomas and Paul concert had been a one shot deal and as I was getting ready to release the album they had done with us, I decided to invite them back to give some "star value" to the tour.

The financial hurdles were imposing. The new jazz club was predicated on a policy of very low membership fees and higher concert prices. Therefore, there was little money in the club treasury to provide upfront costs. If the worst case scenario occurred, that being no audience shows up for any jazz club concerts, I felt sure all the members of the band except Tom and Manny would forego any payment for the gigs. But that still left all of the transportation costs and the salaries for the two New Orleans guests. A considerable sum.

Of course I planned to record one of the concerts for a Jazz Crusade album. It was to be my first attempt at recording a "live" performance. A recording engineer had been recommended to me. His name was Michael Fast. He would become Jazz Crusade's permanent recording engineer and was responsible for the outstanding sound on most of the Jazz Crusade releases.

In addition to the CTJC concerts and my recording, I would still have to come up with more work for the band to break even. With help from other club officials and friends, I booked three additional gigs. It was still not enough and time was running out. There was one possible solution. I could try to sell another recording session.

The major record label featuring traditional jazz in the U.S.A. in 1964, as it is today, was George H. Buck Jr.'s Jazzology/GHB. Buck's catalogue was already extensive and growing all the time. I had just concluded an agreement with him for an album by the famous 1920's blues singer and movie actress Victoria Spivey accompanied by the Easy Riders Jazz Band, our first for a label other than Jazz Crusade. We were scheduled to record it shortly after the tour by the group I was now billing as the International Jazz Band.

I phoned George about the possibility of him buying a concert recording of the band. He said he was interested but he wanted to know if I was going to record them also for Jazz Crusade. He said that would lower his interest considerably for two reasons: first, he felt it might be overexposure of the band and, secondly, he was justifiably concerned about how I would select which session he would get and which I would keep. As an acceptable solution to the second problem, I proposed that we each select a specific date for our recordings in advance. In that way it would be Lady Luck who decided which of us might get a better session. That satisfied him on that point but he was still concerned about the overexposure matter. I could feel my session slipping away like quicksilver through my fingers. I finally agreed to do only one recording of the band. And that one would be for GHB. It was the first, but not the last, time I had to give up a Jazz Crusade recording for financial reasons. In fact, it would happen over and over again during the next few years. At least they were going onto a well distributed and respected label. My relationship with George Buck permitted me to do many recording sessions I would otherwise been unable to do.

With the GHB record deal made, I felt sure I had the backing necessary to go ahead with the International Jazz Band tour. The tour would begin with a CTJC concert on July 17, 1964 and end fourteen days later in Montreal, Canada with a gig Barry booked.

Bill Sinclair wanted to play on this tour and the Spivey recording session. He was stationed in Germany but he had requested a one month leave. He was due home on July 15th. The personnel of the International Jazz Band would be: Kid Thomas, trumpet; Manny Paul, tenor sax, Sammy Rimington, clarinet; Bill Bissonnette, trombone; Dick Griffith, banjo; Dick McCarthy, string bass; Bill Sinclair, piano and Barry Martyn, drums.

The CTJC made up a single flyer to announce all three of their concerts. All three were to be held at new locations untried by the club before. I had to decide which one of the three I wanted to record. I decided to record the second of the three dates. That way the band would have at least three opportunities to play together prior to the recording and, if anything went radically wrong, we could possibly have one more shot at a recording on the last CTJC date. Two days before the first concert, we had done all that could be done to insure the success of the tour. I sat back and waited for things to go wrong. I didn't have to wait long.

The day before the first gig I received a telegram from Sinclair that his leave had been delayed for up to two days because of a military concert he had to play in Germany. He would not be home until Saturday, July 18th. I placed an urgent call to Bud Larson. He agreed to play the first CTJC job.

Manny Paul never cared much for flying so he and Thomas decided to take the train from New Orleans to New York. They were then going to take a bus to Bridgeport. They would arrive late in the afternoon of the 16th. Thomas missed the train. He called me and said they would take the next one out but wouldn't arrive until the next day. . . the day of the first concert. They called me the day of the concert from Grand Central Station to tell me they had arrived and their bus was leaving for Bridgeport. The next call from Thomas was to tell me that the bus had broken down. It was almost 4:00 p.m. and they hadn't gotten out of New York yet.

The concert was scheduled for 8:30 p.m. at the Yankee Silversmith Inn in Wallingford, about an hour drive from my house. Once the bus got on its way again it made good time and was in Bridgeport before 6:00 p.m. Tom called again to say they had arrived. In order to save time I told him to grab a cab to my house on Grey Rock Road while we packed the cars with our equipment. That way they might at least have a few minutes to grab a sandwich at my place before heading out for the job. A half hour later they still hadn't arrived. The phone finally rang again. It was Tom telling me that they were at Grey Rock Road and nobody there ever heard of me! He put the owner of the house on the line who told me he was at Gray Rock Road in the town of Fairfield. Mouldy Dick jumped into his car and retrieved them.

Fortunately there had been no travel problems with Barry and Sammy. They were settled in and ready to play. We were to meet Griff and Bud at the Silversmith. Mouldy pulled in with the two beleaguered New Orleans musicians. We gave them food to eat on the way and we were off to Wallingford.

We arrived just in time to set up and get started. I was gratified to see the place was so full that they had to open a second dining room which adjoined the main one to handle the overflow. The restaurant's young owner, Robert Atwood Myer, had gone out of his way to help with our promotion of the event. He had not even required a rental fee or minimum bar tab. He put up posters in his public dining room notifying his regular clientele of the concert. A considerable number of them joined the club as they entered.

As the band assembled on the bandstand to begin, Mouldy came over to me and said we would have to wait a few minutes more before starting.

Without even thinking to ask him why, I waved him back to his bass saying that we were running late enough and it was time to begin. He went back and picked up his bass.

Our emcee for the tour, Jack Guckin, started us into the "Introduction Blues, a musical device we sometimes "borrowed" from Billie and DeDe's Preservation Hall Jazz Band. As each bandsman was introduced by name he would begin to play, joining those already announced. We learned quickly, to our delight, we had what we called an "up crowd." The solid and loud reception they gave each band member assured the success of the concert. We whipped into "Hindustan," Tom's favorite opener. During Manny's third or fourth solo chorus, Mouldy Dick stopped playing, lay down his bass and walked off the stage! He weaved through the packed tables to the hallway and walked into the Men's Room. Manny didn't know what to make of it. About halfway through my solo, he sauntered back into the room to the cheers and laughter of the audience and band members. Up he came onto the stage and started playing again just as if nothing had happened. At the end of the song I called him over.

"Well," he said over the mike, "I told you to wait for a minute before we started. When you gotta go, you gotta go." He got another round of cheers.

On future gigs when Mouldy told me to wait, I waited.

Our second concert was an outdoor event for the Milford Jaycees. We were to perform a two hour family concert in the Milford bandshell. Sinclair had arrived from Germany so the advertised band was now intact. Admission to the concert was free. It would have been a lot of fun except it turned out to be one of the hottest days of the year. After the first one hour set, we were all covered with perspiration. On the break I sat on the grass beside Thomas.

"I'm really sorry about this heat Tom," I said.

"Don't pay it no mind, Bill. It's the same old soupbone."

I didn't understand the remark and asked him what he meant."

He replied, "What it means, Bill, is everything's always the same in life. Nothing changes. You can put it in the soup today, make stew with it tomorrow, bake it the next day. . . but, it's the same old soupbone."

We had a couple of days off before the next concert. It gave us a chance to get to know each other. None of us had ever met Barry or Sammy before. Sinclair had not met Tom and Manny, or any other New Orleans musician for that matter. On one of these evenings we went to Savin Rock, an amusement park filled with thrill rides. Tom and I were not about to get on a roller coaster but the others, led by Manny Paul, proceeded to take on every hair-raising ride in the place. Sammy loved them all. When he would get off of one that was particularly thrilling, he would run over to me and Tom and yell, "You must try it. It's diabolical!" They finally talked us into going on one ride with them. It was called the Watercoaster. It was only a short ride. Seated in a roller-coaster like car, you went through a dark tunnel, up one steep hill and then down the other side into a water filled trough at the bottom. They stuck me and Tom in the front seat and off we all went. As we climbed the hill, I glanced at Kid Thomas. He sat there staring straight ahead, his jaw set like it was sculpted. Over the top and down we rushed. An impact wave splashed over us and drenched us both. As we wiped ourselves off, with everyone laughing at the soaked Living Legend, Tom finally cracked his jaw and smiled.

"Shoot man, that wasn't nothin'."

On Wednesday, July 22nd, we played a job for a church group in Westbrook, over an hour's drive from home. We took three cars. When we arrived, Barry came over.

"Bill, have you got my drums in your car?"

"No," I replied, "they were in Griff's van weren't they?"

"They're not in there."

The drums were nowhere to be found. I was afraid we would have to do the job without Barry. Then Griff got an idea. This was a school auditorium wasn't it? Maybe there was a band room. We found the janitor who reluctantly led us to the band room. From the marching band drum equipment Barry managed to jury rig a drum set. He used big practice sticks and had to kick the bass drum with his toe but he got by very well, thank you.

We got home very late from the post-gig party and there, on the front lawn, sat Barry's forgotten drum set.

The next evening was the second CTJC concert. This one was at the Actor's Colony Inn. It was the one to be recorded. Mike Fast was already there when we arrived. He had the stage miked and was ready for a balance check. We had plenty of time and we ran through a tune for him until he was satisfied with the levels. We had decided to eat at the inn that night so we sat down to a light supper and watched for the crowd to appear. It never did.

Few things are more disappointing to anyone in the music business than to be faced with a small turnout. But here it was staring us in the face. I could hardly believe it. One of the reasons I had picked this concert for the recording was because I thought we would pull a big crowd to it. By starting time there were only a few dozen fans in the dining room. It was a massive room which made it look like even less. If it hadn't been for the recording, we could have packed up and gone home. Why this one concert flopped I don't know. It might have been because it was midweek. Perhaps the restaurant was too far off the beaten track. Whatever the reason, we were stuck with it now. The recorder was ready to roll.

The musical results of the concert are well documented on the two record set that was issued of the performance on GHB. Despite the low turnout, the band played fairly well but, if those fans who like that recording could have heard the Yankee Silversmith concert, they would be amazed at the difference a good crowd made in that band.

There is a personal aside I should interject about that recording. I hadn't used any sort of nickname since my teenage days when I played drums under the name Bill Cozy (after Cozy Cole). And if I had used one, the last one I would have had the gumption to use would be "Big Bill," implying as it does a comparison to my mentor Big Jim Robinson.

On a friendly whim, Jack Guckin introduced me on the blues opener as Big Bill Bissonnette. I was stunned. I even thought about redoing the opener at the beginning of the second set and told Jack so. He said, "Don't worry about it Big Bill. Jim won't mind a bit." To add to my embarrassment, George Buck spelled it out on the album cover. Later on, after Jim had heard about it and started calling me by the name also, I felt better and better about it. But it was Jack Guckin who was to blame.

There was a little more excitement that night. It should be remembered that all of the Riders held full time jobs all during the 1960's. Working day after day and playing night after night took its toll on all of us. After the concert, as Mouldy Dick was driving Thomas home, he fell asleep at the wheel. As the car swerved off the road, Kid Thomas yelled, "MOULDY!" Dick snapped awake and got the car back under control. Thomas never uttered a word about it again after that night. He also never rode with Mouldy Dick again. After he dropped Thomas off at my house, Mouldy drove home and turned off his ignition. He awoke the next morning still in his car.

Manny Paul snores. No, that is not sufficient. Manny Paul's snoring was a thing of awe, if not beauty. The first time he and Thomas came to town, I put them both in the same bedroom. As they were only to stay over for two nights, there was no problem and Tom put up with it. But when I called Tom about the International Jazz Band tour, the first thing out of his mouth was that he would not share a bedroom with Manny. I understood. Even sleeping at the far end of the house, Manny's barrage came through the walls like a jet breaking the sound barrier. I tried to stick him on Barry. No luck. Barry had already found out the hard way in England. Poor Manny was nonplussed about his ordeal. I finally bought a studio bed and put it in my basement room. There encased in 12" cement blocks underground, Manny, and the rest of us could sleep in peace.

A problem was brewing about an upcoming job. Jack Guckin had arranged for the International Jazz Band to play a concert in Hartford for the Unity Charity Church Association, a black congregation. As the publicity for the gig started to build, the minister of the church called Jack to tell him that a militant faction within the church was calling for a boycott of the concert and attacking the minister for scheduling a racially mixed band for the concert. At one point the minister even suggested that he should cancel the concert. Jack pointed out to him that there had been good press coverage of the event and that a good turnout could be expected even without the support of the black separatist faction. The minister agreed. Jack thought the problem was solved.

Unknown to us, as we finished up our last weekend jobs for the jazz club, the Unity Church situation was deteriorating. We arrived at the Hartford High School auditorium looking forward to a concert during which we planned to mix in many of the wonderful black spirituals from the South. Guckin met us as we arrived.

"Listen, Bill," Jack warned me, "there may be a big problem here. These separatist guys have gotten together and are planning to picket the theater. How do you think that is going to go down with Tom and Manny?"

"I don't think there will be a problem with them," I replied. "But let's not say anything about it and hope for the best. How effective do you think the picketing will be?"

"It doesn't look good but the advance ticket sale has been pretty good. But I don't know what people are going to do when faced by a picket line."

I decided it would be better to not mention the situation to any of the bandsmen. We were going to play the gig no matter what happened anyway. I didn't see any point in making a bad situation worse. As the band prepared to start, I peeked through the closed curtains. The auditorium was about a quarter filled. It was a big place so the crowd looked smaller than it was. But looking down aisle after aisle, I did not see one black face in the audience. The boycott was an obvious success. The band went on as scheduled and received a warm response from those in attendance. However, I noticed that Jack Guckin introduced the band, not the minister as originally planned.

We didn't meet the minister until after the concert. As we were breaking down the equipment and awaiting our payment, Jack came over and said the minister wanted to see the whole band in his office at the church. Jack and I thought he just wanted to congratulate the band on its good performance and pay us. We were wrong. He did want Tom and Manny there in particular, but not to congratulate them.

We drove to the church and parked in the minister's little parking lot behind the church hall. We were ushered into a large, dimly lit office. There were chairs pulled around a massive wood desk behind which sat the minister. He waved us into the chairs and, with no cordialities or small talk, launched into a speech about how he had tried to cancel the concert when word of the boycott reached him. He related how he had been talked out of it by Guckin. He talked on about the picket line out front and how his poor church was now being strapped with a huge expense because of our insistence on going through with the concert. He was, he said, in danger of being ousted as minister because of us. His eyes passed repeatedly from Tom to Manny as he spoke. Finally he said he could not afford to pay the band for the gig!

I realized as soon as he started this fire and brimstone sermon that I had made a monumental mistake in not briefing the band about the events leading up to this incredible outburst. None of our men, save Jack and me, knew what the hell he was talking about. They were hearing all of this for the first time slanted exactly the way the minister wanted it. They looked at me in wonder. Tom's lower jaw jutted out. Manny and Sammy seemed totally mystified. Barry and Griff sized the situation up immediately and saw the scam coming.

My thoughts raced. Where would the loss of this money put me on the balance sheet? Would I still be able to pay the band if I lost it? I could hold him to the contract of course, but how would Tom and Manny react if I went to the mat with this guy and insisted on payment right now as agreed? That was the question alright: how would Tom and Manny react? It was obvious to me why the minister insisted on their being there. He thought he could appeal to their racial consciousness to swing the tide in favor of my deferring payment. Had it worked? If there was one thing I did not want to do, it was to alienate Tom and Manny. I kept glancing at them as the minister talked to see if I could pick up any clue that might reveal their feelings. Tom's jutting jaw proved he was pissed. But at whom? Me or the minister? I caved.

"You know sir," I said, "we have had an expense here also. I don't think it is fair for you to expect us to play for nothing because some of your people undermined the concert."

He was ready for me. "Well, I understand that of course. I am prepared to give you some compensation for your trip up here."

Jack spoke up, "there were quite a few people out there tonight. I don't see how you could have lost any money."

The minister retorted, "well there were a lot of expenses that you don't know about. I'm not going back to my congregation and tell them you wouldn't cooperate and left us holding the bag. I will give you one half of the money we agreed to and that's all. Take it or leave it gentlemen."

Well there it was. Half a loaf. Sounded almost Biblical. For half of the money I could get out of this mess. I could still pay the band and it wouldn't break the budget. And at least Tom and Manny would know that I tried to work it out with the minister so that he and his church wouldn't get stuck "holding the bag."

I took the money and the minister finally decided it was time to tell us he really enjoyed the concert. We walked out into the darkened parking lot. As the guys climbed into the vehicles, Tom walked over to me. "Bill, man, I wants to talk to you in private. Come over here with me."

He led me over to a big car parked in the lot. He looked angry. I wondered if I had made a bad situation worse by not writing off all of the money. Tom was a God-fearing and moral man and maybe felt I should have gone along with the minister's first request. I decided before he spoke that I would walk back into the office and hand over the rest of the money if it would placate Tom.

He was angry. But not at me. "You see this car? It's a brand new Cadillac, Bill. You see those plates on it? Those are clergy plates, man. Shoot, Bill, that man just took you good. He's got plenty of money to pay for what he bought."

I was astonished. "Tom, I felt he should make good too. I did what I did because I didn't want to offend you or Manny because of it being a black church."

"What's that got to do with it, man? What's that got to do with it? You done your job. You does your job in this life Bill and you gets your pay. That's the way it is Bill. Shoot, I'm surprised at you talking stuff like that. You think he don't collect his pay every week? He does for sure. And a new Cadillac to boot!"

We climbed into the car and headed for home. I learned a lesson from Kid Thomas that night I would never forget. It was one of many of life's lessons I learned from my black New Orleans friends.

This was the end of the Connecticut tour for the International Jazz Band. We broke even on it. The new Connecticut Traditional Jazz Club made enough to continue as a club. We made a recording which would ultimately end up as a two record set. Jazz Crusade didn't get a session. All in all, it was an ambitious undertaking that turned out alright. We had met Barry Martyn and Sammy Rimington face to face. Meeting Sammy was an event that would have long range implications for both the American and European jazz scene. And we still had one more gig to play. Our one and only venture into Canada.

Barry and Sammy flew to Montreal to make last minute arrangements for the gig Barry booked for us. Four more of us were going to drive up. Griff and Mouldy were not going because of their day gig commitments. Thomas, Paul, Sinclair and I all squeezed into my little four-seater Corvair and set off for the border several hundred miles distant. It was around midnight when we reached the border crossing point. Normally there is nothing easier than crossing between the U.S. and Canada. It is the longest unguarded border in the world. Usually you are asked where you are going and if you are carrying any contraband. Then off you go.

We were all tired and edgy by the time we arrived. That may account for our problems. We passed through the U.S. customs station with no hassle. The guard on the Canadian side asked where we were going.

"Montreal," I said.

"Purpose of visit?

"We're members of a jazz band. We're playing at a jazz club there tomorrow night," I bragged.

That was exactly the wrong answer. "Where are your work papers?" the guard asked.

"Oh, it's not a job like that. We are just doing a gig with some friends. We'll be going back to the U.S. right after we do this one concert."

"You can't work in Canada without work papers. Where are you fellows from?"

I replied, "This guy and I are from Connecticut. The other two are from New Orleans."

"Not me," Thomas chimed in, "I'm from Algiers."

"Algiers?" responded the guard, "You aren't an American?"

"Sure I'm American, Man!" Thomas replied.

"I thought you said you were from Algiers," the guard said.

I could sense things were not going well. "Algiers is a town in Louisiana," I said.

"Let's see your passports."

None of us had passports with us. They are not a requirement to pass between the U.S. and Canada.

"How about birth certificates?" the guard asked.

"Shoot, man, I don't even have a birth certificate," Thomas replied.

"Park your car over there and come inside," the guard ordered.

We still had a long drive ahead of us and this guy was about to break our stones. On the way in I whispered to Thomas, "Tom, don't say anything more. Let me handle this please."

Tom said, "sure Bill."

I spoke to the guard. "Look this is no big deal. Why can't you just let us go through and we'll be back in the U.S. tomorrow?"

I spent over an hour trying to explain how simple all of this was while another guard went through our luggage piece by piece. He pulled an article from Tom's bag.

"What's this thing?" the guard barked at Thomas.

"That's a slapstick, man. Ain't you never seen no slapstick before?"

The interrogation centered on Thomas, the black Algerian. They asked him his nationality. I almost fell over when he replied, "Creole." If Tom is Creole, I'm Chinese.

Barry had given me a phone number to call in Montreal when we arrived. I asked if I could call my friend who might be able to clear this thing up. They granted me permission. Barry was not there. I told the party who answered what the problem was and asked to have Barry call back. After an hour, we still had not heard from him. We had to get some sleep. I finally told the guards we would return to the U.S. and come back in the morning.

We threw our stuff back into the car and headed back across the "no man's land" between the two countries hoping to find a motel. When we pulled into the U.S. customs station, we were immediately pulled over and invited inside. Oh no! Not again. Apparently the Canadians called the Americans about the suspicious characters who were on the way. We went through the whole business again. We showed them driver's licenses and other forms of I.D. but they would not let us back into the U.S.!

"Listen, we have to get some sleep. Can't we go to a motel and try this all again tomorrow? I pleaded.

"There are no motels around here."

"Do you have some bunks or something here we can sleep on?" I asked.

"No. You'll have to sleep in your car."

My little Corvair coupe? It was just about big enough for us to sit in. We had no choice. We went back out to the car. Thomas was fuming mad. He didn't even get into the car. He paced up and down outside until the sun rose. Unfortunately for Sinclair and I, Manny went right to sleep and the stillness of two countries was shattered by the magnificent wail of his snoring.

The next morning, we took another crack at the border. We drove up to Canadian customs. A different guard greeted us. We tried to bluff our way through as tourists but he knew who we were.

"You're the fellows who caused the commotion last night, aren't you?"

I guessed we were.

"We got a call this morning from the mayor's office in Montreal to let you chaps through. You must have friends in high places. Enjoy Canada."

Yea. Right.

Barry must have pulled some strings because we were on our way again. . . until my fan belt broke, the car overheated and we spent an hour at a garage while they fixed it. Well, no day is perfect.

We finally made it to Montreal. It was worth the trip and the trouble. We played for a marvelous, young dancing crowd. Of all the jobs we did with the International Jazz Band, Kid Thomas liked this one best. It was the dancing that did it for him. After a good nights sleep, we drove back to Connecticut. Barry and Sammy returned home to England from Canada. And the International Jazz Band was history.

For all the headaches, the International Jazz Band tour was both a musical success and a watershed for the Jazz Crusade. There would be no turning back from my goals now. I had irrevocably decided that I wanted to be a part of this music's heritage. As long as that fire burned within me, I would focus all of my abilities on studying it and the men who played it. I was no longer an observer. I wouldn't quit now until I became one of them.

Not like them. One of them.

JAZZ CONCERT

featuring

THE

INTERNATIONAL JAZZ BAND

The World's Foremost Traditional Jazzmen

Assembled From Over 24,000 Miles!!

from New Orleans: from England:

KID THOMAS -trumpet   **BARRY "KID" MARTYN**
(Direct From His Record-Breaking   (England's Leading Jazz Drummer)
World Tour)

EMANUEL PAUL   **SAMMY RIMINGTON**
(Tenor Man With The Famous   (Clarinetist With Ken Colyer's Jazzmen,
"Eureka Brass Band")   England's Leading Traditional Band)
also:

Bill Bissonnette Trombone,   Bill Sinclair Piano
Dick "Grif"Griffith Banjo   Dick McCarthy String Bass

FRIDAY JULY 17 8:30- 12:30
YANKEE SILVERSMITH INN   reservations: CO9-8771
Route 5, Wallingford, Ct. Merrit Pkwy Exit 66

THURSDAY JULY 23 9 - 1
ACTORS COLONY INN   reservations: RE 5-2511
179 Roosevelt Drive, Seymour, Ct.

SATURDAY JULY 25 9 - 1
HILLANDALE COUNTRY CLUB reservations: 268-8691
Daniels Farm Road, Trumbull, Ct (JAZZ CLUB & HILLANDALE members & guests ONLY)

Tickets Good For Any Of The Above Dates

PRESENTED BY THE

CONNECTICUT TRADITIONAL JAZZ CLUB
P.O. Box 6050, Bridgeport, Ct. WRITE FOR MEMBERSHIP INFORMATION

TICKETS NOW ON SALE THROUGH JAZZ CLUB OR AT DOOR OF CONCERT

General Admission $2.00   C.T.J.C. Members $1.50

International Jazz Band
Connecticut Traditional Jazz Club advertisement
1964

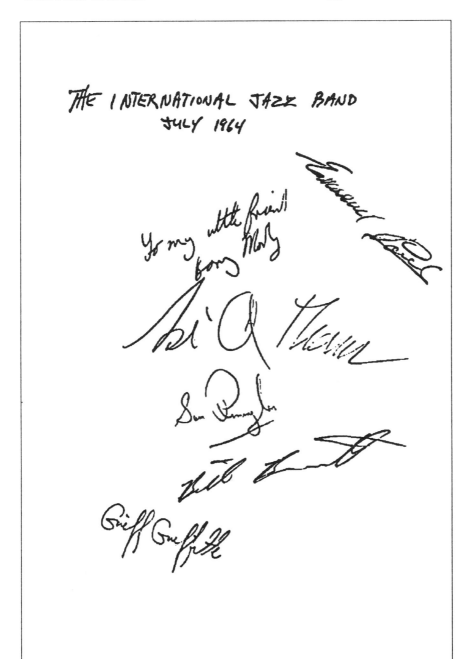

**Autographs of most
International Jazz Band members
1964**

9. Yankee Silversmith

As a result of the huge success of the Yankee Silversmith Inn concert by the International Jazz Band, Bob Myer signed the Easy Riders up for a long term run on Friday nights. In the budget were adequate funds to bring in guest stars on a regular basis, both from New York and New Orleans.

During the 60s, there were still many good oldtime jazzmen living and working in the New York area. Among the top ones we were to use on the Silversmith and other gigs were: Jimmy Archey, trombone; J.C. Higgenbotham, trombone; Zutty Singleton, drums; Freddie Moore, drums; Edmond Hall, clarinet; Herb Hall, clarinet; Tony Parenti, clarinet; Hank Duncan, piano; Bud Freeman, tenor sax; Victoria Spivey, vocalist; Henry Goodwin, trumpet and Henry "Red" Allen, trumpet.

You may wonder why I didn't record more of these New Yorkers. Certainly there was a wealth of talent there. The problem was with the New York local of the American Federation of Musicians. Recording scale, the minimum fee paid to a local's member for making a recording, was over three times higher than that for New Orleans musicians. There were several reasons for this. New York was the recording capital of the world. Top musicians in all fields of music congregated there and recording sessions represented their most lucrative source of income. Thus, the scale was abnormally high. The black local in New Orleans on the other hand was controlled by jazz musicians. Clarinetist Louis Cottrell was the president and trumpeter Alvin Alcorn was its vice-president. The recording scale was much more reasonable, a subject which I will cover with more clarity a little later in its proper context. The bottom line was that, although we were playing on a weekly basis with these wonderful New York men, I was never able to record them. The sole exception was Jimmy Archey who did one Jazz Crusade album, but not with the Easy Riders Jazz Band.

Of the many New Yorkers we used at the Silversmith, Edmond Hall and Jimmy Archey became the favorites of both band and audience. We used them frequently.

Jimmy Archey's career went back into the 1920's. He had recorded with the King Oliver and Luis Russell bands. He was an unusually short man standing five foot or less. One night at the Silversmith, the bandsmen were gathered around a table on break having a snack. One of the fans in the audience walked over to the table opposite Jimmy.

"Mr. Archey," he said, "I have been a fan of yours for many years. I just wanted to shake your hand." He extended his hand across the table and continued, "please don't bother to stand up."

Archey extended his hand in return and said, "I am standing up."

Archey showed me the many tricks he liked to do with his plunger mute. Nobody could "talk" with his trombone like Jimmy. He was to the plunger mute what Jim Robinson was to the "wa-wa" mute. I have loved working with these two mutes ever since learning the techniques from those two masters. When Archey or Higgenbotham came in, I usually played drums on the gigs.

Edmond Hall reminded me of George Lewis. Not in his playing style which, while New Orleans, was more complex, but in his personal manners. He was soft-spoken and highly articulate. Hall, of course, had played with all of the greats in New Orleans, Chicago and New York. He started his career with, of all people, Kid Thomas around 1915. He had gigged with Buddy Petit and the legendary trumpeter Chris Kelly. He left New Orleans for New York and has lived there since the 1920's. He played with the Eddie Condon band which he ultimately left to join the great Louis Armstrong band of the late 1950's. I had dreams of recording him reunited with Kid Thomas and Zutty Singleton. It was one of those things I kept putting off until Edmond suddenly died in 1967. Of all the sessions I DIDN'T record, this is the one I regret most.

The only white New Yorker we used at the Silversmith was tenor saxophonist Bud Freeman. We used him only once and that was in the fall of 1964. He took a train up from New York. I agreed to drive him back to the city after the job. We played the gig and he enjoyed it a lot as did we. On the hour and a half drive back to New York, we talked about the Austin High Gang and other early white bands. Then we made the mistake of talking about the upcoming presidential election. I was a strong Goldwater supporter. Bud was the quintessential "New York Liberal." By the time we reached 42nd Street, Bud was no longer talking to me. As I dropped him off, I thanked him for doing the job and extended an invitation for him to return in the near future. He said, "no thank you." We never played together again.

He won the election.

THE RIVERBOAT
CONNECTICUT

Presents

Armchair Excursions

On Board
For Your Enjoyment

THE EASY RIDERS
New Orleans Jazz Band

With Visits To
OLD SILENT MOVIE HOUSES
PLACES AND EVENTS OF INTEREST

Yankee Silversmith Inn

Exit 66 — Wilbur Cross Parkway

Route 5   Wallingford, Conn.

Sailing Time 8:30 P.M.

Every Friday Night

To Book Passage Call

269-8771

Fare $1.75

C. T. J. C. Members $1.25

**Flyer for Easy Riders Jazz Band
Yankee Silversmith Inn
Autographed by Edmond Hall**

10. The Queen In The Palace

Victoria Spivey had been all but forgotten by the early Sixties. That in itself is incredible when you consider her background. She had sung with the King Oliver Band. She had recorded with Louis Armstrong, Red Allen, Zutty Singleton, Luis Russell, Pops Foster and other great jazzmen. She was featured in an MGM black musical entitled "Hallelujah" directed by no less a cinematic master than King Vidor.

It was because of the diligence of Len Kunstadt, a record dealer and editor of the blues magazine Record Research, that Victoria was "rediscovered." He had already recorded her with some prominent 1960's blues instrumentalists. Len was familiar with my work in promoting jazz and had contacted me about using Victoria on one of the CTJC concerts. He brought her to hear Tom and Manny on their first visit. She liked what she heard. Len and I discussed the possibility of Vicky recording with the Easy Riders Jazz Band. There was much to commend it. The albums she had cut for Len up to this point were all contemporary in nature. The concept of returning to her roots recording with a New Orleans style band was exciting. The question was one of financing the project. At the time we first discussed it, I was just getting ready to cut the first tracks with Thomas and Paul. Len had put all of his money into Victoria's previous recordings. We would have to find a sponsor for the recording. I thought of George Buck. This was before he agreed to do the International Jazz Band session. I had been talking to Buck about issuing an album by the Riders. As all he had to go on were our first two Jazz Crusade albums, he was not particularly excited about recording us. Maybe an offer of Spivey with the band would change his mind.

I called George and proposed the session to him. He was indeed interested. As this was to be our first album for him, he stressed the need for a much better recorded sound than our first two albums on Jazz Crusade had. We discussed tunes and decided on a panoply of classic blues including: "Careless Love," "Sister Kate," "Mama's Gone Goodbye" and others. We scheduled the recording session for sometime in August or September.

We hired Victoria on our Silversmith job a few times to familiarize ourselves with each other. Jack Guckin was getting very excited about the upcoming session. He had seen Victoria in "Hallelujah" and was better versed in her early career than any of the rest of us. He came to the Silversmith and was enthralled by The Queen. He volunteered to write the liner notes for the album. I told him I would be happy to have him do so.

"Where are you going to record it and who is doing the engineering?" he asked.

"I don't know yet Jack. I have been so damn busy on the International Jazz Band tour that I haven't had the time to think about it."

"Well I have an idea about it I'd like you to consider. There is an old theater in Meriden called the Palace. It has been closed for years and they are getting ready to tear it down. At one time it was the most beautiful theater in the area. Top names played there like Al Jolson.

"I checked the place out and there is still electricity hooked up to it. It's just got to have great acoustics. I can get it for almost nothing for you. I think it would be just right for the Spivey session."

"It sounds almost too good to be true," I replied. "Now I have to do something about the audio."

"I think I can help you there too," Jack said. "There is a new company in Connecticut that has just introduced a new line of high quality microphones. They've been trying to sell them to our station. They just might be interested in doing the recording for you to show off the mikes."

"Great. Check them out and let me know. I would like to do the session before Sinclair goes back to Germany."

With help like that, the session came together without a hitch for a change. The theater would be available and the recording company agreed to cut the session, state-of-the-art, for the cost of the tape we used in return for having their microphone in the album cover photo.

Even though the songs we would be doing with Spivey were all standard to our repertoire, we worked them over and over again to get arrangements that would spotlight both Spivey and the band. This would be the first album to feature the band's new personnel line-up. Vigorito had done a few tracks on the Thomas/Paul album but he was so new to the idiom that this album was really his debut. Sinclair hadn't been on the Thomas/Paul session. Griff had settled into the New Orleans style beautifully.

I concentrated on Vigorito. During the International Jazz Band tour both Fred and Noel had the opportunity to see top flight New Orleans men in action on their respective instruments. Unfortunately, neither of them availed themselves of the opportunity. It was discouraging but I still held out hope that Fred would succumb to the New Orleans sound. For the Spivey session, I asked him to study the Bunk Johnson recordings of the tunes we would be doing. Bunk had done them all and that lyrical style of his would go down nicely next to Spivey's hard-edged interpretations. Fred did his homework well, as always.

On August 9, 1964, the Spivey session was underway. It took the engineers over an hour to mike Vicky and the band. But the sound that resulted was well worth the effort. In addition to the Spivey numbers, we planned to fill out the album with some instrumentals. Among them were: "Rose Room," "Get Out of Here" and "Mama Inez." We decided to do all of Victoria's tracks first to make sure we got them just the way we wanted them.

The session went slowly but steadily along. We started with "Careless Love." We did two takes of it. Fred pulled off the Bunk Johnson solo beautifully. Guckin had been listening in on the headset when he did it. After the take, Jack said, "You'll never do it like that again. Don't even bother to try."

We went on to "Sister Kate" which I wanted to do early in the session while my chops were still up. The soaring Jim Robinson parts that I wanted to include are tough enough even when your lip is good. I was afraid if I waited too long into the session I simply would not be able to hack it. We did it in one take. No one in the band noticed that, during the take, Vicky stepped up to the mike and sang the tag along with the band at the very end of the number. It hadn't been planned. She asked for a playback and watched us as the recording came to its end. When we heard her come in and tag it with us, we all gave her a cheer. She did it on several other numbers later in the session.

We took a break. Victoria said she had a slight headache and was going to buy some aspirin. Griff went with her. They returned a few minutes later with the aspirin. Victoria reached into her large handbag and lifted out a fifth of gin! She uncapped it and carefully dropped in a few aspirin tablets. Needless to say, this caught the attention of the hard drinkers in the band. Mouldy was the first to saunter over to her.

"Is that what you take for a headache, Vicky?"

"Oh yes. It works wonders."

"I'll bet it does," Mouldy replied.

Griff looked at the bottle as its contents took on a sour milk look. "It looks pretty potent to me."

Sinclair, the biggest boozer in the band, just stared.

Finally, when its consistency met the Queen's strict standards, she passed the bottle around. There wasn't another complaint about headaches for the rest of the session. But I'll bet there were a few the next morning.

By the time we finished with Spivey's numbers, several hours had elapsed and the band was showing the strain. We still had the instrumental tunes to do but Victoria was due back in New York so she left with Len Kunstadt. We rushed through the remaining numbers. None of them turned out very well. We were just too tired out. The important ones with Spivey were better than I had hoped for. I was satisfied. We packed it up and went home. A few days later I received my copies of the tapes. I played them through alone in the quiet of my home. The Spivey things were fine. The rest was basically trash but I picked out enough to fill the album and sent them off to George Buck.

We played often with Victoria after that session. She even did a concert with Kid Thomas and the Riders. She did many more contemporary blues albums but she never again recorded with a New Orleans style group. The album received generally good reviews when it was released a year later on GHB. By that time we had replaced the instrumental tracks we cut that day with later tracks recorded with Sammy Rimington replacing Noel on clarinet. Those new tracks were cut at the Moose Lodge Hall. The band was in rare form as the album attests. I think I can safely say that Art Pulver never played better drums than he did that night. He was hot as a pistol and drove the band along through "Bugle Boy March," the best single track ever recorded by the Riders in my opinion, with imagination and tasteful power. Fred and Sammy were superb on "Four Or Five Times" and I got in some old fashioned "circus-style" tromboning on "That Teasin' Rag."

Front Cover - Record Research Magazine
featuring Victoria Spivey and the Easy Riders Jazz Band.
November 1964

1965

deceased

ISRAEL GORMAN, clarinet

PAPA JOHN JOSEPH, string bass

BOB "FEW CLOTHES" LEWIS, bass drum

JOE "PROF" ROBICHAUX, piano

LESTER SANTIAGO, piano

11. George Lewis

George Lewis was more than a legend in his time. He was the living, breathing embodiment of black New Orleans jazz. During the Dark Age of jazz which spanned the period between Bunk Johnson's death and the beginnings of the Great Sixties Jazz Revival, it was the Lewis band alone which stood between survival and demise of the music.

He traveled the length and breadth of the land playing on college campuses. He made record after record. His was the hottest of the hot bands. It had power and drive unmatched in later years by the other revivalist bands. In the many competitions in which the band participated, it simply blew their rivals away.

Some current historical revisionists have acted as apologists for the exquisite violence of that great band. They don't understand why the Lewis band wasn't more subtle, more genteel, more - well - British. Some excuse it as being some sort of misunderstanding between George and his drummer, Joe Watkins. Others point out that George played more gently and quieter in his final years. They fail to notice that George, frail in the best of years, suffered grievously during those last years; his strength and drive sapped. George's playing was phenomenal in all of its various moods. But the fact remains that, when George led his own band for two decades, it was a powerhouse band. The hottest band on Earth.

It was that band and the Kid Thomas band of the early 60s, another dynamo outfit, upon which I based the sound of the Easy Riders. Therefore, it should come as no surprise that the project at the top of my list was to record George Lewis with the Riders.

The opportunity arose in January of 1965. George was finishing up some work on the road with Kid Thomas. He was free for a week before he had to leave for Europe. I invited him to Connecticut for three days. We scheduled two concerts with him for the Connecticut Traditional Jazz Club. We planned to record the first of the two on Tuesday, January 26th.

In the past, our largest turnouts had always been at the Ambassador Restaurant in Hamden. It was a big, modern restaurant located in a shopping center. We hadn't used it for the International Jazz Band tour because a labor dispute at the restaurant had resulted in a strike at the facility. In early

January the strike was still going on. I stopped in to talk to the manager to see what the prospects were for a settlement by the end of the month. I was assured that the negotiations were nearly concluded and they expected to have the picket lines down within a week. I decided to risk it and booked their main dining room for the 26th. We then booked the Post Lodge Restaurant in Larchmont, New York for the second concert on the 28th.

We began our publicity. Because George was well known in the area from his previous concert for the Dixieland Society, the advance ticket sale was brisk. It was one of the few concerts we ever held that was sold out in advance. We didn't offer advance tickets to the second concert because that restaurant was so small we felt no need to push it. The Ambassador room sat 350. But, as the date drew near, we were beginning to wonder if we would be seating anyone. The strike continued unabated.

I repeatedly called the restaurant and received the same assurance: the strike would be over any day. On the Sunday before the concert, an article appeared in the New Haven Register saying that the concert was in jeopardy because of the strike. Our ex-friends from the Dixieland Society were creating a little mischief for us. But it got my phone ringing. Ticket holders and club members wanted to know what was going on. I told them all that the concert was on. The day before the concert I received a call from the restaurant management. The strike was settled.

George arrived the afternoon of the first concert and we discussed the program. I wanted the concert to be a mix of his familiar repertoire and other numbers he had not recorded before. He told me had just completed a series of recordings for Tom Bethell's San Jacinto label. Tom had been producing some of the best recordings of the period. His goal appeared to be to recreate the sound of the American Music recordings of the 1940's and he was succeeding. He used George on virtually all of his sessions. George mentioned that he had recorded "Jambalaya" for Tom and liked the number very much. We decided to open the concert with it. I suggested several Duke Ellington Jungle Band numbers. These were: "Creole Love Call," "Mood Indigo" and "Saturday Night Function." George knew and liked them all. Of course we would include Lewis standards like "Burgundy St. Blues" and "Ice Cream." I added the tune George called "Porkchops." This tune has probably been recorded under more different titles than any other jazz piece. The reason for this is that its original title was "Kiss My Little Brown Ass" and no record company, Jazz Crusade included, was going to put it out under that title. It had been the victory tune of the jazz battles in the early days of Storyville.

Before leaving for the concert, I played George some of the tracks from the Victoria Spivey session. He was particularly impressed by the Bunk-like sound on "Careless Love" and "Sister Kate." I mentioned to him that we would have the following night off and could listen to some playbacks from the tapes we were on the way to cut. I was inviting Mouldy and Griff over also so the four of us could select album tracks.

The restaurant was packed. Behind a sliding wall adjoining a smaller dining area there was a meeting of area businessmen in progress. Mike Fast was setting up his recording gear when we arrived. He and I discussed the acoustics of the room. He had never recorded there before and I had warned him of the deadness of the room. He ran several extra mikes up close to make sure he could pick up George and Griff.

The concert began and I announced that the opening number, "Jambalaya," had been written by the late country star Hank Williams. The band jumped into it and got the concert off to a great start. At its conclusion the crowd went wild. As they cheered, I commented into the mike, about Hank Williams, "If he wasn't dead before, he's dead now." Since the release of that record many fans of the album from that night's concert have asked me what I meant by that remark. As my opening comments about Hank Williams had been edited out, it is no wonder so many would be baffled by such a curious remark. Now you know.

As Sinclair was back in Germany, I decided to use Noel Kalet on piano just to give Mouldy his requisite left hand to read. We deliberately kept the mikes off of him as he was not much of a pianist. As a reward for his yeoman service, I invited him up front for a treat few, if any, clarinetists have enjoyed. We featured him in a duet with George on "St. Phillip St. Breakdown." It was without doubt Noel Kalet's grandest moment in jazz. He rose to the occasion and did himself proud standing next to the master. It brought the house down.

It would be braggadocio to say that every number played at that concert was topflight. The recording shows this to be incorrect, but there was a feeling of excitement that ran through this concert that made it an extraordinary event. The recording shows that too. Vigorito was starting into his Kid Thomas phase and played strong all night. For my part, I like "Porkchops" and "Corrine, Corrina" the best.

After the first set the restaurant manager approached me with a problem. "The people in the adjoining dining room are complaining that they cannot conduct their business meeting because of all the yelling and cheering in here." I suggested to him that he tell them that if they would make a one hundred dollar donation to the jazz club, we would slide back the wall between the two dining rooms and they could join our party. They thought it was a great idea and the wall was removed. It solved the problem, added about a hundred people to our audience and a hundred bucks to the jazz club treasury.

Both George Buck and Sonny Faggart of Pearl Records were interested in the George Lewis concert recording. I had decided to get two albums out of the concert tape. I also had promised one track exclusively to the CTJC for use on their annual club record. We had done 27 numbers at the concert. Some current Lewis discographies have put the number at 26 but they overlooked "Burgundy St. Blues." As I needed cash for a series of recordings I was planning to do in New Orleans, I decided to sell both albums for as much as I could get. Lewis and I scrapped six of the numbers as being unacceptable takes. I edited the albums and sold one each to George and Sonny. George paid a little more and, therefore got his pick of the two albums. I gave "Bill Bailey" to the jazz club for their album.

Griff, Mouldy and I enjoyed a quiet evening with George the night after the Ambassador concert at my home. We listened to some of the playbacks and were generally satisfied. George regaled us with stories from his past and answered some questions I wanted cleared up.

"George, I have heard that you turned down a major label recording contract in the 50's. What's the story behind that? Is it true?"

"Yes, we could have recorded for RCA Victor but they wanted me to replace one of my men and I wouldn't do it."

"Who was the man?"

"Howard," George replied. "You know Howard had quite a drinking problem then. He wasn't very reliable. They didn't trust him to be able to play. But I couldn't do it ."

George's most vivid recollection was one he had told me before and repeated for Mouldy and Griff. It was the story of the murder of Evan Thomas. Evan was one of the best, and most powerful, trumpet players in Louisiana. He didn't often come into New Orleans, playing mostly in Texas and western Louisiana. He was so renowned that he frequently used Bunk Johnson as his second trumpet man. One night in 1933 Bunk and George were playing a dancehall job with Evan in Rayne, Louisiana. Evan was drunk out of his mind, as he often was, and flirting with the ladies in the hall. Suddenly, in George's words,

"This man comes out of the audience waving a razor in his hand. He starts cursing Evan for flirting with his wife. Evan sober up just like that, man, and jumps off his chair and grabs me by the shoulders and holds me up in front of him to protect himself. This man jumps up onto the stage and reaches right around me and cuts Evan's throat with that razor. I feels Evan's hot blood squirt all over the back of my head. I screams and Evan dropped me on the floor and goes running out into the street. I was so scared, man, I couldn't move. There was blood, so much blood, I didn't even know if I was cut or not myself. Evan, he die right there in the street."

As George concluded his account of the event, we sat transfixed looking at him. All the terror he must have felt shown forth from his eyes as if it was happening right there in the room with us. I still feel the eeriness of it as I sit and write about it now, over twenty-five years later.

George talked about many things that night. One subject that automatically came up was his years with Bunk Johnson.

I asked, "Was Bunk really as cruel a man as people claim, George?"

"Well let me tell you something, Bill. I don't speak bad of no man. All I can tell you is this: if there's such a place as hell, Bunk's in it."

The next evening we played our second concert with George. The crowd was much smaller and George spent most of his breaks talking to fans. It was a nice ending to a much too short visit by the greatest of all New Orleans jazzmen.

I was to record George once again a few months later in New Orleans. These would be the only two times I recorded him. I have frequently been asked why I didn't record Lewis more than I did. It was certainly not out of lack of respect or friendship. We had in fact become close friends. Everybody else was recording George. He has been recorded more than any other New Orleans jazz musician with the exceptions of Louis Armstrong and Sidney Bechet. Because there were so few of us recording in those waning days, there was a real danger that other deserving reedmen would never get their chance in front of a recording mike. Brilliant players like Albert Burbank, Polo Barnes, Capt. John Handy and Manny Paul deserved some records too and nobody was doing it. And there were others, most notably Israel Gorman, who were virtually ignored. Israel died before I got to him. If it hadn't been for Ken Mills, Israel might have been missed completely. It was always a tough call on who to do next. But George Lewis was everybody else's "next" and that is why I didn't record him more.

The Connecticut Traditional Jazz Club Presents

THE GREAT NEW ORLEANS CLARINET

GEORGE

LEWIS

and the

Easy Riders Jazz Band

THURSDAY   8:00 P.M.

JANUARY 28th

POST LODGE RESTAURANT

Boston Post Road, Larchmont, N.Y.

Admission $2.00

For Reservations Call (914) TE 4-2203 or TE 4-8177

GEORGE
LEWIS
JAN. 28
THURSDAY
8 P.M.

George Lewis and the Easy Riders Jazz Band
Connecticut Traditional Jazz Club flyer
January 1965

12. New Orleans Recordings

I had been putting money aside for over a year, saving up to be able to do some recording in New Orleans. The impetus for it was that I wanted to record the Kid Thomas band. I also wanted to do an album with Thomas, Lewis and Robinson in the front line. The rhythm section I was thinking about for the session was Joe Watkins on drums, Creole George Guesnon on banjo, Slow Drag on bass and Lester Santiago on piano. I doubted I would have the money to do more than that.

As I saved, both of the pianists I wanted to use, Lester Santiago and Joe James, died. During that same period, the first Jazzology Jazz Poll was published. I was exceptionally pleased with the results because the Riders and its individual members did very well in their respective categories. But the thing that struck me the most was the similarity between the major category winners and the band I was planning to record. Louis Armstrong aced out Thomas for first place on trumpet. Josiah "Cie" Frazier came in on top of the drum division and Don Ewell led his nearest rival on piano by a two-to-one spread. The thought popped into my head to do an album with the major category winners. I was still short of money and, though I knew Ewell slightly, I didn't know where he was or whether he would be available at reasonable cost. But I did know who would know and might just be able to solve the money situation at the same time.

I phoned George Buck once again. By this time I had sold George three recording sessions: the Spivey session, the George Lewis concert and the International Jazz Band concert. I told him I planned to record two or three sessions in New Orleans and, as usual, I was short of cash. I told him that one of the sessions I wanted to do was the Jazzology Poll Winners. He asked about Armstrong. I said I would use Thomas instead but, in all other categories I planned to use the winners including Don Ewell if I could track him down and if he would do it at New Orleans recording scale plus his travel expenses. George became very excited about this idea. He said Don was in Florida and that he would personally contact him and talk him into doing the session.

I told him about the Thomas band session I also wanted to do and that I would like to do a third one if possible with Robinson and Albert Burbank together. I hadn't forgotten Burbank's friendliness to me on my first trip to New Orleans five years earlier. I explained my offer to Buck: I would sell to him at a bargain price all of the alternate takes from my three sessions. I would try to vary tempo and solo arrangement as much as possible and to include at least one exclusive number by each band in the alternates. He agreed. Now you may wonder why I just didn't offer George his own numbers instead of alternate takes on my material. The reason is that when recording in New Orleans at that time, union rules permitted you to do several takes of each number at no additional cost to insure you got a good recording. But, as you added tunes, you were charged for each addition. Therefore, by slipping through that loophole and offering George alternates, I didn't increase my overall costs and still stayed within the union guidelines. In short, my deal with George gave me the loot to add the third session.

While George contacted Ewell and got his agreement for the session, I began calling the musicians about the dates. I asked George Lewis to make the arrangements with Cie and Drag. I called Thomas, Big Jim and Albert myself. Thomas, of course, made all the arrangements for his own band's recording. I asked him who he planned to use on piano now that Joe James was gone. He said he would like to use Octave Crosby. I wasn't a big fan of Octave's playing but I wanted Tom to finally do a recording just the way he wanted it. I agreed to Octave but asked Tom if he would mind adding Creole George to the lineup. He was happy to have him. I asked Tom to call him. He said, "You know Guesnon's a contrary man, Bill. I think you should call him yourself." I was afraid he was going to say that. Creole George was indeed notorious about recording. If you caught him with the right approach and in the right mood, he would cut off his arm for you. But, if you were unlucky enough to catch him in one of his funks, he would cut YOUR arm off for you.

I waited a few days after talking to the other musicians before calling Creole George. I wanted to make sure that word of the recording sessions would be spread around and that he would have heard about them. He had already been bragging to everybody about winning the banjo category in the poll. I felt sure that when he heard there was going to be a recording featuring the winners and that all of the others had already been contacted about doing it, he would expect, and want, to be included. I had also been told he would demand extra money for it. That was something I wanted to avoid. Some other producers usually slipped him a few extra bucks in order to get him and there were some hard feelings among the other musicians about it. But I did have something to offer him when I finally called.

"Hello Bill," he said over the phone, "I been wondering when you were going to call me."

"I guess you've heard that I was coming into the city to do some recording, George."

"Yeah, I heard. How come you didn't call me when you called all them other guys?"

"Well I wasn't sure I would be able to afford to use a banjo on the record, George."

"What you mean? How can you do a poll winners album without the main winner?" he said with that famous George Guesnon humility.

"Well, all I can pay is scale you know. I really want you on the session but you're all winners and you all have to get the same pay."

"Thomas weren't no winner. How about that?"

"You shouldn't talk mean about Tom like that, George. Let me tell you something. I'm doing two more sessions while I'm in town and the first thing Thomas said to me when I called him about one with his band was that he would like to use Creole George Guesnon on banjo."

"Well I didn't mean him no harm, Bill. You know that. And you don't go telling him I said he weren't no winner either 'cause he a winner alright. I just meant he didn't win that poll like Armstrong and me did. That's all I meant to say."

I slipped him the prize, "Maybe I could use you on all three sessions George. You'd be the ONLY musician to be on ALL three."

"Well that's more like it," he replied.

"Then you'll do them for scale to help me out?"

"Sure, Bill, you know me!"

The third session was still going to be a budget buster. I figured I would use Robinson, Burbank, Guesnon, Drag and Ewell. I still wanted to record Joe Watkins, one of my favorite drummers and singers. I had to take him off the original session because Cie had won the poll. I thought I might like to use Pete Bocage or Kid Sheik on trumpet but I just could not come up with the dollars for this third recording.

Then an idea struck me which would save the price of three musicians and put the session back in the schedule. I could do what we did so often in Connecticut. If I played drums on the date and listed myself as leader, I would save the price of two musicians because the leader gets double pay. I had thought about bringing along one or two of the Riders on the trip anyway. If I could get Fred to come along, I could use him on trumpet on the Robinson/Burbank date. He was coming along really well in the style but I was still hoping he would take more of an interest in the music itself. This might be just the thing to do it. I ran it by him and he was interested in making the trip. The third session came together.

About a week after Santiago died, I received a call from Leonard Brackett to inform me that Papa John Joseph dropped dead while playing a gig in Preservation Hall. Someone in the audience threw five dollars into the kitty to have the band play "When the Saints Go Marching In."

Instant legend had it that Papa John made the remark, "this song gonna be the death of me yet." At the conclusion of it Papa said, "that took it all out of me," and slid to the floor dead. Papa John died at the age of 92, the oldest active jazzman in New Orleans at the time of his death. If it hadn't been for Grayson Mills, Papa might never have been recorded. One man can make a difference.

Leonard Brackett and Sonny Faggart, who were partners in Pearl records at the time, were helping me with the arrangements for my New Orleans recording sessions. I wanted to record at Preservation Hall. They obtained Allan Jaffe's consent. They also took care of finding recording equipment and engineers. I asked them to speak to Bill Russell about engineering the Jazzology Poll Winners session. He said he would. They also arranged to have Dick Allen and Paul Crawford share engineering duties on the other two sessions. I particularly wanted Bill Russell to do the Poll Winners album. It had been Russell, in the 1940's, who first called the world's attention to some of the artists who would be on this recording: George Lewis, Jim Robinson, Alcide Pavageau and Kid Thomas Valentine. He is unquestionably the most respected figure in the field of New Orleans jazz. Trusted implicitly by all of the black musicians, he produced classic recordings he alone could have produced. He has dedicated his entire life to the promotion of those musicians.

I knew that Preservation Hall would not give me as good a sound as some other locations in New Orleans. Other producers had been using San Jacinto Hall with good effect. My own preference, sound-wise, would have been Artisan Hall where George did his great concert session released on Decca records. But, the poll winners album was becoming more than just another recording session. I wanted it to be a memorial to what was going on in New Orleans in the Sixties. I wanted to bring all the forces that were combining to make the Great New Orleans Jazz Revival a reality together on one grand recording session. Allan Jaffe and his Preservation Hall represented the rock solid foundation upon which the Revival stood. By 1965, it had become the Mecca to which all turned in their daily prayers. I wanted it represented on this special session and the way to do that was to record it there. It was designed to be an historic recording. It was.

Late in the evening of April 20, Fred and I landed in New Orleans to be met by Leonard and Sonny. On the way in from the airport, they reported that all was in readiness for the next day's session. I had decided to begin with the Robinson/Burbank session because, frankly, it was the least important of the three. If anything was going to go wrong, I wanted it to happen on that session to give us a day for corrective action. We dropped off our bags and headed for Bourbon Street to catch Albert Burbank at the Paddock. He was in fine form. At the break he came over to the table and sat down. I was startled when he did it. How things had changed since 1962 when I first met him in this same club. He played one more set and we bade each other goodnight. He wanted to get a good night's sleep for our Noon start at Preservation Hall the next day.

I had had a busy day and here we were at 3:00 a.m. sitting in a bar with Sonny and Leonard. I should have been trying to sleep also but I knew it was useless to try. I had waited so long for these sessions to happen. It was a dream about to come true. I did manage a few hours sleep. At 7:00 a.m., Sonny and I were sitting in the French Market having coffee. This was the first time I had met Leonard and him in person. We had corresponded and talked on the phone. We had exchanged courtesy copies of our record releases. Neither of them were musicians. Both had become enchanted with the music and were tired of being merely spectators. They started their Pearl label specifically to record Jim Robinson. They even named their label after Jim's wife, Pearl. Jim got a big kick out of that of course, which was just what they intended. They had no overt sense of trying to make history. Like me, they were doing their recording out of a sense of fun and compulsion. Each of us felt compelled at some point during the Sixties to quit. Then someone would say, "Gee wouldn't it be great to do a session with Earl Humphrey on trombone?" And we would be off and running again. We anxiously awaited each others new releases to see what bizarre combination of musicians and songs would come out next. I think the only two who did have a sense of history were Grayson Mills and Tom Bethell. Tom took his sessions on San Jacinto more seriously than anyone else took theirs. He knew precisely what kind of sound he wanted. He was after that 1940's American Music feel. He always seemed frustrated when the musicians tried to interject solos into his ensemble oriented recordings. I don't recall with certainty, but I don't think he ever did a recording without George Lewis on it and, at most, one or two without Robinson, Guesnon or Cie. With Tom, his personnel decisions were basically limited to which trumpet player he would use next with his San Jacinto house band. Having said all that, it is important to add. . . it worked. Tom produced some of the finest sessions to come out of the city in the Sixties. I just wished he had more fun doing it. But, as I knew, satisfaction was often more enjoyable than fun. Now Leonard and Sonny, on the other hand, did some fine sessions also. But, with them, it took several days of sobering up before they knew it!

I woke Fred up around 9:00 and took him on a walking tour of the Quarter while we waited for the session to begin. We ended up in Ye Olde Ice Cream Parlor having a pre-session banana split. I asked him how he felt. He seemed confident. I couldn't decide if it was due to youthful arrogance or just plain ignorance. I sure as hell was nervous. This was to be my first recording on drums. I would be using a composite set made of components of the Preservation Hall house set, Sammy Penn's set and my own cymbals which I brought from Connecticut.

Don Ewell had already arrived in town and he was at the hall, along with Dick Allen and Paul Crawford, when we arrived. Both Dick and Paul were jazz historians of the first rank. In addition, Paul was, and still is, a highly regarded trombone player. The hall quickly filled with jazz celebrities, both players and non-players. If you had set off a bomb in the hall that day, you could have stopped the Revival dead in its tracks. Besides the band and the engineers, there were, wandering in and out, Kid Sheik, Sammy Penn, Punch Miller, Bill Russell, Allan Jaffe, Sonny Faggart, Leonard Brackett and a small army of foreign jazz fans.

Don Ewell was very unhappy with the piano in the hall. Fortunately he had played there the night before. Allan graciously, and unhesitatingly, decided it was time for the old relic to go and he bought a piano on the spot and had it delivered in time for the recording session. Drag was racing to and fro and stammering untranslatable comments to all who would listen. Guesnon arrived. Smiling! He was as happy to see the new piano as Don was. Burbank came in, greeted everyone, and quietly pieced his Albert system clarinet together. Jim shuffled in. He greeted me with a big grin. I hadn't seen him since '62. He looked around and said, "Who ya'all using on the drums?" I told him I was going to play the session. His eyes opened wide. "You play drums, too? You tough, man. TOUGH!"

Unlike the upcoming Thomas band session, I picked the tunes for the Robinson/Burbank and Poll Winners sessions. On the session we were now starting, that had given Fred plenty of time to get familiar with the tunes and various recordings that had been done of them in the past. Until this session, Fred had been playing a lot of Bunk Johnson stylings. He surprised me and everybody else on this afternoon by blowing a hot Kid Thomas horn throughout the session. This suited the session perfectly and both Jim and Albert played hotter and hotter as the afternoon progressed. After hearing a few playbacks on break, I was sure it would be a better session than I had envisioned. We mixed up the tempos on alternate takes to make sure Buck would get some different material. Actually I had deliberately picked many of the tunes because they were ones that could be played either fast or slow. It was a happy session. Everybody had a good time making it. We spent about three hours at it. Vigorito blew a great gig. In my opinion, he could have become the Sammy Rimington of the trumpet if he had been seduced by the music. His head and heart led him in a different musical direction. It was a loss to New Orleans jazz and a gain for only Fred knows who. But, on the day of this recording, he ran with the thoroughbreds.

When it came time to release the album, I struggled with a title for it. I had always referred to it as the Robinson/Burbank session and that was my first thought for the title. The more I thought about the session, the more I remembered the fun I had trading quips with Slow Drag, who stood right beside me throughout the session. Drag had never been given top billing on any of the hundreds of albums he played on. But, he was always the first bass player called when a recording session was being planned. I decided to honor him on this album. During the session he kept saying to me, "Good bunch, Bill, good bunch," referring to the band. I called the album Slow Drag's Bunch. He got a big kick out of it and bragged about his "bunch" all over town. Sadly, when it was reissued, it became Drag's Half Fast Jazz Band. I guess even George Buck is entitled to a lapse in taste now and then.

It will always be Slow Drag's Bunch to me.

Jim and Pearl Robinson with Bill
Bissonnette at their home in New
Orleans: 1965.

The late trombonist Jack Teagarden
and Bill Bissonnette chat during
intermission of jazz concert in San
Antonio, Texas: 1961.

Catalog page
Jazz Crusade
1965

13.   Jazzology Poll Winners

On April 22, 1965, jazz history was in the offing. Everybody in the hall knew it. As that magnificent band assembled, the air in the room was one of anticipation and jubilation. There was only one problem. Drag had not shown up. We thought maybe he had forgotten about the session, though, if he had, it would the first time in the hundreds he had done. Leonard and Sonny went searching for him while Allan made numerous phone calls to find him.

We decided to make a recording test while we waited and the band swung into "Sentimental Journey." Bill Russell patiently relocated his mikes until he was hearing all he wanted to hear in his headset. There was still no Drag. My time was running and the union man who was sent to oversee the session, while sympathetic, told me I'd better get recording. I reluctantly started without him and we made the first actual take on "Journey."

As we finished it up, a cheer went up as Drag came stepping into the hall. His face was a mess. He had bruises all over his head. We crowded around to find out what had happened. It was difficult under the best of circumstances to understand Drag's speech and now he was speaking even faster and more jumbled than usual. What we did catch was that Drag had been mugged on the way home from the hall the previous night. All of his money had been stolen. It was lucky that he was alive. It took awhile for everyone to calm back down. I asked if Drag wanted to be excused from the session, all the while trying to remember who was his runner-up on the poll in case I had to replace him (that wouldn't have helped me because it turned out to be Pops Foster who was in California and who I wouldn't meet for another four years). Drag said he was okay and definitely wanted to play on this record. And play he did, beautifully, strongly. Some thief in the night was not going to spoil this event. In future days, Drag always carried a gun with him; an old relic that, if fired, probably would have blown up in his hand. There would have been adhesive tape from his fingers hanging from buildings a block away!

We did a second take on "Journey" with Drag in attendance and then the party really got going. "Lil' Liza Jane" is a little two chord romp that is good to get away on. The band romped into it and halfway through it everybody who had been sitting in the carriageway just outside the hall talking as they often did had come inside and was intently listening. Something fabulous was happening here. This band was sensational. Every man in it was showing every other man in it why he had been voted the best on his axe. It just got hotter and hotter as each chorus raced by and when it ended there was dead silence in the hall as musicians, historians, record producers and fans alike looked at each other in stunned tribute to the music they had just heard. It was unbelievable. Then Kid Punch let out a low whistle through his teeth and everybody broke out laughing. The outcome of the session was no longer in doubt.

"Ciribiribin" is basically "Bill Bailey" with class. Thomas led the band into it with gusto. It is seldom Tom hits his stride right at the top of a session. But he knew all too well that he was the only one on this album who was not a Jazzology Poll Winner and he was going to take care of that little matter right now. "Ciribiribin" has some of the hottest Thomas on record. He owns this track from beginning to end. It would be insane to try to rate the players on the Poll Winners session. Everyone of them played way over their heads that sparkling afternoon and that is saying something when you're dealing with the best of the best to begin with. But, if I had to pick even a marginal "Most Valuable Player," it would be Thomas. He played with a fury and passion I believe to be unparalleled during the Sixties. It's equally futile to think what, if anything, the trumpet winner, Louis Armstrong, might have brought to that session. But it is unfortunate no one ever managed to record Louis in with a band of his peers from New Orleans. The very thought of an Armstrong/Lewis/Robinson front line leaves one breathless. But, when the next year's 1965 Jazzology Jazz Poll results were tabulated, Kid Thomas had swept past Armstrong into first place; his selection for the album totally vindicated. He approved.

One of the most interesting aspects of the session was the way the titular leadership of the session flowed back and forth between Tom and George Lewis. It was an uncanny, almost unnerving thing. I would call the next tune and one or the other of them would take it upon himself to count it off. They never spoke about it, they just did it. Tom would use his usual "count-off," a loud stomp on the floor to let the band know it was time to make some jazz and then two stomps on the one and three of the measure and off they went. Lewis had a strange way of kicking off a tune. He would give the traditional get ready stomp. Then he would lightly tap-off seven beats in time, hesitate briefly and then kick, "go."

One,two,three,four,five,six,seven --- thump.

For those trivia lovers among you, Don Ewell was listed as leader on the Poll Winners date so that I could pay him the double fee for coming in from Florida.

Another strange thing I noticed was that there was never any discussion about keys. Some of these songs were not run-of-the-mill tunes the New Orleans bands usually played. A few times Don turned on his stool and asked, "key?" When he did this either Tom or George would blow a few quick starting notes for him. He would nod and turn back ready to begin. There was almost no discussion of any kind between takes. I would give them a brief rundown of what I wanted as to solos and tempo and they went to work.

There were a few false starts here and there but essentially this session went into the can without a hitch. They were all familiar tunes but ones which few of the musicians were associated. I selected "Home Sweet Home" for a personal reason: John Howard Payne, the composer of it, was my great-uncle. He had written the tune while sitting drunk in a bar and immediately sold the rights to it for $25.00 in order to keep the booze flowing. When you think about how many kitchens in America have signs hanging in them with "Home Sweet Home" written on them, you get a feel for how much royalty money he threw away on that bender. Now that I think about that, I wonder if I should have honored him by including it on the session.

It was a breathtaking session in every way. Each tune topped the one before it. When it was over, everyone in the room came up to me and thanked me for letting them be involved. Even Bill Russell, who has heard everything this music has to offer, told me he thought this was something very special.

Guesnon was beside himself with joy. "You got a great recording here, my boy. I want about 25 of them when you get them."

"Okay, Bill?" asked Jim Robinson. "Did you get what you wanted?"

"It was great, Jim. Absolutely great."

Kid Thomas kidded, "Did I cuts the mustard with all these here winners, Bill? I tried my best to keep up with them all."

"Thomas, you're the winner of the century and you know it too," I replied and he grinned.

I walked over to Cie, who was breaking down his set. "Cie, I've heard some great drumming in this town, but what I heard today was the best."

"I heard you did some fine drumming yourself here yesterday partner. I thanks you for letting me record for you, Bill."

"What did you think of the session, George?" I asked George Lewis.

"It was mighty fine, Bill, mighty fine. Yessir."

I thanked Don for coming in and doing the gig. He too seemed well pleased with it. He said he was going to stay on for a couple of more days in New Orleans to play at the hall.

We gathered around Drag one more time to see how he was feeling. Allan asked him if he wanted to take a few days off from the hall. He would be there that night Drag assured him.

You'll notice that, whenever possible throughout this book, I have tried to quote the New Orleans musicians to the best of my recollections. I do not do that with Drag. There is no writing on Earth, no keys on a typewriter, that can convey Drag's way with speech. . . if that's what it was. His manner of communication was a cross between several languages mixed with laughs, stutters, sputters, stammers and whistles. And each meant something. As you got to know him, you could usually figure out what he was trying to tell you. But it was a language that has yet to reach the point of being reduced to written form.

And what were the results of the Jazzology Poll Winners session? Did it reach historical proportions? Judging by the accolades it received, the answer has to be an unqualified yes. As the first reviews rolled in after its release, it became obvious that this was not just one more recording session. Downbeat Magazine gave it its highest 4-star rating. Billboard Magazine selected it as the jazz, "Pick of the Week," and as one of the best jazz albums of 1965. The New York Times radio station, WQXR, devoted an entire edition of its award winning jazz program to playing every track on the album. America's leading jazz critic, John S. Wilson, wrote it up in glowing terms in several journals including High Fidelity magazine. The New York Times listed it among its Top Ten jazz albums of the year. In addition, the Times published a listing of what it described as the Fifty Best Jazz Albums of All Time. Included was the "Jazzology Poll Winners - 1964" on Jazz Crusade.

As a result of all this publicity, the orders rolled in. The United States Information Agency ordered one hundred copies for placement in USIA libraries around the world; the biggest single retail order Jazz Crusade ever received for an album.

One of the most intriguing consequences of the album's reviews was a phone call from RCA Victor's top jazz A & R executive, Brad McCuen. He invited me to his home in Connecticut to talk about the Poll Winners session. My first impression was that he might have in mind re-recording the band for RCA. I didn't know that they bought outside sessions. But, buying my session was what he had in mind. He congratulated me on the album, a copy of which sat on a coffee table in his den. He asked me how much it cost to produce it. I evaded the question and asked what sort of deal he had in mind. He said RCA would reimburse me for my costs plus a modest profit. Of course, he suggested, I must have already made my money back from my sales so I would come out way ahead on the deal. He had no comprehension of how small those sales were.

"What about royalties?" I asked.

"For who?"

"For the musicians and me," I replied.

He seemed surprised that I brought up the subject. That surprised me considering he must deal in royalties all the time.

"No, we couldn't pay royalties," he said.

"Why don't you just record the band yourself?"

"In order for me to do it, I would have to fly the whole band to our New York studios. By the time I paid transportation, hotel expenses and studio time, it would cost too much to produce this kind of a session. What you did was unique and there is no guarantee that I could get the same result. I probably couldn't."

"Well, I CAN guarantee the quality of my session so why don't you just figure out what it would have cost you to produce it and we'll take it from there."

"I can't authorize that kind of money to buy a session," he said. "I would like to put this session on RCA for the welfare of the musicians. Think of the prestige they would get from having it on a major label like ours."

I couldn't help thinking what Kid Thomas might say if he heard this, "Prestige? Shoot man, Bill. Prestige don't put no chitlins on no table, Bill. No sir."

This guy sounded like he had worse budgetary problems than Jazz Crusade. I almost suggested to him that he call George Buck to help him out with his session financing. And speaking of that, he also asked me what I had in alternate takes. When I told him that I had already sold the alternate takes to another record company, he said I would have to get them back. RCA could not permit the alternate takes of one of "their" sessions to be released on another label. What he didn't know just yet was that there was no way RCA was going to buy this session. The more we talked, the more I realized that this was not a deal I wanted to make. I had tried for many years to buy on LP the Victor Bunk Johnson records of the 1940's. It was impossible to get them because RCA had never re-released them in America (and has not to the day this is being written). I began to wonder what would become of my beloved Poll Winners if I sold it to him. Six months on the market and then withdrawn for fifty years while jazz collectors yearned for it? He was probably right when he said that an RCA release of the session would result in sales of tens or even hundreds of thousands of copies. What good would that do me or the musicians if there were no royalties? And what good would it do for jazz fans, and most importantly young jazzmen, ten years in the future who wouldn't be able to get a copy because it had been discontinued?

The bottom line was the only way I would sell this session was if there was enough money in it to significantly enhance my own recording plans and that there be some guarantee that the session would remain available to collectors. He was unable to assure me on either point. I kept the session. But, it was nice to be asked anyway. I would have future dealings with Brad

McCuen and they would be equally unsatisfying.

So, the Jazzology Poll Winners was itself a winner. It is infrequent in any field to take an idea, turn it into a plan which becomes a project and which is carried through to fruition without a glitch resulting in a perfect success! In jazz this is almost unheard of. But here it was. Even the album cover photo was great.

JAZZOLOGY JAZZ POLL
1964 - 1965

1964	1965	1964	1965
TRUMPET:	**TRUMPET:**	**BASS:**	**BASS:**
1.LOUIS ARMSTRONG	1.KID THOMAS	1.DRAG PAVAGEAU	1.DRAG PAVACEAU
2.KID THOMAS	2.LOUIS ARMSTRONG	2.POPS FOSTER	2.POPS FOSTER
3.KID HOWARD	3.BILL DAVIDSON	3.-------------	3.JOE BUTLER
4.DOC EVANS	4.KID HOWARD	4.BOB HAGGERT	4.BOB HAGGERT
5.BILL DAVIDSON	5.DE DE PIERCE	5.MILT HINTON	5.S.MANCIAPANE
TROMBONE:	**TROMBONE:**	**DRUMS:**	**DRUMS:**
1.JIM ROBINSON	1.JIM ROBINSON	1.CIE FRAZER	1.CIE FRASER
2.KID ORY	2.KID ORY	2.SAMMY PENN	2.SAMMY PENN
3.LOUIS NELSON	3.LOUIS NELSON	GEORGE WETTLING	3.GEORGE WETTLING
4.TURK MURPHY	4.TURK MURPHY	3.JOE WATKINS	4.ZUTTY SINGLETON
5.GEORGE BRUNIS	5.VIC DICKENSON	4.PAUL BARBARIN	5.PAUL BARBARIN
CLARINET:	**CLARINET:**	**NEW YOUNG ARTIST:**	**NEW YOUNG ARTIST:**
1.GEORGE LEWIS	1.GEORGE LEWIS	1.CHARLIE DEVOR	1.BILL BISSONNETTE
2.EDMOND HALL	2.EDMOND HALL	2.MIKE POLAD	2.SAMMY RIMINGTON
3.PEE WEE RUSSELL	3.PEE WEE RUSSELL	3.BILL BISSONNETTE	3.CHAS.BORNEMANN
4.ALBERT BURBANK	4.BOB HELM	4.TREVOR TECHO	4.FRED VICORITO
	TONY PARENTE	5.-------------	5.TREVOR TECHO
5.LOUIS COTRELL	5.ALBERT BURBANK		
		NEW JAZZ BAND:	**NEW JAZZ BAND:**
ALTO SAX:	**ALTO SAX:**	1.HALL BROTHERS	1.HALL BROTHERS
1.JOHNNY HODGES	1.JOHNNY HODGES	2.EASY RIDERS	2.EASY RIDERS
2.CPT.JOHN HANDY	2.CPT.JOHN HANDY	3.QUEEN CITY	3.HAPPY J.B.
3.PAUL DESMOND	3.HAROLD DE JAN	4.SALTY DOGS	4.JELLY ROLL
4.HAROLD DE JAN	4.BENNY CARTER	5.BOLL WEEVIL	5.EL DORADO
5.ADE MUNSBOURGH	5.ADE MUNSBOURGH		
		JAZZ BAND:	**JAZZ BAND:**
TENOR SAX:	**TENOR SAX:**	1.GEORGE LEWIS	1.GEORGE LEWIS
1.BUD FREEMAN	1.BUD FREEMAN	2.KID THOMAS	2.KID THOMAS
2.MANNY PAUL	2.MANNY PAUL	3.LOUIS ARMSTRONG	3.TURK MURPHY
3.COLEMAN HAWKINS	3.EDDIE MILLER	4.TURK MURPHY	4.HALL BROTHERS
4.EDDIE MILLER	4.COLEMAN HAWKINS	5.DOC EVANS	5.EDDIE CONDON
5.------------	5.ANDREW MORGAN	6.EDDIE CONDON	6.BILL DAVISON
		7.FRANZ JACKSON	7.HAPPY J.B.
PIANO:	**PIANO:**	8.JIM ROBINSON	8.LOUIS ARMSTRONG
1.DON EWELL	1.DON EWELL	9.------------	9.EASY RIDERS
2.EARL HINES	2.ART HODES		
3.WALLY ROSE	3.ALTON PURNELL	**FOREIGN ARTIST:**	**FOREIGN ARTIST:**
4.ALTON PURNELL	4.EARL HINES	1.KEN COLTER	1.KEN COLYER
5.KNOCKY PARKER	5.WALLY ROSE	2.CHRIS BARBER	2.CHRIS BARBER
		3.SAMMY RIMINGTON	SAMMY RIMINGTON
		4.MONTY SUNSHINE	4.KENNY BALL
BANJO:	**BANJO:**	5.KENNY BALL	5.BARRY MARTYN
1.GEORGE GUESNON	1.GEORGE GUESNON		
2.EMANUEL SAYLES	2.EMANUEL SAYLES	**OTHER EASY RIDER AWARDS:**	
3.JOHNNY ST.CYR	3.DANNY BARKER	15.DICK McCARTHY(NEW ARTIST)	
4.DANNY BARKER	CLANCY HAYES	15.BILL SINCLAIR(NEW ARTIST)	
5.CLANCY HAYES	4.JOHNNY ST.CYR	11.SAMMY RIMINGTON(CLARINET)	
		16.BILL SINCLAIR(PIANO)	
		12.DICK GRIFFITH(BANJO)	

Jazzology Jazz Poll - major categories
Comparison of 1964 - 1965 results

The Best of Jazz: A Discography

The recordings in this basic discography are limited to those long-playing discs that are currently available, as listed in the Schwann LP Catalogue. The headings of sections are not intended to be exact, but simply to serve as guides to general areas of jazz. When two label numbers are given, the first indicates a monophonic disk, the second is stereophonic. For free reprints of this list, write to Dept. D-4, The New York Times, 229 W. 43d St., New York, N. Y. 10036.
— JOHN S. WILSON.

TRADITIONAL JAZZ

Louis Armstrong—Story. Columbia CL 851/4 (4 disks)
    A Rare Batch of Satch. RCA Victor LPM 2322
    New Orleans Nights. Decca 8329
Sidney Bechet—Jazz Classics. Blue Note 1201/4
    Bechet of New Orleans. RCA Victor LPV 510
Bix Beiderbecke—Story. Columbia CL 844/6
Eddie Condon—Legend. Mainstream 56024, 6024
Wild Bill Davison—Blowin' Wild. Jazzology 18
Johnny Dodds—With Kid Ory. Epic 16004
Eureka Brass Band—Atlantic (S) 1408
Firehouse Five Plus Two—Story. Good Time Jazz 12010/13
Great Jug Bands—Origin Jazz 4
Jazz at Preservation Hall, Vol. 2—Billie and Dede Pierce, Jim Robinson. Atlantic (S)1409
Jazzology Poll Winners—Jazz Crusade 2004
Bunk Johnson—Bunk and Lu. Good Time Jazz 12024
    Legend. Mainstream 56039, 6039
George Lewis—Concert. Blue Note 1208
Jelly Roll Morton—King of New Orleans Jazz. RCA Victor LPM 1649
    Stomps and Joys. RCA Victor LPV 508
    Immortal. Milestone 2003 and Mainstream 56020, 6020
Albert Nicholas—With Art Hodes. Delmark 207, 209
Red Nichols—Story. Brunswick 54047
King Oliver—Epic 16003
    In New York. RCA Victor LPV 529
Kid Ory—Favorites. Good Time Jazz 12041/2, 10041/2 (2 disks)
Tony Parenti—Downtown Boys. Jazzology 11
Pee Wee Russell—A Legend. Mainstream 56026, 6026
Muggsy Spanier—The Great 16! RCA Victor LPM 1295
Thesaurus of Classic Jazz—Nichols, Mole, Dorsey, Venuti, Lang. Columbia C4L 18
Lu Watters—San Francisco Style. Good Time Jazz 12001/3 (3 disks)

"Fifty Best Jazz Recordings of All Time"
partial listing - Traditional Jazz
New York Times - 26 November 1967

14. Algiers Stompers

Almost anything would be a letdown the day after the Jazzology Poll Winners session. Anything that is except Kid Thomas and his Algiers Stompers. I knew the band would sorely miss the bawdy-house piano of Joe James. He was as integral a part of the Thomas rhythm section sound as had been Lawrence Marrero to the Lewis band's. And just as the Lewis band never sounded the same without Lawrence, I was sure the same would happen to the Thomas band as a result of Joe's demise. But with the addition of Creole George, I felt confident this would be a hard-driving session.

I had requested only two tunes of Tom. They were "Gettysburg March" and "Summertime." The others were up to him as were the arrangements. I was surprised by some of his selections. I hadn't expected "Stardust," "Clarinet Marmalade" or "Alexander's Ragtime Band." He also chose "Algiers Strut" which surprised no one. Tom claimed authorship of this hot little number but a close listen to it reveals it is nothing more than "You're All I Want For Christmas" given a wonderful Thomas mauling. Tom had done such a great job on it just a few years earlier on Riverside that I felt it was redundant. But, as Manny Paul was not on that session, I didn't mind and the finished product stood up well against the earlier one. Curiously, the Riverside producers did not think the saxophone was an appropriate musical instrument for the playing of New Orleans jazz so they missed out, intentionally, on Manny, Capt. John Handy, Harold DeJan and others.

This was my first opportunity to meet and record my favorite New Orleans drummer, Sammy Penn. I had seen and heard him in 1962, and I admired his too few recordings greatly. I hadn't met him personally before this day. We became instant, fast friends for the rest of his life. Next to - no, along with - Jim Robinson, Sammy Penn became the closest friend of my life. It was also the first, and only, time I recorded Tom's great trombonist, Louis Nelson and bassman Joe "Kid Twat" Butler, recipient of New Orleans' most obscene nickname.

There was no question of who was in charge of this session. Tom's was the most disciplined band in the city. When Thomas stomped his foot, all discussion stopped instantly and bandsmen grabbed their instruments. The problem with Manny Paul wasn't getting him ready to play. It was stopping him once he started. Like most saxophonists (Polo Barnes excepted) once Manny got to blowing, he would continue until someone put their foot on his throat and pried the horn from his grasp. The band had dozens of tight arrangements. As I hoped, Tom had included his "In the Mood" arrangement we had so much trouble with during the Riders session.

The music flowed easily and smoothly. The only discussion was about the key for "Stardust" which Thomas quickly established as Db; the original Hoagy Carmichael key. They tore through "My Blue Heaven" with total abandon. The whole session was completed in under three hours, long breaks included. Guesnon always enjoyed working with the Thomas band because they were so professional in every regard.

Tom's band was playing that night in the hall so Sammy left his drums in place with the exception of his snare drum which he carefully packed away. Twat lay his bass down beside the piano to await the evening performance. Sammy and I sat down in the outer carriageway and talked for over an hour. Various people came by to say hello or congratulate Sammy on the session. I can't describe how much I liked him in just the space of an hour or so. Maybe it was because I didn't hold him in awe the way I did Robinson, Lewis or Thomas. And yet I was making many friends in New Orleans that I didn't hold in awe. Even Creole George who made others quake in their shoes, never intimidated me. There was just something about Penn that was different from the rest.

He asked me first about my drumming. He wanted to know what drummers I admired. As he was on the top of my list, I didn't have to put on an act for him. I told him straight out that he was my favorite followed by Joe Watkins, Gene Krupa, Zutty Singleton, Baby Dodds, Sid Catlett and Chick Webb. He shook his head in agreement with each trapster I mentioned.

"You know something, Bill," he said, "I was surprised when I didn't do better in that poll all the fellows been talking about." He didn't say it with any rancor or jealousy that I could determine. He seemed genuinely surprised, that's all.

"Sammy! You did come in second after all. But, I was disappointed too. I voted for you."

"You did? Sho nuff, you did? I guess Cie just the better drummer. That's what the poll said."

"He's a hell of a drummer, Sam. No two ways about that."

"Bill, I been wanting to ask you something."

"What's that, Sam?"

"I been seeing how you been bringing Thomas and Paul up to Connecticut. I been wondering if maybe you could include me along one of these times. I sure would like to go to Connecticut for you."

I said, "There's nothing I would like better than that, Sam. The next time I bring anybody up, you're coming too. . . on one condition."

"Oh, oh, Bill, you know I'll do anything to make that trip. What's the condition?"

"You've got to start giving me drum lessons just like Jim does on trombone."

"Why sure, Bill, sure. I'd be mighty pleased to do that."

Kid Sheik had been around for all of the record sessions, wandering in and out. You always knew he was near by his cackling laugh. He came over where Sammy and I were sitting and asked if he could see me alone for a minute. I excused myself and we walked toward the back of the walkway.

"Bill, I just wanted you to know that I'd be pleased to come to Connecticut and play with your band like Thomas done any time you want me."

I had released an album by Sheik that had been recorded by Barry Martyn in England. Sheik had also been the first of the New Orleans musicians to befriend me back in 1962. I promised him an early trip up. I had been planning to bring him up even before he asked. I always liked Sheik's playing. It's not attention getting like some of the others but it had a simple haunting quality I liked. It reminded me a lot of Bunk but apparently no one else thought so or he would have been in front of recording mikes twenty hours a day. Sheik and Big Jim were very close friends. I had been thinking about bringing them to Connecticut together and would do so the following year.

The thing that was the most interesting was the effect these three recording sessions had on the local musicians toward me. Up to then the musicians knew who I was or had at least heard about Tom and Manny's trips to Connecticut. But there were only a few I knew personally. Within the first few days after the recording sessions, I was sought out by musician after musician wanting to meet me and discuss future recordings and trips to Connecticut. I was suddenly the most popular guy in town. I'm sure they had visions of trips and albums dancing through their minds but it went further than that. They knew instinctively who their friends were. Instinct bred of a hundred years of apartheid. Word passed from mouth to mouth about who really cared about them and who was just trying to use or abuse them. If you were black and lived in the Deep South, you didn't place your trust in a white man frivolously. Your very life could hang in the balance. What I found was once you made a bond with a few of the musicians you were as good as gold with all of them. . . except Creole George Guesnon.

As I was paying Guesnon, in cash, of course, for the Thomas session, he surprised me with an invitation to his home the next afternoon. I told him I was having dinner at Jim Robinson's house with Leonard and Sonny but I would come by earlier, on my way there. I didn't ask if there was a specific reason for the invitation. If there was, I had no doubt he would get to the point of it soon enough.

We spent the evening at Preservation Hall except for a one set side trip to the Paddock to hear Albert Burbank and thank him again for a great session. I asked him if he would be interested in coming to Connecticut in the future. He said he would be if I could give him good advance notice so he could arrange for the time off from his steady gig at the Paddock.

The next day I got side tracked from my visit with Guesnon because Leonard was doing a recording session himself with George Lewis and a group of white dixielanders who played at a dixie sing-a-long spot called Your Father's Mustache. Leonard asked me to play drums on the session. Free of course. I couldn't pass up a recording session with George Lewis so I went along. But I just couldn't get into any kind of a groove with the rest of the rhythm section. I knew it. They knew it. And so did Leonard. After a few takes, we agreed that he should give Cie a call which he did. I missed out on the recording session but that was better than messing it up for everyone else. I stayed to listen to a few takes with Cie just to learn how one plays to fit in with a dixieland band. The humor of the situation struck me. Here I was, a white man, studying Cie, a black man, to figure out how to play with a white band! Had my life gone astray somehow? Screw it. I didn't want to play that honky music anyhow. I cut out for Guesnon's.

I apologized to Creole George for being late and explained the cause of it. I told him I had at least a few hours as Leonard had his work cut out for him at the recording session before he could get over to Jim's house. George talked non-stop for over an hour. He complained about this and that and everything in between. I must say that many of his complaints seemed valid except for the harsh terms in which he always put things.

His major gripe of the day was about one of the paintings from the Preservation Hall series. He said he had posed for a painting which came out particularly well. For some time it hung in the hall which was the purpose of the painting George thought. Then he went to play one night and the painting was gone. He asked Larry Borenstein what happened to it. He said Larry told him that they alternated the paintings in the hall to accommodate all of the musicians getting a chance to have their pictures displayed. His picture was in storage for the time being. Guesnon then said that, after a passage of some time, he had gone to New Jersey on a tour with George Lewis. The fellow who booked them invited the band to his home after the performance. George described the house as being a very rich home. As they sat in the living room talking, the host invited George into his den to see something special. George walked into the den and there, hanging on the wall, was the painting of him I have just described. Guesnon was non-plussed. How did he get the painting

George wanted to know.

"I saw it hanging in Preservation Hall and bought it," the fellow told him.

"And how much did you pay for it?"

"I got a real steal on it," the fellow told George, "It was only a thousand dollars."

George was going into a rage as he concluded his story. "You know how much I got for sitting for that painting? NOTHING! Not one red cent!"

If the facts were as George stated them, he certainly had a right to his anger. The fellow obviously bought the painting because it was of Guesnon. It was not some painting he picked off the fence in Jackson Square. But, it was the lie that was the knife in the back.

George's distrust (or was it disgust?) of the white man had deep roots, some justified, perhaps some not. He didn't bill himself as "Creole George" for nothing. He was Creole and he wanted everybody to know it, blacks and whites alike. But, it left him out of both worlds in his mind. He felt trapped in the cross-fire. He was a man without a race in a society where racial issues dominated. He knew his facts. HIS facts. He could tell you the history of Reconstruction and how things got to where they were through segregation from Lincoln forward. What he couldn't tell you was what he could do about his own predicament. I visited Guesnon many times. I'm not sure to this day whether I ever gained his complete trust but a few startling things happened which I shall describe in their place that make me feel I did.

Finally he got to the purpose of my visit. "Listen, Bill, I got a tape I want put onto an album and I want you to be the one to put it out."

Well, this was interesting. I asked him what was on the tape.

"It's me. Just me playing and singing some songs I wrote myself. If you take them, they'll make you a rich man. These are wonderful original songs written by me, Creole George Guesnon." As he spoke his name, "Creole George Guesnon," you could hear the hero worship in the words. This strange man was his own role model.

"Gee, George, I'm really proud that you would want me to do this. The problem is that all I put out on Jazz Crusade are jazz albums," I replied.

"But, these will make you rich. And I'll tell you what, if you do this just the way I want it done, I might have some other tapes for you that are right down your alley."

Now he caught my attention. There had been rumors around New Orleans for a long time that Guesnon had some jazz tapes that he had privately recorded right in his home. Several people had asked him about them and he always denied it. I felt I was on the trail of something important.

"What are these other tapes, George?"

"Oh, I can't rightly say about them now until you put out this other one.

But they are something nobody else got."

"I have to know the whole deal, George. I'm not putting out an album just on your word that you got something more. I have to hear what you got."

"Well, then, I guess we can't do any business," he said. "I guess maybe you're not the right man to do this after all."

Our meeting was at an end. He showed me to the door. It was just as well as I was now running late for dinner at Jim's anyway. I turned at the door.

"George, let me take the tape you want released and I will listen to it. Then I'll get back to you about it. But, I can't promise anything." He went to a drawer and took out two five inch reels of quarter inch tape and handed them to me as I left.

Dinner at Jim's was always a culinary delight. Pearl Robinson was just as good a chef as Helen Mares in her own fashion. The style of dinner was strictly oldtime New Orleans black. Pearl did not sit with us at the table as we ate although there was plenty of room. She sat in a straight back kitchen chair about ten feet away and watched. As soon as one of our plates started getting a little light of food, she was up piling more on. It was a bottomless mound of food. When you finally finished, there was just as much food on your plate as when you started. When we were through and adjourned to the front room, Pearl sat by herself at the table and ate. Once in awhile Leonard or Sonny would try to lure her into the conversation. But this seemed to make her so uncomfortable that they soon stopped. Jim was oblivious to it all. He just kept chatting away.

It was just custom and, custom notwithstanding, Jim Robinson loved his wife Pearl very much. He was never quite the same after she died. While she lived, he philandered every chance he got, even into his seventies, but he still loved her. She was HIS woman and that was that. Pearl agonized about losing Jim to another woman. She worried especially when he came to Connecticut because of the name of my band. Jim used to tell me, "Bill, you know what Pearl say to me when I comes here? She say, 'why dose boys call theirselves Easy Riders anyhow. Must be some monkey-shines happening when you wit dose Easy Riders.'"

Two musicians who made an impression on me during this trip were Polo Barnes and Punch Miller. I met them both in 1962 and liked them. This time I listened closely to their playing at the hall and got to know them better. I filed both of them away in the back of my mind for future sessions.

One other musician I had to seek out on this trip because he wasn't playing while I was in town was Israel Gorman. I had hoped to record him also. He was one of my favorite clarinet players. I realized a few months later that what I should have done was add him to the line-up on the Algiers Stompers session. Had I done so, it would have been his last recording. He died in 1965 during the big hurricane that struck New Orleans.

15.   Rimington Joins The Riders

In August of 1965, Sammy Rimington returned to Connecticut for another short tour. He had promised Griff when he went home from his first visit that he would try to locate a Vega banjo for him. He brought it with him to Griff's delight.

Sammy only stayed a week, during which we managed to use him on our weekly Silversmith gig twice, feature him at a Moose Hall concert which was recorded and cut a record session. It was at the Moose Hall concert that we recorded the tracks that ultimately became the instrumental sides on Buck's Spivey album.

The other recording session we did that week was a strange one. I don't know what got into me when I was picking the tunes for it. They included: "If I Ever Cease To Love," "Ory's Creole Trombone," "Java" "The Sheik of Araby" (with a kazoo solo by yours truly!), "Early Hours" and other weirdos like that. The album was never released. George Buck now owns the rights to that session and I think it questionable whether it will ever see the light of day. We recorded it in the banquet room of the West Haven Motor Inn, where we later recorded one of the December Band sessions.

As the week drew to a close, Sammy said he wanted to talk to me about something important. I was thunderstruck by what he had to say.

"I want to come to America to live. I'm sick of the jazz scene in England. There's no sincerity or understanding of the music there. I'd like to move to Connecticut and join the Easy Riders."

Sammy was playing with Ken Colyer's Jazzmen at the time so I was surprised at what he said about the British scene. We all greatly admired the Colyer band. But, Sam's unhappiness with the jazz environment in England as a whole was understandable. Colyer's was the only band to make a serious impact on American jazz musicians. Chris Barber was popular for a short time after Ken left the band but, as Barber shifted away from the "Colyer sound," interest in his group faded fast. Barry Martyn's band was beginning to be noticed but it wouldn't be long before he left England also. Sammy indicated that he and Colyer were not getting along and it would be best for both of them if he left.

This was an interesting development for sure. For all of our playing and recording, we were still a part-time band. Every member made his living outside of the music.

"Sam, I'd like to have you in this band so much I can taste it. I just don't see how you could make a living playing here. I'd be happy to have you move in with me so you wouldn't have any expenses to speak of."

The more I spoke, the more I convinced myself that we might be able to pull it off if Sammy wanted to come bad enough to take the risks with me. I thought about how Mouldy, Griff and Sinclair would react when I announced that Sammy Rimington was joining the Easy Riders Jazz Band. God, they would die. Then I thought about how Noel Kalet would react. Well, that's life, I thought. It was time for Noel to go anyway. I knew it and he knew it too. When it happened, he took the news well. Noel had played competently and never let the band down while he was with it. He just had different musical interests than the rest of us.

My thoughts returned to putting this thing together. "Sam, you know we might just be able to work it out. I wonder what's involved in bringing you into the country. I don't think you can just come in as a tourist and stay forever."

"I'd be happy to stay with you and Carol for awhile," Sammy said. "I might be able to make some extra money teaching guitar."

I knew some of the music school owners in the area and Sam was a good guitarist. Perhaps. . . son of a bitch, this might just work!

"Listen, Sam, I think we could do it. I will have to see about getting you some work papers or something from the State Department. You'll probably have to sign something for them. But there is one thing I want you to understand: I have a great admiration for Ken Colyer and I won't steal you from him. If I am going to do this, I want you to know that I have to write to him and ask his permission."

"That's alright," Sammy replied, "He will not try to hold me back. After all, he came to America also to learn about this music. I'll talk to him before you write and there will be no problem with him."

Sinclair had just been released from the army. He decided, and I agreed, that he should not continue as co-leader of the Riders. He didn't want responsibility and I had firm concepts of what I wanted the Riders to sound like. I called him and asked him to drop over. Then I called Mouldy and Griff and invited them too. Sammy was as "high" about telling them as I was.

"Wait until we tell them," he said, "they won't believe it!"

Pulver and Vigorito lived quite a distance from me so I decided to inform them both by phone after I told the others. I was a little concerned about how they would react when they realized that this would spell the end for Noel's participation in the band as they were both friends of his. Sinclair was his best friend but Bill was not one to let sentimentality or friendship interfere with what he saw as his musical goals.

When Sam and I broke the news to Griff, Mouldy and Bill, they were incredulous. It took us a while to convince them we were serious and not just putting them on. After a million questions, they finally grasped it. None of us could foresee what this would mean for us or our band. What it ultimately did mean was that we would have an incredible year of great jazz ahead of us and then a break-up of the band that would leave all of us with a bitterness that would last for years afterward. Perhaps the year was worth it. It certainly was for jazz collectively if not for us individually.

I contacted the State Department through some friends and discovered that Sammy could come only if someone was personally willing to take full responsibility for his financial well-being. He would have to come as my employee.

I wrote to Ken Colyer and told him that Sammy wanted to join my band and, because of my high regard for him, I wanted his permission for Sam to do so. I also asked if he required some time to replace Sammy. I received a prompt reply telling me he would not stand in Sammy's way even if he could. He said Sammy could not have made a better choice of bands and he then gave me some candid thoughts about Sammy that would prove helpful. I'm sorry but I do not choose to share those comments with you in this book. Suffice it to say, they were not derogatory to Sammy in any way. Just leader to leader stuff. He then congratulated me on getting a fine clarinetist for the Riders.

I broke the news to Art and Fred. I think it sealed Fred's fate as far as the Rider's was concerned. For all of his growth and competence in, and assimilation of, the music, he just was not as engrossed with it as the rest of us were. He would last in the band less than three months after Sammy came to stay. He then left and joined the U.S. Air Force where things weren't quite as combative. Pulver stayed on until the break-up that split the band in two a year later. I told Noel that Sammy was permanently joining the Riders on a full-time basis. He understood it was time to go.

For the next several months I had my work cut out for me. Not only did I have to work out the details of Sammy's State Department visa, but I decided to put on a concert to welcome him to America that would eclipse anything we had done before. We scheduled a tour to begin during the first week of December. It was the first tour we scheduled so close to Christmas. We had avoided the month for fear that people would be too preoccupied with the holidays to bother with going to a jazz concert. This would have to be some band to catch their attention.

Yes, it would have to be some band. . . this December Band.

16.   The December Band

Unlike the Jazzology Poll Winners album which had been carefully planned to become a classic of the genre, the recording that resulted from a hot night of jazz on a cold winter's eve, at the Moose Lodge Hall in Stamford, Connecticut on December 3, 1965, was a total surprise to all, participants and fans alike. Critics agree there has never been a New Orleans jazz concert recording to equal it. That something very special was happening became apparent even before the conclusion of the opening "Introduction Blues." A melding of band and audience occurred that approached mysticism. Only the people who were in that room will understand exactly what I mean, although it is somewhat evident on the recording.

No one who was there will ever forget that evening. There were times, such as during Kid Thomas' climax of "Uptown Bumps", or along about the second chorus of Handy's "Ice Cream" solo, that reality took leave of its senses. Waitresses stopped serving and bartenders left their posts to walk to the entrance of the main hall to stare and listen in awe to the sights and sounds of that bandstand.

The emotion reached such heights that, at one point, Handy left the bandstand in the middle of "Lil' Liza Jane" and walked out of the hall into the bar saying he couldn't continue because of the tension. He almost threw up from it. But, he couldn't stay away and, within minutes, he was back doing things to a tune I introduced as the "Kid Thomas Boogie Woogie" that would prompt me to change its name on the album to "Handy's Boogie."

Even those numbers that became out-takes on my Jazz Crusade release became an outstanding album on the Center label. With the exceptions of a "Saints" finale and "Burgundy St. Blues," I don't recall a number that didn't end up on an album. How did it come about, this incredible evening of jazz?

It was a celebration party to welcome Sammy Rimington, the Easy Riders Jazz Band's new clarinetist, to America. Having become disenchanted with the British jazz scene, which had already begun its long decline, Sammy left home simply to be able to play in a hot band. He could have gone with virtually any New Orleans style band in the world. He chose the Riders. It was our intention to throw him a party he wouldn't soon forget.

The idea for it came about in a discussion I had with Bill Sinclair. I asked Bill to suggest his "dream band" for Rimington's first tour as a regular. He instantly recommended Jim Robinson, Kid Thomas and Capt. John Handy. I agreed it was a great combination. I said there had to be one addition to the lineup. When I was in New Orleans, I promised Sammy Penn he would be on the next Connecticut tour.

Bill replied, "Penn would be great. I thought you would want to play drums if Robinson came up. Aren't you going to play at all?"

"I have the feeling this band might be able to struggle along without me," I kidded.

"Do you really think you can get them all to come together, even Handy and Jim?"

Bill had never met any of the musicians he suggested except Thomas. Handy was the only one I had doubts about. I knew him slightly but we hadn't talked much. He was an extremely shy man when it came to dealing with strangers. He hadn't mentioned a desire to come and tour like so many others had. I asked Kid Thomas to recruit him. I felt confident he would come when he heard about the company he would be in.

I approached the new Connecticut Traditional Jazz Club governing board with the proposal after informing them that Rimington was moving to Connecticut to join the Riders. Both the news of Rimington's move and the tour band floored them. It would be an expensive undertaking I told them and I didn't expect them to foot the bill. I would get enough other work for the band to keep their costs down. I requested that they take two concerts. They were excited about the prospect of having so many great names perform for the club but, they were worried about the timing of the tour. I agreed it was risky but, I told them I wanted it to coincide with Rimington's arrival. It was early enough in the season so snow probably would not be a problem. The concern was the proximity to the holidays. They took the two concerts and requested that I schedule them as early in December as possible.

As the meeting ended, Jack Guckin took me aside. "Maybe I can help you," he said, "I've been thinking about doing a privately sponsored television special on New Orleans jazz. I talked to my station about it and they have zero interest in it. Maybe now is the time for me to move on it. This sounds like a helluva band. I can feel it running down my leg just thinking about it. How much would it cost me to get these guys into a TV studio for an hour video taping? An afternoon would be fine so it doesn't bump one of your concerts."

"Jack, it will cost you whatever you want it to cost you. You've supported me in everything I've done in this music. Do the best you can for us but, any number you come up with, the band is yours," I replied.

Once again I called George Buck to offer him a concert recording. But this time I was determined I would not cut myself out of doing one also as I did with the International Jazz Band. I wanted that opening night concert at the Moose for Jazz Crusade and I was intent on keeping it. I described the band to George. Like Guckin's, his leg must have been getting damp too at the thought of it because he agreed instantly to take the final concert for GHB.

We picked up an additional gig at New Haven College for the Student Center. Bud Larson's modern jazz group was booked for the same affair; a jazz battle between Traditional and Progressive jazz. The tour was fully booked with my costs guaranteed in advance. I would be able to relax and enjoy one of my own productions for a change.

I phoned Kid Thomas and he assured me all was set with Handy. He said Robinson and Penn were spreading it all over town that they were heading to Connecticut for "Big Bill." I told him I had booked all I was going to on the tour and they could expect to be in Connecticut from December 2nd through the 7th.

Rimington arrived several days before the Moose Hall opener. When we told him what we had in store for him, he could hardly believe it. I arranged for Mike Fast to record both CTJC concerts. Mike had become a real fan of the band and had even taken up drums.

Because of earlier problems with musicians getting from the New York airports to Connecticut, I decided that, on all future tours, I would pick up the New Orleans guests at the airport myself. It was a pain in the ass but, as I always used late night, cheapie flights, it was at least tolerable. Rimington went with me to meet the plane. There were warm greetings all around as we packed their bags into my station wagon. This was the only time, of his many trips to Connecticut, that Sammy Penn brought his complete drum set. The night was cold and clear. The weather forecast for the next night's concert was for more of the same. We drove to my house and found room for everybody to bed down.

On December 3rd, I took the day off from work to spend with my guests and to attend to last minute details. The other members of the Riders all went to their day gigs as usual. The first time Griff, Mouldy and Sinclair ever met Robinson, Handy and Penn was a half hour before the concert at Moose Hall. And this in the midst of setting up for the gig. It amazes me to this day that these eight musicians, unknown to each other until the minute they unpacked their instruments for the job, could walk onto a bandstand and create jazz history together in front of several hundred jazz fans who were now filling the hall.

There were important people in the room. John Hammond of Columbia Records strode in: the man most responsible for the career of

Louis Armstrong and innumerable other jazzmen. Brad McCuen of RCA Victor arrived, perhaps looking for another Jazzology Poll Winners style session. Victoria Spivey arrived on the arm of Len Kunstadt of Record Research magazine, there to report the event for what turned out to be a cover article. Connecticut Congressman Donald Erwin was working the crowd. And there were many musicians from New York and Connecticut.

I was to emcee the concert. When the band was ready, I walked out onto the bandstand. Seated offstage and directly below me was Mike Fast making last second adjustments to his array of dials. He looked up and nodded. I glanced at the entrance and saw Sinclair at the head of a column which would put onstage, in order: Bill Sinclair, piano; Dick McCarthy, bass; Dick Griffith, banjo; Sammy Rimington, clarinet; Sammy Penn, drums; Capt. John Handy, alto sax; Big Jim Robinson, trombone and, "last but not least, probably the world's greatest jazz musician, Kid Thomas Valentine."

I could see Sinclair's nervousness clear across the hall. He looked terrified. Not to worry, Bill, I thought. If you can just make it across the room without blowing lunch, this sucker's in the bag. I pushed the switch on the mike and said, "I'm not going to make any announcements or anything. We're going to get right to the music. . ."

As I introduced each man, they stepped onto the bandstand and started to play. It wasn't just Sinclair who was nervous. Penn carried himself with his usual aplomb but he was chewing the tip of his cigar to a juicy pulp as he walked up. Handy seemed bolted to the floor when I called him out. I watched as Big Jim gave him a nudge. I could see Jim mouth the words, "Go on, Handy." It would take more than this crowd to frazzle Jim Robinson. He came out smiling and waving to the audience with those massive hands. He stepped onto the stage and gave a little hip-shuffle to the music before sitting down.

And then came Kid Thomas. He strode into the room and leapt onto the platform facing the rhythm section, his back to the crowd. He then raised his horn to his lips and swung around directly at the audience and let go with a blast that stunned everyone. I looked at Mouldy as he broke into a big grin that told me everything was going to be alright.

On they went. Brilliant chorus after brilliant chorus; like a diamond starting to glisten as each facet is cut. Each musician topping his previous solo. For a jazz fan it was thrilling, maddening. I kept glancing down at Mike Fast for his reaction. Professional that he was, he would just nod his head now and then, assuring me that he was getting it all. Never before, or again, would I see the Riders in such a state. They were working like bastards to keep up with the titans from New Orleans and loving every minute of it. Griff was yelling, screaming, at the highpoints. There were so many, he was hoarse at the end of the night. Mouldy and Rimington would look over at each other and break up laughing like kids at the mischief they were doing.

So many highlights. So many moments that just couldn't be eclipsed. And, then, eclipsed. Handy sitting there, never standing, not even on his solos, blowing hot, Hot, HOT. Big Jim taking Handy's cutting session challenge on "Ice Cream" with a chuckle and two brazen return choruses. Top that Jim! Sho'nuf I will, Handy! Sammy Penn pushing his mighty foot into the bass drum, the cigar dangling dangerously from his smiling face; never losing his cool or his ash. Thomas jumping up with his tambourine and banging it against his hip in rhythm, pushing Handy along. Jim jumping up next to him and dancing in place while waving his handkerchief at the crowd. Rimington's leg jerking uncontrollably as he stomped the floor on his solos. All leading up to. . . what?

And then it came. A moment frozen in time for anyone lucky enough to have witnessed it. A moment even the recording machine couldn't possibly capture. It came in "Uptown Bumps." The old riff on "Bucket's Got A Hole In It" started simply enough. Rimington and the rhythm section playing the verse. Sensuously. Bodies started swaying in the crowd. It must have been this way half a century ago in New Orleans I thought. No whites present then to be sure, but it must have been just this way. The band came in on the chorus, dirty, lowdown and lovely. Rimington took it back from them as Sinclair let out a scream lasting half a chorus.

Then Jim. The old time Jim. The American Music Jim. The Bunk Jim. The other horns joined in on the "Uptown Bumps" riff behind him as Kid Shots had twenty years before. Then it was Handy's turn, the same John Handy that young Earl Bostic used to sneak in on and listen to for ideas. The "temperature," as Kid Thomas used to call the tempo, going up. Sinclair in next bringing it back down, softening the edges. Trying to keep it from getting pornographic. Setting the stage for an ensemble that never came. Sinclair started into another chorus. That's when it happened, this black magic.

Suddenly there was a sound. A strange, haunted sound. Heads snapped up and looked around. What was it? It came again and all eyes focused on its source. It was Kid Thomas, still seated, a plunger mute caressing the bell of his horn. One eye closed. The other staring, who knows where?, over the top of his derby mute. A man possessed. He wailed again. And again. An unearthly wail from heaven, diverted through hell. Fire and brimstone on pearly wings. Voices in the crowd began crying out, "THOMAS! THOMAS!" He jumped to his feet, threw the plunger aside and lifted his horn towards the ceiling. No. Through the ceiling. Through the roof. Through the ionosphere to the stars and beyond. Was someone up there? Listening? None of the other musicians stood. There was no standing beside this man now. Let him go. They started riffing under him and listening to the magic. The Thomas horn blazed. It was as if this man's whole life had been lived to play this one chorus. Energy charged the room. People began cheering him long before he was ready to finish. And when he did finish, the whole room rose to its feet, audience and band alike, and exploded into applause. Thomas stood there looking around the room, his trumpet clutched in his hand. Finally, as if to end it, he dropped the horn onto its stand and sat down.

And that was that.

— — — — —

The next afternoon the band trouped to Hartford for Guckin's television taping. It was held in the same studio as our first recording with Kid Thomas and Manny Paul. Guckin had been at the concert the night before. He laughed as he said, "Just do it exactly the same as you did it last night." Fat chance! Three cameramen stood at the ready to add the visuals television demanded. The audio guys were putting microphones everywhere. I wondered what Mike Fast would think if he saw all of this high-class state-of-the-art audio stuff. A sound check was made and played back. Guckin thought it sounded fuzzy. He went into the control room where the audio engineers were seated. They assured him everything was okay. They said it was just that the studio monitor speakers were getting old and that was where the problem lay, not in the recording. He asked them to double-check everything. They did, then offered him a headset and replayed the tape. It sounded fine through the phones.

The taping began. Everybody was comfortable and the music flowed like fine wine. After the first couple of numbers, Jack asked for a video playback so the band could see how they looked. They all got a kick out of it. But, Jack could still hear the fuzziness in the audio. He didn't like it. He walked into the video control room, which was separate from the audio, and mentioned his concern to the technician in charge of the overall production.

"It sounds great to me Jack. It's those damn speakers."

Jack needed an hour of good, solid New Orleans jazz in order to have a chance of selling his program. The band repeated several key numbers. He ended up with a couple of hours of material in the can. The visuals were stunning. WTIC-TV, owned then by the Travelers Insurance Company, was the leading TV station in Connecticut with the best equipment and technical people. Jack has really got something here I thought as we packed up to leave.

He agreed, "Yeah, now I have to edit it into a usable program and decide what kind of commentary to add to it. You know, this business with the audio is still bothering me. I don't understand why I can hear static in the track and nobody else does. I mean these guys are pros and if they say it's a clean tape, it must be a clean tape. But, I'm a pro too. And damn it, I hear static."

I asked if he was coming to the college jazz battle the next day.

"No. I think I'll study this tape tomorrow. I'll see you at the West Haven Motor Inn gig Monday." He gave me a check in payment for the taping.

It is interesting to note that of these four "New Orleans" jazzmen who made up half of the December Band, not one of them was born in New Orleans. Handy lived, and died, in Pass Christian, Mississippi. Jim Robinson's birthplace has been given as either Deering or Deer Range, Louisiana. Thomas was from Reserve, La. And Sammy Penn came from Morgan City in Louisiana.

Penn's career had been tied to Tom's since the 1930's. At the time of the December Band tour, the few recordings he made had all been with Thomas and would continue to be with rare exceptions. The two most notable of these exceptions were his two recording sessions with Punch Miller for Jazz Crusade in 1967 and 1969. He treated Thomas with deference. Tom was his leader.

Sammy Penn was one of the heaviest drinkers of the New Orleans coterie of musicians. He had a tendency to rush his tempi when he was drunk and had to be closely supervised to prevent his reaching that state; a job Kid Thomas saw to when Sam played with the Algiers Stompers.

Beginning with the December Band tour, and continuing through over a dozen tours with me, I became more and more responsible for controlling Sam's problem. It was a difficult situation for me because most of the Riders were two-fisted drinkers also and it was only natural that they keep passing the bottle to Penn as well. Add to that the many fans and well-wishers who were constantly offering to buy him a drink and you can see the potential for disaster. I never knew Sammy to turn down a drink. Neither Thomas nor I drank.

The first time I had to face the problem was when Tom came to me to complain that he had "talked" to Sammy about it and Sammy boldly told him that, now that he was in Connecticut and "working for Bill," it was none of Tom's damn business. Fortunately it happened at a party the evening of the television taping when the band wasn't playing. I didn't know how to handle it. Here was Penn, a man who had already become a close friend. A man older than my father. A man I idolized as a musician. Finally, a black man from the South who had spent decades listening to white men tell him what he could or couldn't do. My first inclination was to ignore it. That's basically what I did with my own sidemen. None of them were sloppy drunks. As long as they played well and didn't become obnoxious or offensive, or at least more so than usual, I figured, like Sammy said to Thomas, it was none of my damn business. Sammy certainly never got obnoxious. It was worse. The drunker he got, the more lovable the old bastard became! But Tom's warning about it affecting his playing scared me. What if he ruined a gig or, worse, Buck's recording? For the first time I had to face up to actually disciplining one of the New Orleans musicians.

It was a watershed decision that would have far-ranging implications on my relationships with musicians, both black and white. I was fearful that I might get the reputation of being a martinet. Allan Jaffe was already becoming thought of in this way, rightly or wrongly, by many of the Preservation Hall players. It would take him years to dispel this image, which, to his credit, he did. On the other hand I thought it might strengthen my hand with my own sidemen. If they saw me acting the part of a strong leader even with the New Orleans men, perhaps it would help if I ever had to do it with one of them. Unexpectedly, just the opposite occurred. Some of the Riders took offense when I treated the New Orleans guys as sidemen. But, the New Orleans men respected my doing so.

I talked to Penn and explained to him that I was concerned that his drinking might wreck one of the recording sessions and that it would hurt his reputation. I bluffed him by telling him the only way he was going to make it past Cie to that coveted first place in the Jazzology Jazz Poll was to continue making great recordings.

"One screw-up on a recording, Sam, is all it's going to take for you to drop out of second place." He understood instantly. He also sensed the true concern I had for him and for what I was trying to accomplish. There would be times in the future when it got away from him and he got smashed. My little talk wasn't about to put him on the wagon. When it wasn't important, I just looked the other way. But, he always tried to be at his best for recordings.

Much more importantly, he and Thomas quickly spread the message throughout the New Orleans jazz community that I was someone to be fully trusted and accepted as one of their own. This was a status I wanted and nurtured. I would never claim to have reached musical parity with my New Orleans friends. But I do claim with certitude that I achieved equal standing with them as a member of that coterie. The only other white musician to do so, I think, was Barry Martyn.

This accomplishment entitled me to all of the perks of membership. I could now be harangued by George Guesnon, scolded by Kid Thomas, kidded by Jim Robinson, lectured to by Alvin Alcorn, upstaged by Eddie Sommers, fathered by Sammy Penn, mothered by Polo Barnes, preached to by Punch Miller, raise hell with Kid Sheik and finally be forced to listen to the symptoms of every disease known to man as contracted by that supreme hypochondriac Sing Miller.

It also meant that I could more effectively control the Jazz Crusade sound. If the sound of the Jazz Crusade releases was different from those of my colleagues, and many have said it was, I think it is because I approached my recordings from a jazzman's perspective. You have to have a different outlook on the job of the musicians when you have actually sat beside them and played with them than you have by being a spectator. It doesn't mean my albums were better than the rest, some were, some were not. I could list a dozen sessions produced by non-musicians that I would have murdered for just to get the rights to release them on Jazz Crusade. But, still, my sessions WERE different. They had a different feel to them. I instinctively knew what ensemble sound I would get from a certain combination of musicians that hadn't been tried before. I knew precisely how a band's sound would vary if recorded in a studio or in the Moose Hall. I was seldom surprised at the overall results of a recording. I was ALWAYS surprised at the minor things that could affect the quality of the result. One musician could, and frequently did, make the difference between a mediocre and a great session. Get a drummer on a bad night and you've lost the session. Which leads me back to where I began about keeping Penn off the bottle.

On the afternoon of December 5, 1965, a Sunday, over 300 students packed the Student Center at New Haven College. In the December Band, they would be hearing a musical style that, to them, would be new. Bud Larson, once the New Orleans jazz fanatic who taught me to be the same, would open the concert with his modern jazz group. Larson now played valve trombone. It was a far cry from the Kid Howard style trumpet he once played. He was the only member of his band who realized what they were up against. Battle of the Bands duels are fun but meaningless exercises. You get to test your mettle but you seldom prove anything, particularly when the competing bands play totally divergent styles. Nevertheless, we figuratively tied the wagons together and had at it.

Bud's band played a superb set. I'm sure it was state-of-the-art because nobody in the audience seemed to comprehend what the hell they were trying to accomplish musically. I guess that's what you want to happen when you're on the cutting edge of your music. Big Jim was enthralled with the valve trombone Bud was playing. He told me he had seen such horns in New Orleans in his youth and asked me if I thought he could easily master it! I suggested he not even try. Handy understood what he was listening to and seemed to enjoy it. It wouldn't have taken much to get him up on the stage with them and start jamming.

Thomas didn't like modern jazz. He thought it was, "a lot of foolishness." Penn stood to the side of Bud's drummer watching and nodding his head in approval every time Bud's drummer looked over at him. Sammy was grinning and chomping on his cigar. The drummer was obviously trying to show this old-timer his stuff. Sammy would just grin and nod. Finally he walked over to me. I asked him how he liked the boy. He smiled and leaned his head close to mine. "He ain't no Cie, Bill. That's for sure. Everything's alright, Bill, alright."

The December Band opened with "Hindustan." The slaughter went on for an hour. This is the way it must have been for Hannibal at Cannae. I had heard college concert recordings by the 1950's George Lewis band. I had been amazed at the great audience response on those records. I even surmised that some of the applause had been dubbed in. Could kids really go that crazy for this kind of music? I had my answer this day as I listened to that same, noisy, unrestrained applause. I had brought along a pile of Jazz Crusade albums that featured Thomas, Jim and Penn. They sold like hotcakes after the concert. Yes, these kids loved what they heard. Then why is it, I thought then and wonder still, that New Orleans jazz is the least commercial music in America? Below country blues, opera, barbershop quartets (!) and even below dixieland. How can it be? But, it is.

That evening, after the concert, Mike Fast brought over the tapes from the Moose Hall concert for us to hear. All eight members of the band were present and listened carefully. The tape was magnificent. Nobody thought the excitement of that night could have been captured on tape but here it was. Handy was slightly under-recorded for which Mike apologized to Cap. The problem, Mike said, had been caused by Handy's proximity to a very loud table of fans. When he boosted the gain on Cap's mike, the table noise came up with it. He moved the mike in on Handy as tight as he dared but still Handy was soft. But you could hear him and the problem was minor compared to the overall sound Mike achieved.

As the first few numbers rolled off the lead reel, the band tried to be as objective, and even critical, as possible but they were soon swept up with the excitement of the session and our alleged "evaluation session" turned into a celebration party with everybody laughing and congratulating each other. Even Tom, who was usually brutally critical of himself on record, seemed delighted with the results. When he heard the playback on his "out" choruses of "Uptown Bumps," he broke into a big smile as the band once again applauded him. Same old soupbone, man.

I walked Mike to his car. "Great job Mike. The best yet. I hope Buck's session goes half as well tomorrow night. If it does George will be one happy man when he hears it."

He replied, "We'll get a good clean sound at the inn but it is a dead room compared with the Moose. It will give us a more conventional sound. You seem to like that boomy Moose Hall sound but it's a bitch to record in."

"Get used to that Moose Hall sound, Mike. You're going to be making many recordings there."

I learned of the Moose Hall through a machinist friend of mine where I worked in Stamford. He was a member of the Moose Lodge. He booked their dances and one day, when a dance band he hired backed out at the last minute, he asked if I could throw a band together to bail him out. I told him my band was a jazz band. He was desperate and had to have something. I brought a small group in and played his gig. It was successful and I was really impressed with the big sound of the room. In return for my small favor, I asked if we could hold a jazz club concert there. They didn't allow outside groups in but he made an exception for me. After that first December Band concert, they let us come anytime we wished.

The last concert by the band was a sellout. Word of Friday night's stunning concert spread quickly and almost everybody who attended that first concert returned, friends in tow. The band was just as "up" as at the earlier concert and the crowd went wild again. Mike's recording went smoothly. He took great care setting up Handy's mike and every note Handy played was faithfully captured on tape. Many new tunes were added to give Buck material they hadn't already recorded. The session was more relaxed as this was the fourth time the band played together. Once again there were many unforgettable highpoints but, it was Handy who stole the show. On one number, after he completed his solo, he suddenly yelled, "I ain't done yet!" and started soloing all over again. His "Cap's Blues" brought the house down and required an encore. . . which he was happy to supply. George Buck honored his outstanding performance by giving him leader status on the three album set he released.

On one of the band's breaks, Jack Guckin asked me to step outside into the hall for a minute. He broke me the only piece of bad news of the entire tour.

As soon as we were alone, he turned to me. I could see something was wrong by the look in his eyes. He said, "The audio's crap. My tape is worthless."

"Oh no," I replied. "Are you sure, Jack?"

"I spent all day with it yesterday. I told those guys there was a buzz on the audio but they insisted it was only the speakers. It's junk man. I could have cried when I heard it."

"The band's going back home tomorrow, Jack I don't know what I can do. I'll refund your money if you want but it will leave me short on paying the guys."

"No, it's not a matter of money goddamn it. It's just that the goddamn video is beautiful and the band played great and it's all shit now."

The December Band tour brought the pivotal year 1965 to a close. The band had not been billed as the December Band. That was a name I selected when I released the album. I tried several other names before I chose it. It had a nice layering of meanings. The fact that the concert had been held in December served only to give me the thought. "It's a long time from May to

September." The "September Song" ends there. The September of the lives of our four New Orleans guests had long since passed. For them, the summer and fall had been no big thing. They had spent those life seasons living under a repressive social system that brought them no good. Now they were entering their winter. And yet winter sometimes is a wonderland. Particularly December. For them winter had become warm fireplaces, pure snowfalls and Christmas. A Merry Christmas. And soon, too soon, it would be over for them. All of that was hidden in the name December Band.

Like another band name I had invented, the International Jazz Band, the December Band name would be "borrowed" in future years, always without permission, by people too unsophisticated to understand its full meaning. It was flattery by imitation I didn't appreciate.

As the December Band's New Orleans contingent awaited their flight home, we decided to have breakfast in one of JFK Airport's super-expensive restaurants. Kid Thomas sat staring at his menu while the others ordered. Finally, the waitress turned to him and asked, "Is there something you'd like, sir?"

Thomas, who raised poultry in his backyard, replied, "Yes, ma'am. I'd like to see the chicken that lays these $3.00 eggs!"

DIRECT FROM NEW ORLEANS
TWO CONCERTS
Kid Thomas - Trumpet
Jim Robinson - Trombone
John Handy - Alto Sax
Sammy Penn - Drums

featuring: Sammy Rimington, Bill Sinclair,
Dick McCarthy & Dick Griffith

Friday, Dec. 3, 1965 - MOOSE LODGE HALL
119 Main St. STAMFORD, CT. "45 Minutes From Broadway"
Monday, Dec. 6 - WEST HAVEN MOTOR INN
Exit 42 Conn. Turnpike

8:30 P.M. - 12:30 A.M.

Adr. $2.50   CTJC members $1.00

pre   ɔy the   Connecticut Traditional Jazz Club
P.O. Box 152, Wethersfield, Conn.

December Band Flyer autographed by Thomas, Robinson, Handy and Penn.
1965

(PHOTOS BY ANDREW P. WITTENBORN)

ISSUE 73
JANUARY, 1966
record research 35 cents

NEW ORLEANS JAZZ AT THE LEGION OF THE MOOSE - Len Kunstadt

FRIDAY, DEC. 3, 1965 - MOOSE LODGE HALL, STAMFORD, CONN.

Direct from NEW ORLEANS came KID THOMAS, trumpet; JIM ROBINSON, trombone; JOHN HANDY, Alto Sax and SAMMY PENN, drums and with the stalwart support of EASY RIDERS JAZZ BAND Sidemen: SAMMY RIMINGTON, clarinet; BILL SINCLAIR, piano; DICK McCARTHY, bass and DICK GRIFFITH, banjo; the sounds of native New Orleans jazz captured the delight of an eager, most appreciative audience.

Under the auspices of the dedicated CONNECTICUT TRADITIONAL JAZZ CLUB this native American music had an opportunity to be heard in all its sincerity and simplicity. Kid Thomas is a remarkable old-timer whose shading of Keppard and Dominique in ragging; in low-down gutbucket helmet work like Mutt Carey; in the blue curves of Tommy Ladnier indeed make him an exciting musical personality to see and hear. Jim Robinson, they call him 'Big Jim', not because he is of large stature, but he is the boss man of that big round trombone note which makes him the inspiration and model of the younger generation of New Orleans jazz trombonists. And then there is John Handy whose alto sax phrasings stomp back to great jazz saxophonists of yesteryear. And does he stomp and make runs like the legendary Charlie Holmes, Stomp Evans and like Coleman Hawkins used to sound. He may be classified as 'New Orleans' but there is a heck of a lot of the 'hell for leather' Texas technique in his rip snorting, hard hitting, on beat, frivolous playing. The fourth member of these venerable New Orleans jazz men is Sammy Penn, smiling Sammy, with that big cigar (in the Willie, "The Lion" tradition) protruding almost dangerously from the side of his mouth, as he lays down the big two beat sound of the Cottrell, Dodds, Singleton, New Orleans school. He also is an industrious vocalist as he uses the side of a small snare drum to act as a rudimentary amplifier. Sammy Rimington, from Great Britain, and now the clarinetist with the EASY RIDERS, has the facility of Shields and Parenti, the warmth and minor tones of George Lewis and Johnny Dodds - and he complemented the above New Orleans veterans with succinct and admirable teamwork. Dick Griffith is a very fine banjoist who is practically a rhythm section all by himself. 'Slow Drag'-Dick McCarthy certainly pays excellent tribute to the great Slow Drag of New Orleans fame with his almost effortless solid, lazy, heavy bass thumping so essential to New Orleans music presentation. And last but not least is Easy Rider pianist, Bill Sinclair, the anchor man, supplying the key, the chord - and squaring off with easy flowing classic jazz-piano choruses in the manner of Steve Lewis, Richard M. Jones or Jimmy Blythe. Good company, no doubt!

And good music as they followed their opening improvisational blues with LITTLE LIZA JANE, CARELESS LOVE, SMILE DARN YOU SMILE, SOMEDAY SWEETHEART, WASHINGTON AND LEE SWING, LADY BE GOOD, ST. LOUIS BLUES, ICE CREAM, SLEEPY TIME GAL, KID THOMAS' BOOGIE WOOGIE and BUGLE CALL MARCH.

In the audience were such dignitaries as Bluesdom's Victoria Spivey, RCA-Victor's Brad McCuen, Columbia's John Hammond and the Honorable John J. Irwin, a Connecticut congressman who expressed his appreciation with some fine words about the music and its participants - and its value in our society. Also present were key members and officials of the Connecticut Traditional Jazz Club - and other musicians of the up-and-coming Easy Riders Jazz Band including their leader Bill Bissonnette.

So good was New Orleans Jazz At The Legion Of The Moose, that we had to get another 'taste' and on December 8th we were back again to hear the aggregation, this time at the West Haven Motor Inn, right outside West Haven, Conn. They scored again with their music and their audience. Perhaps we can have them score right here in New York City. After all it was just 20 years ago that Bunk Johnson came through with the sparkling New Orleans sound!!

Record Research Magazine - front cover
December Band Issue #73
January, 1966

17.   The Half-way Marker

  1965 was indeed a pivotal year in the Jazz Crusade. The New Orleans Jazz Revival was reaching its peak. Dozens of excellent recordings were being made in New Orleans and elsewhere. The Jazzology Jazz Poll for both 1964 and 1965 showed clearly that the black New Orleans musicians dominated the traditional jazz scene as never before. At least three kitty halls were going full blast in the French Quarter at any given moment. Young musicians were pouring into New Orleans from all around the world. They would form the nucleus for later revivals. Preservation Hall had become an institution under Allan Jaffe's careful tutelage. Other bands across the nation were starting to play the music including the incredibly fine Hall Brothers Jazz Band of Minneapolis. They began importing New Orleans jazzmen as we were doing in Connecticut. New Orleans bands were on the move, touring in England, Europe and Japan. It was a wonderful time to be associated with, what we insiders called, "our music."

  I had recorded three sessions in New Orleans to rave reviews. We had our new jazz club which seemed to flinch at nothing when it came to promoting New Orleans jazz. We had recorded George Lewis with the Easy Riders Jazz Band. Sammy Rimington had shocked the jazz world by leaving the Colyer band to join the Riders. We were planning tours for 1966. And we climaxed the year with the December Band tour. As John S. Wilson summed up the year for Jazz Crusade in a major New York Times article:

  "Bissonnette's crusading fervor is focused on his steaming desire to help traditional jazz survive. . . All of the elements involved -- the jazz club, the Easy Riders, the musicians from New Orleans and England -- were products of (his) crusading zeal. . . Jazz Crusade records, which has now issued 11 disks, has expanded to such an extent that it lost $4,864 for Bissonnette in 1965. . . With the help of youngsters such as Rimmington(sic) and veterans from New Orleans, Bissonnette's crusade has been steadily building in Connecticut."

  In short, though broke, I was on a roll.

Ntl. Register Dec 5 1965

JAZZ BEAT

Emigration In Reverse

By ROCKY CLARK

Now that the farthest-out of our modern jazzmen, Ornette Coleman, has joined the growing number of American jazz musicians to take up residence in what they consider the greener pastures of Europe, it is strange to note that one of England's budding young jazz clarinetists is moving to America.

Sammy Rimington, who visited Connecticut last summer to perform with Bill Bissonnette's Easy Riders Jazz Band, apparently liked what he found here. He has given up his job with Ken Colyer's Jazz Band in London to return to America and settle down in the Bridgeport area to teach music and become a regular member of the Easy Riders group.

Rimington will perform on clarinet with the Easy Riders' rhythm section —Bill Sinclair on piano; Dick Griffith, banjo, and Dick McCarthy, bass — accompanying the four New Orleans jazzmen performing for the Connecticut Traditional Jazz Club tomorrow night at the West Haven Motor Inn.

Shades Of Colyer!

Rimington thus will be emulating his former boss, Colyer, who worked his way aboard ship to New Orleans in 1952 for the thrill of sitting in with such jazz pioneers as George Lewis, Jim Robinson, Paul Barbarin, Johnny St. Cyr and Doc Souchon. (In fact, Colyer overstayed his visa and wound up in the New Orleans jail).

The same Jim Robinson, now 72 years old, will be among the New Orleans men Rimington will be playing with tomorrow night. Big Jim, who has played trombone since 1918 with such groups as the George Lewis and the late Bunk Johnson bands, has been leading his own group at New Orleans' Preservation Hall in recent years.

The other New Orleans men appearing at the West Haven session are trumpeter Kid Thomas Valentine, who toured Japan last year with the George Lewis band; alto saxist John Handy, and Sammy Penn, drummer and vocalist with the Algiers Stompers, who puffs a big cigar as he beats the drums.

The group actually arrives in New Haven today to perform for students at New Haven College this afternoon at 3 o'clock.

• • •

Article announcing Rimington's joining Easy Riders
Jazz Beat - New Haven Register
5 December, 1965

The Photo Artistry of

Andrew Wittenborn

1. Albert Burbank	9. Sammy Rimington,
2. Big Jim Robinson	Capt. John Handy
3. George Lewis	10. Bissonnette, Robinson
4. George Lewis	11. Kid Sheik Cola
5. Henry "Red" Allen	12. Kid Thomas Valentine
6. Zutty Singleton	13. Big Jim Robinson
7. Billie & DeDe Pierce	14. the December Band
8. Sammy Rimington	15. the December Band

Andy Wittenborn first started taking jazz photography in the 1950s while at college. He served as a photographer in the U.S. Army. He joined the Connecticut Traditional Jazz Club in the 1960s which gave him many opportunities to use his photographic skills in the jazz field. Andy is also a member of the Long Island Trad Jazz Society and of the Jazz Photographers Association. He uses a Rolleiflex camera for his B&W jazz photos and does his own lab processing. He also has many 35mm slides.

He is an auto mechanic by trade and owns a one man garage in Briarcliff Manor, N.Y. He is also a railroad fan, mainly Colorado & short lines & steam engines ("I love that beat"). He also owns two antique automobiles: a 1933 Franklin and a 1929 Graham-Paige. His daily car is a 1964 Plymouth Valiant station.

Albert Burbank

Big Jim Robinson

George Lewis

George Lewis

Henry "Red" Allen

Zutty Singleton

Billie & DeDe Pierce

Sammy Rimington

Sammy Rimington, Capt. John Handy

Big Bill Bissonnette, Big Jim Robinson

Kid Sheik Cola

Kid Thomas Valentine

Big Jim Robinson

The December Band

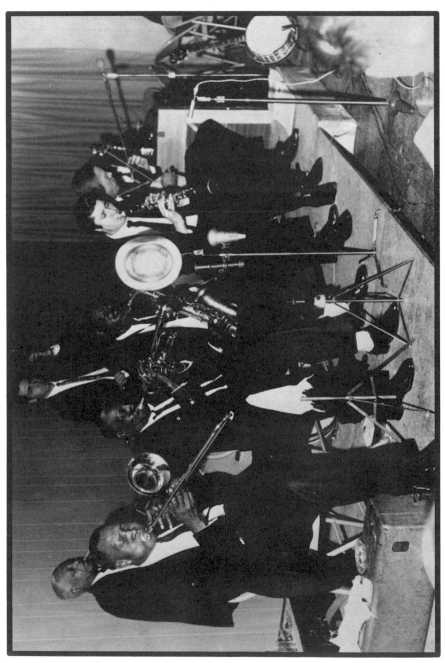

The December Band

1966

deceased

AVERY "KID" HOWARD, trumpet

ISAIAH MORGAN, saxophone

JOHNNY ST. CYR, banjo

ALBERT WARNER, trombone

18. A Busy Year

1966 was to be even more exciting than 1965. In that one year, I promoted seven Connecticut tours by New Orleans musicians including the full Eureka Brass Band, Billie and DeDe Pierce, Kid Thomas (three times), Capt. John Handy, Sammy Penn, Jim Robinson and Kid Sheik. I produced thirteen recording sessions, more than one a month. We started a second, five piece, band called the Mouldy Five in which Rimington was the sole horn player and I played drums. Our two bands held down four separate weekly gigs at the Yankee Silversmith Inn in Wallingford, the Villa Rosa in Woodmont, the Rocking Horse in Hartford and the West Haven Motor Inn. On these steady jobs we featured many New York based jazzmen including Henry "Red" Allen, Edmond Hall, Jack Fine, Vic Dickensen, Zutty Singleton, Tony Parenti, Jimmy Archey, Henry Goodwin and many others. I even tried to arrange recording sessions for the Riders with Coleman Hawkins and Earl Bostic but could never hook up with either.

We also received visits in Connecticut from the Original Osaka Jazz Band, later known as the New Orleans Rascals, from Japan and by the Canadian Black Eagle Jazz Band. We sponsored concerts for both of them. Fred Vigorito left the band after the Eureka Brass band concert to be replaced briefly by Englishman Clive Wilson. Griff and I made a month long pilgrimage to New Orleans, his first as a jazzman, where he began banjo lessons with Creole George Guesnon.

Sammy brought a surprise package with him from England: his bride, Nina. This was a totally unexpected development. I had agreed to put Sam up at my house for however long it took for him to get established in America. He hadn't said a word about Nina in advance of showing up with her. I didn't mind one way or the other, just one more mouth to feed. My wife didn't see it that way and friction developed between the two women instantly. It was no one's fault. Nina tried to be helpful and friendly. The shock of her unannounced arrival on my wife was just too much for her. It led to problems that quickly spread to the band.

And just to ice the year's cake, we finished it with a titanic (in more ways than one) knockdown, drag-out battle that blew the band apart during a recording session. . . with Kid Thomas looking on.

At year's end, the Easy Riders Jazz Band consisted of myself, Griff and Mouldy Dick. Rimington was preparing to leave Connecticut for his long trek to the apex of New Orleans jazz where he resides today. Kalet, Sinclair and Pulver were back together playing dixieland music behind flapper clad Charleston dancers.

Let me tell you about 1966.

the Queen & the Riders

JAZZ FANS: The West Haven Motor Hotel announces
the first of its new series of "Jazz Nights".
  Dine, dance or just listen to The sounds of
New Orleans as the legendary blues singer Miss
Victoria Spivey joins The Easy Riders Jazz Band
for an evening of jazz. Miss Spivey and the
Riders will feature songs from their new hit
record album.
February 11, 1966 (Friday) 9:00 P.M. to 1:00 A.M.
West Haven Motor Hotel, Exit 42, Conn. Turnpike

The Connecticut Traditional Jazz Club Presents

A"SPECIAL FEATURE"JAZZ CONCERT

Starring the renowned master of the tenor sax:

BUD FREEMAN

Direct from his appearance at the NEWPORT JAZZ FESTIVAL

playing with the EASY RIDERS JAZZ BAND.

July 9th, Friday, 8:00 P.M. - 12:00 P.M. at the
YANKEE SILVERSMITH INN, Route 5,Wallingford,Ct.
(Just north of Wallingford Toll Station on the
  Wilbur Cross Highway extension of Merrit Pkwy)
Members & guests: $1.50   Others: $2.00

Postcard Advertisements
1964/65

19.　　　Eureka!

They came by bus from Boston. All eleven of them. Percy Humphrey, trumpet; his brother Willie, clarinet; his other brother, Earl, trombone; Milton Battiste, trumpet; Peter Bocage, trumpet; Oscar "Chicken" Henry, trombone; Emanuel Paul, tenor saxophone; William Brown, sousaphone; Chester Jones, snare drum, Henry "Booker T" Glass, bass drum and Grand Marshal Fats Houston. The Eureka Brass Band of New Orleans had arrived in Connecticut. . . in the middle of one of the worst blizzards of the decade.

Percy had called me to let me know that the Eureka would be doing a concert in Boston. They would be traveling by bus from Boston to New York on February 25th. If I wanted, they could stop off in Bridgeport for one concert on that day. It would be the most expensive single concert we ever put on but I wanted them to come. And I wanted to record them.

Percy and I discussed terms. Percy always drove a hard bargain and we finally agreed on a price which would allow me to record four songs or twenty minutes, whichever was longer. I brought it to the governing board of the jazz club and they approved it in minutes even though it was a budget buster. We would need a minimum of four hundred people in the audience at a higher than normal ticket just to break even. This even after the money I was willing to personally put up for my recording. It was risky business. It would have been risky even in a month when the weather was reliable. February is winter in extremis in Connecticut. We decided to gamble on the weather. We lost.

By the time we picked up the band at the bus terminal in Bridgeport early in the day, there was already several inches of fresh snow on the ground and it was coming down at a rate of over an inch an hour. Several of us took our cars down to meet them. We made arrangements with various club members to put them up overnight and feed them. As Sammy and Nina were still living with me, I would stay the night at my parents house which gave us a total of three bedrooms at my house. I took four of the musicians.

We had decided to have a big spaghetti dinner at my place for the band. In addition, we included Sammy, Mouldy, Sinclair and Griff and their spouses. About two dozen for dinner! The women: Carol, Nina, Fran and Sue did the cooking while we set up additional tables and chairs. Fats Houston settled into my favorite easy chair. When the call for dinner came, Fats didn't move. We called again for him to come to the table. He replied that he couldn't. He had sunk so low into the chair he couldn't get up. It took three of us to pull him out of the chair. This was a man who really deserved his nickname.

The women piled the spaghetti high on three extra large serving trays. Griff, Sammy and I each took one and carried them to the table where the band was seated. As Sammy approached the table he tripped on the edge of the rug and three pounds of spaghetti, sauce and meatballs slid gracefully off of the tray, flew through the air right between Percy and Willie Humphrey and landed in the middle of the table with a loud splat. Everyone just sat there looking as the massive, squiggly mountain of orange stuff settled down and the meatballs stopped rolling around. Sammy cried out, "Oh no! Oh no!" Unfazed, everybody dug in.

The concert was scheduled for 8:00 p.m. About 6:00 p.m. the snow stopped with over a foot of it on the ground. There was no backing out now. The concert would have to go on. The band would have to be paid in any event so we would have to try to make it to the Glorieta Manor site and hope that at least a few fans would show up. Some of the main roads were being plowed as we prepared to leave. The phone rang. It was the manager of the Manor asking me if we intended to cancel. He didn't want to go to the expense of having his parking lot plowed. I told him we were on the way and to make sure the plow got there before we did.

When we arrived, a plow was at work clearing the driveways to the hall. By 8:30, the Riders were ready to go on with our opening set. And to our surprise and delight, the hall was already more than half full with a line of cars outside waiting for the plow to clear additional parking areas. We played until 9:30 when the hall was filled to capacity: over 600 fans had braved the storm. What a magnificent tribute to this band that so many people would go out in such bad weather to see and hear them. They would not be disappointed.

We arranged with Percy to keep the band out of sight in the outer lobby while we played our first set. We were doing a History of Black Jazz in Music. It was the only time we ever did this and it worked nicely. We worked our way through oldies like "Dead Man Blues" and "After You've Gone." Mike Fast was balancing his microphones and setting the sound he wanted during our set. When he gave me the thumbs up sign that he was ready, we ended our set. All of the Riders stayed on the stage for the big event to follow.

I approached the mike and made the announcement all were waiting for. "Ladies and gentlemen," I raised my finger and pointed over their heads to the back of the hall, "the EUREKA BRASS BAND OF NEW ORLEANS!"

The bass drum boomed. The trumpet sounded its call to arms and the Eureka marched into the hall behind the gyrating bulk of Fats Houston, his hat held high in his outstretched arm, his chest ablaze with the Eureka banner. The crowd went wild. People were standing on chairs to get a better look as the Eureka snaked through the aisles. The strains of "Just A Little While To Stay Here" filled the hall and even the Riders members were screaming and yelling as the band climbed the stairs to the huge stage. Sammy and I started playing along with them. There was no way we could stop the compulsion to do so.

We left the stage and Percy greeted the audience. I went down to where Mike was getting ready and sat beside him to make the critical decision of when to turn on the machine for those four precious songs. Jack Guckin was there also trying to help me decide. Mike glanced at me and said, "you know I could flick that switch right now and get this whole set." No Mike. A deal's a deal. Beyond the very fact of recording the Eureka, another thought went through my mind. This was the opportunity to record the three Humphrey brothers together for the first time. There they were: Percy, Willie and Earl together on the same stage.

Percy and I agreed that I would signal him when the recording would begin and I would then take the next four numbers, no matter what they were or how they came out. I had discussed some numbers with him that I wanted. He would try to do them during my twenty minutes. I was dying to turn the recorder on but I was determined to hold off until I thought the band had hit its stride. It was killing me to wait but I did. We did not record the first set at all.

During the break, Griff and I were talking to Chicken Henry. He took us aside and turned to me. "Bill," he said looking very serious, "I'se gonna tell you somethin' nobody else knows. I knows the secret of good trombonin' and good health and I'm gonna tell you it. And you never forgets it. Clean your horn and your bowels everyday and you'll always play good and never be sick." Griff and I looked at each other and back at Chicken who was nodding his head knowingly. And now you know it too. Don't forget it.

Percy was in good form that night. Before the job, Sinclair noticed him taking swigs out of a bottle. Thinking it was booze, Bill cozied up to him and asked him what he was drinking.

"Olive oil," Percy replied.

"Olive oil? You're kidding."

"No man, it's olive oil. I always drink a bottle of olive oil when I'm gonna be drinking alcohol because it cancels out the alcohol and you don't feels it. Want some?"

"Uh, no thanks, Percy."

Percy asked me why I hadn't taped on the first set. "You better get that machine going if you gonna get that tape you want." I told him I would take the first four numbers of the next set. "Just don't forget to turn it off after those four numbers," he said.

The recorder went on. Mike felt confident all his levels were set and he assured me we would get a good recording. The band opened with the "Saint Louis Blues."

And now I am going to tell you a little story which is the most bizarre story I will tell you in this book. You may not believe it but it is the absolute truth. As the Eureka played through "St. Louis Blues," it came time for Earl and Chicken to blow a chorus. Earl stepped up to the mike, raised his trombone to his mouth and, just as he got ready to blow, his false teeth dropped out of his mouth onto the stage! He glanced out at the audience, reached down and picked them up, put them back in his mouth and began to blow his horn just as if nothing had happened.

I had requested a dirge of Percy and he obliged with a beautiful rendition of "Nearer My God To Thee." I also taped "Jambalaya" and "Oh! Didn't He Ramble." This completed my four numbers. We switched the recorder off. The Riders then joined the Eureka onstage for a grand finale jam session. The concert was over. It was a great success in every way. The tapes came out fine including the two Easy Rider sets. It was my intention to put out the session as a concert recording with the Eureka on one side and the Riders on the other. It didn't work out that way. A few months later, my wife and I were divorced. I needed money for my legal fees. I had only one way to raise it quickly. I sold the Eureka Brass Band session to George Buck. It was released two decades later coupled on an album with the great Barry Martyn recording of the Olympia Brass Band.

The morning after the concert broke clear and cold. We took several cars and delivered the Eureka to Kennedy Airport. Fats pranced through the main terminal as if he was leading a parade. . . to the annoyance of the band and the delight of passers-by. An hour later the Eureka was on the way home to New Orleans and we were on our way back to our next adventure.

THE
'EUREKA'
BRASS BAND of NEW ORLEANS

&

THE EASY RIDERS JAZZ BAND

- NINETEEN TOP STARS -
ONE NIGHT ONLY!

GLORIETA MANOR — FRIDAY, FEB. 25, 1966
52 TRUMBULL RD., BRIDGEPORT, CONN. 8:30 PM to 1 AM

ADMISSION: CTJC MEMBERS: at door of concert: $ 1.50
advance tickets: $ 1.00

OTHERS: at door of concert: $ 3.00
advance tickets: $ 2.50

Advance tickets available from:

THE CONNECTICUT TRADITIONAL JAZZ CLUB
P.O. BOX 152
WETHERSFIELD, CONNECTICUT

**Eureka Brass Band of New Orleans
advertisement flyer
1966**

1. BUGLE BOY MARCH
2. DEAD MAN BLUES
3. OVER THE WAVES
4. IN A LONE BEZAUSE
5. SUMMER TIME
6. IT FEELS SO GOOD
7. PRETTY BABY
8. TIGER RAC
9. CLIMAX RAG
10. AFTER YOUVE GONE
11. BELLS
12. NOBODY'S FAULT
13. PEACE IN THE VALLEY
14. LEAD ME SAVIOR
15. ROSE ROOM
16. OVER THE WAVES

CTJC CONCERT WITH EUREKA BRASS BAND 2/25/66

**Griff's play list
Eureka Brass Band concert
25 February 1966**

20.   Redwing

In March we brought Kid Thomas back to do a Jazz Crusade recording session. I wanted a session with just Tom and the Easy Riders. In order to do so, we searched for, and found, supporting gigs to cover the costs of bringing him up. We used him on two of our regular jobs and Art Pulver's wife arranged an interesting concert for the Junior Woman's Club of Cheshire.

The concert was on March 12, the day before the recording session. In addition to Tom, I decided to use Victoria Spivey on the gig. Programmes were printed in advance and I sent one to Vicky so she would know what numbers we planned to do with her. She arrived with Len Kunstadt several hours early to dine with us before leaving for the concert. I was interested in seeing Tom's and Vicky's reactions to each other. I didn't wait long. The first time Spivey uncorked her bottle and took a swig, Tom turned off to her. He didn't like male drinkers and female ones were anathema. And Vicky could chug-a-lug with the best of our men. Tom was properly cordial throughout the evening but she couldn't break through with him. After a few blasts from her bottle, she didn't even try. The concert went very well. We opened with a hot "Bugle Boy March" and then did our "Intro Blues." We featured Vicky on some of the things we recorded with her for George Buck. Sammy did feature numbers on "Lead Me Saviour" and "Burgundy St. Blues." Tom and I each did a few vocals. Vicky added a few suggestive lines to one of her songs and Art heard about it later. But, all in all, it was a fine concert.

The next night we recorded in the Moose with no audience. Mike engineered the session. Things did not go well. Thomas, Sammy, Mouldy and Griff were in great form and saved the session despite lackluster performances by Sinclair, Pulver and myself. Sinclair missed chord changes regularly throughout the session. I was in over my head on several of the tunes and just did fills as best I could. Pulver's foot was following a separate drummer, except he was supposed to be the drummer.

We did multiple takes on everything, sometimes three or four, except for "Everybody Loves Somebody" which I didn't even bother to play on. It was one of the best tracks of the night. . . maybe because I didn't play. We only had this one open night for recording so there was no turning back.

Tom was leaving the next day for home. We finally got the session in the can after hours of laboring with it.

We listened to the playbacks about a week later. I often had Mike hold onto tapes and keep me away from them for awhile after our sessions as "day after" playbacks usually only confirm the opinion you formed on the session. A little distance gives objectivity. I only violated this rule a few times when Mike thought we had something special or the New Orleans guest specifically asked to hear them.

When I did hear them, the tapes were confusing. Mike had preliminarily rearranged the takes to put the ones he thought the best up front. Even some of these were flawed but, perhaps not fatally. The tracks deteriorated in quality too quickly. We listened to them all. Everybody in the band was in on the listening but the final selection, of course, was mine. There were some really outstanding highlights that everyone agreed should see the light of day. There were two in particular. Thomas was brilliant on "I'm Alone Because I Love You." He did some bizarre things on the out-chorus that were stunning; especially in the "channel" as we often called the bridge of a tune. The other was "Redwing." Tom had changed the normal F-Bb key to Eb-Ab. It made a dramatic change in the feel of the song. I announced as soon as I listened to it all the way through that if there was enough material here for an album it would be called "Redwing."

But, I seriously thought about junking the session. There were too many things going wrong. Not any one of them fatal but the cumulative total of them was devastating. Sammy talked me out of killing it. His point was simple: there is some great Thomas here. I knew there was some great Rimington also. It was also the first album Sammy did with the Riders since joining us and I had wanted that to be an especially good release. I spent several weeks listening to the good tracks over and over. I was trying to talk myself into it. I played them for other non-band members who thought they were pretty good. I finally made the finished album edit and played it for the band. Each and every man had a track he wanted cut from the album because of his own playing or because of the wobbly rhythm on otherwise good numbers. I pointed out that if I made everyone's cuts there wouldn't be enough left to put out a 45 rpm single, never mind an album.

I finally decided to go with it. My reservations about it prompted me to economize on the packaging. I put it out in stock record jackets with just basic letter-press printing of the vital information on the cover. I didn't even bother with liner notes. The reviews were mixed at best. Downbeat's Ira Gitler savaged me as usual but he gave both Tom and Sammy high praise. His sense of imagination soared as he critically appraised my trombone playing: "Bissonnette's trombone sounds like a sick cow dying in a hailstorm."

Mouldy read that, looked at me, and said, "Moooooo."

To my surprise, "Redwing" became one of the most popular Jazz Crusade albums. Even in its re-release on GHB, it has sold out its first press run and has been re-printed. It makes me wonder about some of the other tapes I erased back then that I thought were not good enough to issue.

JAZZ CONCERT
PROGRAM
PART ONE

BUGLE BOY MARCH
Welcome
Introduction of Easy Riders Jazz Band Leader
EASY RIDER BLUES
LIL LIZA JANE
CARELESS LOVE - Vocal by Victoria Spivey
A GOOD MAN IS HARD TO FIND - Vocal by Victoria Spivey
ALGIERS STRUT
EH LA BAS - Vocal by Kid Thomas Valentine
BELLS OF ST. MARY
LEAD ME SAVIOUR
ICE CREAM - Vocal by Bill Bissonette

Intermission
PART TWO

JUST A CLOSER WALK WITH THEE
VICTORY WALK
I AINT GONNA GIVE NOBODY NONE OF MY JELLY ROLL
MAMA'S GONE GOOD BYE - Vocal By Victoria Spivey
SHAKY BABE FROM NEW ORLEANS - Vocal by Victoria Spivey
GIRL OF MY DREAMS - Vocal by Bill Bissonette
MILK COW BLUES - Vocal by Kid Thomas Valentine
CONFESSIN

Intermission

BYE AND BYE
I CAN'T ESCAPE FROM YOU
PANAMA RAG
KID THOMAS BOOGIE WOOGIE
BURGUNDY STREET BLUE - Featuring Sammy Rimmington
WHEN THE SAINTS GO MARCHING IN

New Orleans Jazz Concert

By the

Easy Riders Jazz Band

Sponsored by

the

Junior Woman's Club of Cheshire

March 12, 1966

Cheshire High School

Programme
Thomas/Spivey/Riders concert
March 1966

21.   Billie And DeDe

One of our finest tours in Connecticut during the 60's came about by chance and was, unfortunately, not recorded. It was the two week long visit by Billie and DeDe Pierce. I had originally scheduled George Lewis and Cie Frazier for the tour. A scheduling conflict prevented either of them from coming.

The last minute cancellation threw us into near panic. Flyers had already been mailed out to hundreds of fans. Lewis, of course, was a top draw and this would have been Cie's first tour with the Easy Riders. I started placing frantic phone calls to find replacements of similar stature. We didn't want to use Kid Thomas again so soon. He had been here in December and March. The Lewis tour was scheduled for the last week of April through the first week of May. Because of recent trips, I decided against Robinson, Penn, Handy or Paul. I tried to get Albert Burbank but it was too short notice for him to get away from the Paddock. Everyone I called had a problem. We were within two weeks of our start date with no guest stars.

As it was because of a conflicting Preservation Hall Band tour that we lost George and Cie, I decided to call Allan Jaffe for help. I hadn't remembered that it was Mardi Gras in New Orleans the day I phoned. A man answered the phone at Preservation Hall. The background noise was deafening so I couldn't identify his voice.

"Is this you, Allan?" I shouted into the phone.

"What did you say? I can't hear you," the voice yelled back.

I realized it was not Jaffe. "Is Allan Jaffe around?" I yelled back.

"I don't know any Allan Jaffe," the voice hollered.

Had I gotten the wrong number? Certainly everyone at Preservation Hall knew Allan Jaffe. "Is this Preservation Hall?"

"Yes, that's what it is alright," the voice replied.

"Who are you?" I yelled.

"My name's Joe. I'm from Cleveland. A tourist. This place is so crowded, that I got pushed against this wall a half hour ago and haven't been able to move since. So, when the phone rang, I answered it!"

I hung up on my friend Joe. . . from Cleveland.

It took me several days to reach Allan. I explained my plight. He was already aware of it. He asked what he could do to help. I told him I needed two New Orleans musicians to come to Connecticut on short notice because of the conflict with George and Cie. He asked me if I had tried Thomas seeing he was, "practically living in Connecticut anyway." I let the wisecrack pass and told him I needed someone new to the area for this tour. He then surprised me by offering to let Billie and DeDe Pierce come up. They were his main attraction at the hall and on the road. I hadn't even considered them as I knew from previous conversations with them that they would not travel without Allan's consent. I had a high regard for Jaffe, though I can't say we were friends, but I hadn't gone through him for any of our guest stars because I wasn't about to let anyone have a veto power over my bookings. The offer now of Billie and DeDe was, I thought, a magnanimous offer. He asked me what I was prepared to pay. This was the main reason I had hesitated before calling him in the first place. I didn't want him to find out how little pay some of the musicians were accepting to come to play with the Riders. Touring with my band had become somewhat of a status symbol among the New Orleans men. I ignored the question and responded by asking how much Billie and DeDe would cost me. He said he would give me a special reduced price for them because he knew they would like to go to Connecticut with us. So that was why he was offering them, I thought. He asked how many jobs were involved. I told him I really didn't know as we were still trying to book out the dates.

I mentioned that I usually hired the New Orleans people on a weekly rate and that I covered all of their living and travel expenses separately from that rate. I knew exactly how much Allan paid his people on the road because Jim Robinson had complained to me about it. It was substantially more than I paid them but they had to pay for their own food and lodging which sucked up more than the differential. I told him to include in his price the cost of one recording session. He said he would get back to me in a day or two.

The next day he called with a price that bowled me over. It was higher than the wages he paid on the road without even factoring in their paid expenses. As if that wasn't bad enough, there was one firm condition: no recording. Not at any price. My back was to the wall. I had to have somebody and Billie and DeDe would be a good draw. The no-recording restriction stuck in my craw. God, how great it would have been to do a session with them at the Moose Hall. December in May! I accepted his terms, stiff as they were. When I told the band who was coming, they flipped out. I promptly punctured their balloons with the no-recording clause. I never heard so many people say, "Oh shit," in unison.

I got another call from New Orleans a few days later. It was from the English trumpeter Clive Wilson. He had been studying jazz in New Orleans for several months. He asked if he could come along with Billie and DeDe. I really didn't need a second trumpet man with DeDe on the gig. On the other hand, Fred Vigorito left the band after the Eureka concert and we were looking for a replacement for him. We had been using the marvelous black trumpeter Henry Goodwin from Long Island in the interim but it was a long trip for him and rather expensive for us. I discussed Clive with Sammy and he said he might make a good permanent trumpet player if I could live with his "very British" mannerisms. I wasn't sure what he meant by that but a quote from one of the old "Raffles" mysteries popped into my mind, "After all," Raffles said, "if one is an Englishman, it's no crime to be a snob. Is it?" I invited him up..

The tour began, as usual, with a Moose Hall concert on April 29th. We managed to get out a last minute letter to club members informing them of the switch in personnel. We had a full house. Among the dignitaries was New York Times critic John S. Wilson who gave the guests, the band and the Crusade a marvelous half page write-up. Clive did an excellent job in the second chair, never trying to upstage, always complementing DeDe's horn. I was impressed. We did most of Billie and DeDe's standard repertoire: "Peanut Vendor," "My Little Girl," "Indian Love Call" and, of course, their piece de'resistance, "Love Songs of the Nile;" one of my favorite numbers, and which they always did, despite latter comments to the contrary in certain jazz journals, in the original key of Db. The concert was a great success and both of our guests commented on the great sound of the Moose Hall and the fine reception they received.

As we moved across the state, the bandsmen became more and more frustrated that we couldn't record such a great tour. The suggestion was made more than once that we "bootleg" a session, if only for ourselves. Bootlegging was one thing I opposed and never did. (Later, in California, when we inadvertently taped several numbers with Clancy Hayes singing and playing with the band at Earthquake McGoon's, I had the tapes immediately erased.) Even DeDe said to me on the drive home after one of the concerts that he wished he had a tape of it! I knew that if I did such a thing and word of it spread back through New Orleans the Crusade would be over. I had the trust of the musicians and I was not about to jeopardize it. Now, as I sit here a generation later, and think about the music we made on that tour, I wonder if I was right. Most of the New Orleans musicians, including Billie and DeDe, are gone. Even Allan Jaffe is dead. So few recordings. So few. And this was one more of those great sessions that got away. Days beyond recall.

We did two more concerts for the jazz club: one at the Matarese Restaurant in Newington, another at the Moulin Rouge in Ivoryton. We also brought them onto our steady Friday night gig at the Villa Rosa. The crowds were strong all along the route but nothing prepared us for what was to happen when we took them into our regular Sunday job at the Rocking Horse bar in East Hartford.

Jack Guckin had talked a young woman reporter from the Hartford Courant, the most influential newspaper in the state capitol, into going to the Matarese concert. Her name is Barbara Carlson and she brought along staff photographer, Bob Ficks, just in case she found the event newsworthy. She fell in love with Billie and DeDe and went back to her newsroom and wrote a truly inspired article so charming and compelling that it was run in the middle of the front page of the paper on the Sunday morning of our East Hartford gig replete with several magnificent photos.

The Rocking Horse was a small bar where our new group, the Mouldy Five played on Thursday nights just to try things out in public. Believe it or not, we were paid the grand amount of $8.00 per man plus beers and Cokes. If we wanted hard liquor, we had to pay for it. But, occasionally the management would spring for a few extra bucks if we had something special going on the alternate Sunday afternoon gig we did there with the full Easy Riders Jazz Band. They sprung for Billie and DeDe. . . a whole extra hundred bucks.

We arrived for the gig about a half hour before starting time. We expected the usual Sunday crowd of about fifty fans. As we approached the place in our car, we noticed a commotion on the street corner where the "Horse" was located. We thought there might be a fire. It was no fire. It was a double line of people which ran from the Horse's front door all the way down the block, around the corner and out of sight; all waiting to be admitted to see this jazz couple from New Orleans who had made the front page of the Courant. There were hundreds of them.

We entered through a side door and had to force our way through the crowd inside to the little band area. The bar layout was in two sections separated by a service bar. The room we played in sat about forty people with another fifteen at the bar. The other room opposite the bar usually accommodated another fifty. There must have been twice this number packed in. Where they couldn't sit, they were jammed in shoulder to shoulder along the walls and in the aisles. As Billie and I led DeDe through the mob, they all started cheering our arrival. Guckin and the reporter had met us at the side door when we arrived. They couldn't get in! We brought them in with us along with several other regular fans of the band, each carrying a drum case to make them look legitimate.

As we got ready to play, the owner came over to me. "This is unbelievable," he shouted over the crowd noise. I pointed out the girl reporter who was responsible for it and suggested he give her all the free drinks she wanted. He then told me that the ex-world champion boxer Willie Pep had just come in and asked if I would announce his arrival to the crowd. I did so and Pep raised his hands over his head as if everybody was there to see him. I didn't see him again but found out later that they had managed to clear a table for Pep and his party in the outer room, from which he couldn't see the band. He got really mad because they wouldn't throw people out of a "ringside" table for him and stormed out of the place without hearing a note of music. So I guess we took him on points. But, on the other hand, he was the only prize fighter I ever met in my life. Big thrill.

The band rose to the occasion and just knocked everyone out, including ourselves. It was the wildest gig I ever played in my life. For Billie and DeDe, it was more like playing at Preservation Hall than a concert. They thought it was just great. It proved to me the power of good publicity. And good writing. The reporter had compared DeDe in the article with the great stone statues on Easter Island. Thor Heyderdahl couldn't have written it better. And this stone-faced megalith blew hot trumpet!

I have many fond recollections of this tour. The band never played better, nor were the bandsmen ever to be closer as friends and team-mates. Billie and DeDe were two of the most charming people ever to grace a bandstand. They were warm, friendly folks who cooked for all of us most of the time they were in Connecticut. They regaled us with stories about their bouts with alcohol which caused DeDe's blindness. We heard how Allan Jaffe had turned their lives around and made life worthwhile again. They were the ones, the only ones, who talked about the caring, compassionate side of Jaffe and showed me what a complex man he was. I could understand their loyalty to him that never once faltered in all the years they worked together.

We did several jobs with Billie and DeDe which took us to the northern part of our state. Each time we went north, we returned via the Merrit Parkway, a scenic highway which traverses the state north to south. Something mysterious was going on each night as we approached home in the dead of night. Just before I would pull off the highway onto the exit, DeDe would say, "Oh, it's so good to be home." I didn't think much about it the first couple of times he said it. Then I got to thinking about it. DeDe was blind. How did he know we had arrived at the exit before I even slowed down? It was so dark in the shadows of the parkway that, even as I drove, I had to watch carefully so as not to miss it. And here's this blind guy telling me where to turn off! I asked him about it and he just laughed and told me there was more than one way to "see" things. Finally, as I was seeing them off at the airport, DeDe told me his secret.

"I'll tell you how I "saw" that exit, Bill. Just a minute or two before we reached it we crossed over some kind of bridge that made a low humming sound. When I heard that humming I would start counting to myself. When I got to 105, you always turned off. Good trick?"

Good trick.

Dixieland Duo Marching In

Dixieland Duo Here

Billie & DeDe Pierce Rocking Horse write-up
Hartford Courant - front page
5 May 1966

THE NEW YORK TIMES, SUNDAY, MAY 15, 1966.

Young Man With a Horn in Stamford

By JOHN S. WILSON

STAMFORD, Conn.

UNDER the benign, glass-eyed gaze of a stuffed moose head, its antlers surmounted by a brightly neon-lit clock, Sammy Rimmington stomped his foot, waggled his head and blew some of the most exuberantly exciting jazz out of his clarinet that has been heard since that instrument went out of fashion in jazz 30 years ago.

Rimmington, an Englishman raised among the British "trad" bands that pattern themselves on traditional New Orleans jazz, arrived in the United States last December and was, on this late spring evening, celebrating his 24th birthday on the bandstand of Moose Hall, a big, echoing room one flight above Main Street in Stamford, Conn. With him on the stand was Clive Wilson, another young Englishman, a trumpeter and physicist who had just arrived in Connecticut after eight months spent in New Orleans "improving" his trumpet work.

Beside Wilson are two legendary figures of New Orleans jazz — gray-haired Dede Pierce, 62 years old and blind for the past 16 years but still playing a trumpet that throbbed with the clean, emotional power of a young Louis Armstrong, and, at an old upright piano, his wife, Billie, pounding out strong, percussive chords that could cut through any din and shouting the lyrics of classic blues and such forgotten gems of the popular repertory as "Love Songs of the Nile."

Businessmen

Backing them up were members of the Easy Riders Jazz Band, a local group which included an insurance salesman, a house painter, a draftsman and an executive of a company that manufactures speedometers. The lusty, driving way in which this oddly assorted band attacked "San," "Lonesome Road," "Exactly Like You," "Runnin' Wild" roused shouts and cheers from an audience seated around long wooden tables. It even caused impromptu dancing by the waitresses who kept the tables stocked with beer.

The occasion was one of half a dozen concerts presented during the year by the Connecticut Traditional Jazz Club. All of the elements involved—the jazz club, the Easy Riders, the two musicians from New Orleans and the two from England—were products of the crusading zeal of Bill Bissonette, a short, stocky, bushy-haired man who is trombonist and leader of the Easy Riders and, by day, a speedometer manufacturer.

Bissonette's crusading fervor is focused on his steam...

Dede Pierce, right, on cornet, and Clive Wilson, trumpet.

Pierce, 62 years old and blind, plays with the power of a young Louis Armstrong

...what he has described as "this dark period when some of its greatest practitioners are passing from the scene." To do this he has brought many of the surviving practitioners—Billie and Dede Pierce, George Lewis, Kid Thomas, Capt. John Handy, the Eureka Brass Band—north to Connecticut to play for audiences that would have no other opportunity to hear them. (New York has been a closed town for New Orleans jazz since it flourished briefly with Bunk Johnson at the Stuyvesant Casino 20 years ago.)

Bissonette provides opportunities for promising young musicians with New Orleans interests to play with these veterans. He preserves as much of this music on records as he can afford to. And, in the process, he stands up against "all this baloney about jazz being a great art form."

"I like surprise in my music," Bissonette, who is 29, declared after the Moose Hall concert. "That's why we bring in New Orleans people like Billie and Dede. They play what's in them—what they feel and how they feel. That's why I don't want the Easy Riders to get letter perfect. If we get a tune down to it's polished and all the pieces fall neatly into place, we change the key, do it differently somehow, anything to break it up. Or we'll stop playing it. We're a rough and tumble band."

Bissonette's crusade began four years ago when he got out of service and, en route home to Connecticut, spent a month in New Orleans. He had already been indoctrinated in New Orleans jazz and now he was able to sip from the source, living over Preservation Hall where his idol 70-year-old trombonist...

...son's mouthpiece, which he still uses, and a flaming zeal.

With several other traditional jazz enthusiasts, he formed the Dixieland Society of Southern Connecticut and, on his own, organized the Easy Riders and founded a record company, Jazz Crusade, to record the band.

"The band was pretty bad then and I knew it," he admitted. "But I wanted a chronological step-by-step record of the development of a band. At every step forward, we have recorded again. Whenever we bring musicians up from New Orleans, we have a concert and we record. We may not have the best band in the world but we're going to have the most recorded one."

Recordings

Two years ago the Dixieland Society split into two factions: proponents of what Bissonette calls "New York style" (exemplified by Bobby Hackett, Conrad Janis and Yank Lawson) remained in the society, while Bissonette and other New Orleans followers formed the Connecticut Traditional Jazz Club. Jazz Crusade Records, which has now issued 11 disks, has expanded to such an extent that it lost $4,864 for Bissonette in 1965. And the Easy Riders have become a relatively successful semi-professional band which works two or three nights a week. When Bissonette brings the old practitioners up from New Orleans for his recording concerts, however, the band usually reverts to an amateur status.

"We blow for nothing to get the money to pay for the guest musicians," Bissonette explained. He helps to keep costs down by putting up his...

...ing space for the 12 members of the Eureka Brass Band. (On that occasion Bissonette and his wife moved out to her mother's place.)

Rimmington is the only member of the band who devotes himself completely to music. Before moving to Connecticut, he spent five years in the English band of Ken Colyer, who popularized the New Orleans style in Britain 15 years ago. Bissonette first heard Rimmington when he and Barry "Kid" Martyn, a drummer, came to the United States for New Orleans in a musical exchange for New Orleanians Kid Thomas and Emanuel Paul.

"He was the best clarinetist I'd ever heard," Bissonette said, as he offered Rimmington a job even though it meant paying him out of his own pocket.

Since he arrived in December, Rimmington has added to what Bissonette can pay him by giving guitar lessons. "I play unorthodox clarinet," Rimmington explains, "but I was taught classical guitar when I was 11. I'm worse off financially over here, but I feel happier because I have a chance to play with musicians I like. It knocks me out."

With the help of youngsters such as Rimmington and veterans from New Orleans, Bissonette's crusade has been steadily building steam in Connecticut. Now he is beginning to look with interest toward New York. A New York job for the Easy Riders might mean giving up his day job, becoming a full-time musician. Would the crusader go that far?

"Yes," he declared without hesitation. Then he added, not entirely tongue-in-cheek, "I...

Billie & DeDe Pierce Moose Hall concert
New York Times write-up
15 May 1966

22. Very Handy

When Billie and DeDe left, I invited Clive Wilson to stay on with the band for awhile. Capt. John Handy was on the way in for a short tour right on their heels. I put this tour together on the spur of the moment because I had been informed that Brad McCuen was going to offer Cap an exclusive RCA recording contract as a result of his outstanding performance with the December Band. If I wanted to record Handy again I would have to do so before the contract was signed. Booking the tour served three purposes: it was my last chance to record him, it offered the opportunity to bring Handy and McCuen together for the contract signing and it gave me a chance to let McCuen hear Cap with the Easy Riders in the hope that he would consider the band for the first RCA recording with him.

This was the first tour we did completely on our own without jazz club sponsorship. It was too soon after the Billie and DeDe tour for them to do another. At their peak, they only sponsored a half dozen or so concerts a year. We booked Cap on a couple of our regular gigs and managed to hustle up a few other jobs. One was in Larchmont where we had played with George Lewis. Another was in a jazz spot in Waterbury owned by a dixieland enthusiast named Phil Becker. He featured regular Thursday night jazz sessions with imported dixie guys from New York. I heard about his place and contacted him. He had heard about our band. I mentioned that we were a New Orleans jazz band. He thought that meant dixieland so he booked the band when I told him about Cap and the upcoming RCA contract.

As my house was continually filled with visiting New Orleans jazzmen and because of the growing problems with our wives, a friend of Griff's named Ruth Blood offered to take Sammy and Nina in while the Handy tour was going on. This arrangement worked so well that Sammy decided to stay on with her. It was a relief all the way around. Now all I had at my house were Handy and Wilson.

Once Handy took you into his confidence, he was a great cutup. He was always kidding around and telling outrageous stories about the early days in New Orleans. He had played all types of music from bop to rock but his heart stayed pure throughout. He wasn't much of a clarinetist and we were always trying to get him to play it. He would have none of it. Many critical

New Orleans fans in those days considered Handy an aberration on the New Orleans scene. I constantly received letters asking why I recorded him. What the hell does he have to do with New Orleans jazz? Others of us, me included, saw him as a breath of fresh air; a unique addition to the genre. In their otherwise authoritive book, "New Orleans Jazz Family Album," Rose and Souchon, write him off simply as a "rock-and-roll type musician limited to the blues." You have to have your head pretty deep in the sand to dismiss Handy in such an off-handedly trivial manner. Even if he assaults your sensibilities, he must be given his due as a highly skilled, technically competent musician. But he was much more than that. He was a "hot" player, which is more than can be said for about sixty percent of the players listed in the "Family Album." In addition it is a strange state of affairs when he is not accepted as a bonafide black New Orleans jazzman by a couple of white critics and accepted as such by the likes of Kid Thomas, Jim Robinson and Punch Miller. One of these two groups of experts doesn't know what they're talking about. You decide which.

He was also a big help in popularizing the music during the Great Sixties Revival. People were being lured to the music at that time because there were new and exciting things going on. Principal among them were Kid Thomas and Handy. Properly presented on RCA, Handy could have raised the Revival to new heights. Unfortunately that was not to happen. He was miscast, mishandled and misled by people ignorant of what to do with him once they got him. It was a tragic waste of a golden opportunity.

But, just getting him that contract was what was on my mind. We finished up our tour at the Rocking Horse, scene of the Billie and DeDe triumph. It was here that McCuen advised me he was bringing the contract for signing and to hear Handy with the Riders.

The day before, we spent over eight hours in the Synchron Recording studio getting, what was supposed to be, my last Jazz Crusade recording of Handy. It was, in retrospect, a big mistake to go to a professional studio for the taping. I did it for two reasons. First, we had not gotten a good recording of Handy at the Moose with the December Band. The huge wooden structure seemed to swallow up the alto's sound. Secondly, I wanted a state-of-the-art recording in case Handy hit it big on RCA. Maybe then I could sell the session for some serious money to help the Crusade along. We brought Mike Fast along to supervise the session but the studio insisted on having their own man engineer it or they wouldn't guarantee the product. It was done in four track stereo. The band was so spread out that we had trouble hearing each other without headphones.

We did take after take. Nothing seemed to go right. We broke for supper and began again. Mike wasn't pleased with the sound he was hearing through the phones either and tried to advise the engineer. He was rebuffed.

We got some good stuff alright but it was not the great stuff I wanted. When the session was finally over, I took a monaural copy of the tape along with me.

Then we were in the Rocking Horse with Brad McCuen sitting at a front table. There was a good crowd but nothing like the three ring circus a few weeks earlier when the Pierce's had been there. We played a good gig. On our second break McCuen called us over. He produced the contract for Handy's signature and we all applauded as he signed it. A round of drinks appeared and we all raised our glasses. I said, "Tell us, Cap, how does it feel to be a star?"

Cap raised his glass and said, "It's been a long time in coming!"

McCuen made another announcement to the band. He said if it hadn't been for us, Handy would never have come to his attention. He said the music he heard here today was a great sound and we could rest assured that the Easy Riders Jazz Band would be recording with Handy for RCA. It sounded great. It was never to happen. Handy eventually made two albums, out of the five promised him, for RCA. The first was with a black Harlem swing band. The second was with some New Orleans men and, mysteriously, with a couple of the ex-Riders. Both albums flopped commercially and Handy's contract was cancelled. McCuen left RCA shortly thereafter to make country music albums in Nashville. Nobody stepped forward to take the blame for Cap's misfortune but a sinister force was at work undermining the Riders for personal ambition. Handy went on to make several more excellent albums. For Jazz Crusade.

Clive left with Handy for New Orleans. We were once again in need of a trumpet player. But there was no rush. We had already booked Kid Thomas for a return trip in June.

After they left, I listened many times to the Handy tapes. I was really unhappy with the sound. I discussed this with the studio people. We got nowhere except into arguments. The upshot was that I refused to pay them for the balance due on the session and they locked up the master tapes. I finally edited the monaural copy I had. I cut out virtually all of the solos except for Handy's and released the session in a limited edition release which accounts for its rareness today. As a postscript I should add that in the 1980's I recorded again at the same studio. By this time it had changed ownership and its name to Trod-Nossel. I told the new owners the story and they said that the original masters of that twenty year old session probably still existed somewhere in their vaults. They conducted a search for them with negative results. Perhaps someday they will surface and I will take another listen to them with the objectivity a generation gives.

23. Thomas & Penn On Tour

Here he was again! Connecticut really was becoming a second home for Kid Thomas. Before the Crusade was over, Thomas would make over two dozen tours with me. Adding it up, we would spend almost a year of our lives together between 1964 and 1969. With him was Sammy Penn for his second trip. He would also make many trips to Connecticut and California. We were to become as father and son. In the darker days, which lie just ahead, when money and support were in short supply, I would sometimes call Sammy and ask if he would come to Connecticut with no advance money guarantee. As long as I could scrape together plane fare, he would come, a smile on his face. I always managed to pay him. I don't think it would have mattered to him if I had not.

Regarding this tour, according to both Tom and Sammy, there had been a confrontation with Allan Jaffe about their coming. The Thomas band had been doing more and more road work billed as the second Preservation Hall Jazz Band. Thomas hadn't mentioned to Allan that he and Penn were coming to Connecticut once again. And, without checking with Tom, Allan had scheduled his band for an out of town tour which conflicted with my dates. When Allan gave him the Preservation Hall tour schedule, Tom told him about the cross booking. Allan asked him if he had a contract for my tour. Tom told him he never needed a contract from me. Allan suggested that the lack of a contract gave Tom and Sammy a valid reason to cancel their Connecticut trip. Both men flatly refused. The argument got heated. Tom told Allan to never book him again without first getting his permission. Allan said he just might not book him again at all. When Allan told Penn not to accept any more road work without checking with him first, Sammy just smiled and said, "When Bill calls me, I goes. That's it."

There was justification on both sides as I saw it. Allan was certainly doing a lot for these musicians. On the other hand, he wasn't doing it as a hobby. He was making a very good living at it. He was intelligent, hard-working and an extremely good businessman. The promotion of Preservation Hall was done with skill and competency. By trying to control the bookings of the musicians who played at the hall, he was protecting his "product."

But, the musicians, at least the more independent of them, didn't see themselves as product. They saw themselves as free agents. They had been playing their music long before there were any kitty halls. The halls were one more gig out of thousands. Now, finally, a small measure of fame and success had come to them. They wanted to enjoy it without someone, anyone, telling them where, when and with whom they could play. And if that screwed up somebody's schedule who should have cleared it with them in advance, that was too damn bad.

With the exception of Icon Hall, the later kitty halls were riding the coat-tails of Preservation Hall. This is a normal business gambit. Success always breeds imitation. Jazz fans like to look only at the artistic aspects of the music without realizing that it is also a business. Playing at a kitty hall one or two nights a week wouldn't feed Jim Robinson's family. Jim Robinson played jazz for a living, my friends. Neither does a half empty kitty hall pay the rent on the place. Preservation Hall was, and is, a business. There was no profit sharing at Preservation Hall. Don't be under the misapprehension that the kitty is divided up among the musicians. The musicians are paid union scale whether five people walk in or five hundred. In the Sixties a business war raged between kitty halls. And their stock in trade were a few dozen black musicians whom they could make or break and who could make or break them. The closing of Icon Hall was not done because the New Orleans police were ever vigilant of the public safety as relates to "proper egress."

So, I guess, if you are the owner of a little mom and pop store, you side with Allan Jaffe on whether Thomas and Penn should go traipsing off to Connecticut on their own. But, if you own a trumpet. . .

Those few of us with our little record companies were only tangentially involved with the kitty hall wars. Each of us had outside sources of income. I know of no one who made his living recording New Orleans jazz. Unfortunately, my situation was different because I also had a band and I was taking a big cut out of the hall's most important commodity: the musicians time. And I didn't take it by the hour like the other recording companies. I took it by the week. The only time I ever lost a tour because of it was with Lewis and Cie. And, even in that case, Allan supplied me with replacements. I didn't have to cancel any dates. All I lost was a recording session.

We began the Thomas/Penn tour at Phil Becker's Restaurant in Waterbury. He must have liked the Handy gig we did for him as he booked us again. The place was full and we had a happy opening night. The crowd was responsive and I thought Becker must have been completely satisfied. At the end of the night he handed me a folded check which I slid into my pocket without looking at it. When I arrived home, I opened the check and saw, to my astonishment, it was made out for exactly half the amount we had agreed upon. There must be some mistake. I called the restaurant and caught him in.

"Phil? This is Bill Bissonnette. I just looked at your check and it's made out for the wrong amount."

He replied, "It's made out for what you were worth. That was the worst band I ever heard. Those two guys from New Orleans don't know what dixieland is all about. I don't know where you dug them up but I ain't paying out good money for guys who play that shit. The only decent musician in that whole ragtag group is that skinny limey on clarinet. If that's the kind of crap you're offering, don't bother me again." With that he hung up.

I guess he didn't like the band.

Nevertheless, I wasn't about to let him off the hook. A contract is a contract and rudeness is rudeness. I phoned him again the next day and we engaged in a. . . uh. . . vigorous exchange. I finally told him I was going to the Federation of Musicians with my contract and he could forget about having any union musicians play in his club until the money was forthcoming. This time I hung up in his ear. A few days later a check for the balance arrived in the mail. I never offered him another band. But, you knew that, didn't you?

The next night we played a concert in a boat shed at the Essex Yacht Club. It was a huge barn-like building, open at both ends and half full of boats. There was still room left over for a couple hundred jazz fans and curiosity seekers. We planned to record that concert and the one the following night. I was hoping for three or four good albums from the two nights. Mike Fast cringed when he saw the place.

"I hope you don't think you're going to get a good sound in this cavern," he said.

"Of course I do. What's the point of having a genius for an engineer if you can't record in your everyday, conventional boat shed?"

It became academic because the band's performance was one of worst of any I can remember; second only to one we would soon do with Big Jim's Little Six. And, wouldn't you know it, the crowd in the shed loved it. There's just no accounting for audience reaction. It was one of the wildest crowds we ever played for. They were yelling and whistling and cheering continuously whether anything was happening or not. Musically, there was nothing happening at all. Penn had somehow managed to get himself almost falling down drunk. Thomas was pissed out of his mind about Penn's condition. To cap it, Sinclair had what even he admits was his worst night of the Sixties. All of it spilled onto the tape. Listening back to it was almost as bad as living through it. Still I salvaged two mediocre tracks which I used on the "On Tour" album only because of the great crowd reaction.

We did the second recording on the following night at a concert in Huntington, just up the street from Griff's house at the Grange Hall. Griff booked the gig. It was a small hall and there were only about fifty in attendance but we had a ball. We were on a raised stage. We played a strange mix of things including several dixie tunes like "Honeysuckle Rose," "Tin Roof Blues" and "Ball The Jack." Becker must have gotten to me.

Penn was still drinking but, this time, just enough to crack his headache from the previous night and put a happy glow on his face. Sam tended to rush his time when drunk. The more I drinks, the faster I goes. You can hear it to its extreme on the boat shed recordings. He rushed a bit the night at the Grange also but just enough to keep us scuffling to keep up.

There was a long staircase that led to the basement room of the Grange Hall. The way to more booze was down this staircase as Penn well knew. On one of the breaks, Penn, Rimington and Griff started off the top step together. Penn missed the step and flew off into space. He hit the steps about halfway down and went tumbling head over heels the rest of the way down onto the wooden floor with Rimington and Griff in terrified pursuit. I had just come down the stairs and turned at the commotion to see Sammy Penn come bouncing down the steps. He landed with a loud thud in a sitting position on the old board floor. We all rushed to him certain that he must be hurt. There he sat, cigar still clenched tightly between his teeth. As we tried to help him up, he grinned and said, "I believe I can make it by myself." He got up, hobbled over to the bar and medicated himself with his favorite pain killers.

I guess the moral of this story is: The Penn is mightier than the board.

Sorry.

The recording at the Grange was much better than that of the previous night but still much of it was unusable. We were not going to make my goal of several albums but the one that I pieced together is one I have always enjoyed listening to. I was now convinced that great recording sessions were acts of God.

We played jobs at the Rocking Horse and the Alpine Inn in North Haven (which is also where the album cover shot of the Very Handy album was photographed). On Monday evening, we found ourselves on the Dolly Madison riverboat. We got there by being auctioned off in a charity fund-raising drive. It sounds like something Jack Guckin might have gotten us into and it was. He talked a bank into hiring the band for the night and then auctioning us off for the night on the riverboat. The job would hardly be worth mentioning except that one of the aristocratic women on board asked Thomas how many times he had played on riverboats.

"Not many lady. The last time I played on one, somebody yelled fire on one side of the boat which caused everybody to run over to the other side. The boat tipped over and sank. I don't like no riverboats, lady. No suh!"

We finished up the tour with a farewell party at the Rocking Horse. Tom was in great spirits. He pulled all of his many tricks out of the "gimmick bag" he always carried. For "Milk Cow Blues" he went full out, dressing up in his woman's dress and baby bonnet. He spent most of the night with his handkerchief on his head, a sure sign Thomas was having fun. Several times he jumped up onto his chair for ride-out choruses. He saved the best for last. As we swung into our last number, Thomas disappeared into the crowd as he often did, usually to pop up somewhere out in the audience at the end of the last solo to blow it out. This time he vanished. Everybody in the band was looking out over the crowd trying to spot where he would jump up but he was nowhere to be found. The rhythm section played on and on while first we laughed and then began to get concerned about his absence. Suddenly the door of the Ladies Room swung open and out marched Kid Thomas Valentine, legend of jazz, with a shawl over his shoulders, a woman's feathered hat on his head and blowing "Tiger Rag" at the top of his power!

And people ask me why I spent all that time and money promoting jazz.

TRADITIONAL JAZZ

from New Orleans:

Kid Thomas - Trumpet

Sammy Penn - Drums

&
THE EASY RIDERS JAZZ BAND

Here they are again! The world's greatest jazz trumpeter: Kid
Thomas and the happy, singing, cigar puffing drummer: Sammy Penn.
Here is the schedule of events:

Thursday, June 23: Phil Packer's Restaurant, Waterbury, Connecticut
Great food, no door charge or cover. 9:00 P.M.

Friday, June 24: The Boat Shed, Essex Yaucht Club, Essex, Conn.
Outdoor concert in the boat shed. Great Sound!8:30 P.M

Saturday, June 25: Huntington Orange Hall, Huntington Green, Conn.
Dance/Concert for those who wish to dance as well
as listen. Bring your own drinks. Tickets available
now from 135 Grey Rock Rd., Ept.Ct. Limited space.
so get your tickets early! 9:00 P.M.

Sunday, June 26: The Rockinghorse, Franklin Ave, Hartford, Conn.
The swingingest place in Connecticut. Great fun
place. 8:00 P.M.

Monday, June 27: Private Party, Dolly Madison Riverboat
SORRY!

Tuesday, June 28: Back to the Rockinghorse
for a slam-bang farewell party for Tom and Sammy.
Don't miss this one because our farewell sessions
are always the best of the bunch. 8:00 P.M.

The farthest South we will go is the Huntington session and the
farthest North is the Rockinghorse. We have allowed as much time so
you may plan well ahead on these. Hope to see you at your favorite
place. Come prepared for some fun! Kid Thomas is back!

featuring: Sammy Rimington,

Bill Bissonnette Trombone,   Bill Sinclair Piano
Dick "Grif"Griffith Banjo   Dick McCarthy String Bass

Kid Thomas/Sammy Penn "On Tour"
Tour schedule
June 1966

Jazz Greats Slated for Shelton

By MARILYN WEBB

SHELTON—The Grange Hall on Huntington street will ring out with the one and only jazz beat, straight from New Orleans, on Saturday at 9 p.m.

SHELTON

Famed New Orleans jazz men, Thomas Valentine and Sammy Penn, will be on hand to fortify the authentic New Orleans sound and entertain the local folk like they've never been entertained before.

Sammy Penn and Kid Thomas are Negro musicians who were there when the New Orleans jazz was born. They will be playing with "The Easy Riders" led by Bill Bissonnett. This band is dedicated to the promotion of jazz in Connecticut. They have belted out rhythm and blues on every entertainment media from stage to recordings and TV.

Easy Riders

Members of the Easy Riders group featured Saturday night are Sammy Rimmington, a former clarinetist of Ken Colyer's Jazzmen in England; Bill Bissonnette, trombonist responsible for carrying on the highest traditions of New Orleans jazz by founding a state-wide jazz club; Dick Griffith, banjo man who turns in admirable performances on "High Society" and other New Orleans favorites; Bill Sinclair, who plays a hearty piano and is a commander of New Orleans classics; and rounding out the group, Dick McCarthy giving grandeur to the American past with his string bass.

The Easy Riders band and Kid Thomas were recently reviewed in The New Yorker, the New York Times and Down Beat. Down Beat hailed Kid Thomas as the "world's greatest jazz musician," having his best moments in fast driving ensembles." Jazz fans and critics have been receiving the Easy Riders with vigor and spelling out fantastic promise.

Long-Time Musician

Kid Thomas was born Feb. 3, 1896, in Reserve, La. His father was a musician and gave him the choice of playing any instrument in the house. In 1915, he got his first professional job playing trumpet on a skiff that took passengers across the river. Today he leads the Algiers Stompers of Bourbon Street. He often plays 14 or 15 hour jobs and commences with the same powerful tome he had at the start of the job.

The cohesive element in the original jazz sound to be presented in the Grange hall is the drumming of vigorous Sammy Penn. Though he's "no spring chicken" and was in New Orleans when the Creoles joined up with the Uptown Blues Men, he can beat out a swinging rhythm so his equal would be hard to find.

The two famous New Orleans jazz men are joining the Easy Riders for a seven night concert tour. They'll be at Phil Becker's in Waterbury on Thursday, the Boat Shed in Essex on Friday, the Rocking Horse on Franklin avenue in Hartford next Sunday. June 27 they'll give atmosphere to a private River Boat party in Hartford and June 28 they'll return to the Rocking Horse.

Kid Thomas/Sammy Penn at Huntington Grange Hall
Bridgeport Post
19 June 1966

24.   The Mouldy Five

By the Summer of '66, the tours were coming so fast and furious, you might think we had time for little else. That wasn't the case at all. In addition to our weekly Riders gigs and our day jobs, we started a separate band. We called it the Mouldy Five because, well, it was mouldy and there were five of us. It served a few functions the Riders did not such as giving me a chance to play drums again and providing Sammy Rimington a little more freedom to "run with the ball" now and then. It was strictly a fun group and we did little professional work with it. All of us needed an outlet from our music so we turned to. . . more music.

The band played every Thursday night at the Rocking Horse and quickly acquired a good following there. It was the type of group wherein we could experiment with the New Orleans idiom, sometimes bouncing off the very edges of it. We did some ragtime, ballads, Jimmie Noone and Johnny Dodds things, and even some mouldy interpretations of modern numbers. The band's repertoire quickly passed the one hundred mark and we were adding a half dozen or so new tunes every week.

Getting my chops up on drums was not as difficult as I thought it would be. When Penn was in town, we did quite a bit of wood-shedding on my set. He had been taken with my set and started using it when touring in Connecticut. He particularly liked the sound of my side tom tom. I was picking up on many of his trademark gimmicks. I became his protege on drums as I was Robinson's on trombone. This is a polite way of saying they didn't mind when I stole their stuff.

Both Sammy and Bill enjoyed being able to take longer solos in this group. Griff and Mouldy liked the harder driving rhythm section with me bumping them along on the skins. We decided that the group was good enough to put on tape. We discussed what selections to do and couldn't reach a consensus. We finally decided to record the band's whole repertoire; all hundred and fifty tunes. We figured we would do it just as we did on the job. No second takes of anything until we did every number at least once. By the time we started doing this a schism had developed in the band. But, before we split up, we managed to get in one night of recording with the Mouldy Five. On that session we recorded a representative sixteen numbers. At that rate, we could have recorded the band's full repertoire in about ten sessions. At least we got these few. It was better than nothing. They have since been issued on GHB.

Sammy was now living in an apartment in New Haven. Nina had just had her first child and she would bring the little girl to the Rocking Horse sessions. Sammy still didn't have a car which was a nuisance as somebody in the band had to pick him up for every job. One night we took up a collection at the Rocking Horse to buy him a cheap used car. Each member of the band then put the tap on friends and fans alike. We came up with a couple of hundred dollars and bought him the cheapest car we could find at a Bridgeport used car lot. Within a month Sammy blew the engine on the way to the Rocking Horse. I had a friend tow it back to the place we bought it and we complained to the owner of the dealership. He asked me what I expected from a cheapo car like that and refused to help us. We got up a high-powered delegation of fans and bandsmen and invaded the showroom during the busiest time of day. We explained how we had taken up the collection to buy the car, how Sammy was a newcomer to the country, how his wife just had a baby, the whole bit. Then we told him if he didn't make good on the car, we were going to spread the word to every jazz fan in Connecticut about what a crook he was. He threatened to sue us if we did and one of our lawyer fans in the delegation invited him to do so by all means. And be prepared to have our other friends on the newspapers and television news shows plaster it all over the state. The guy capitulated and gave Sammy another car which lasted longer than the band.

And about that trouble in the band. It is time to start addressing it. It is difficult to do because each of the band members recall it differently. I think we have all spent the last twenty-five years trying to forget about it and we have apparently succeeded. But there is no doubt about some things. Mouldy, Griff and I were on one side. Sinclair, Pulver and Rimington were on the other. The crux of the problem lay in simple conflict of interest. We all had spent several years building a following for jazz and for the Riders in Connecticut. We worked hard at it, as you know from what you have already read. Now Bill, Art and Sammy started taking outside work with some of the ex-Rider sidemen. That would have been okay except, not only were they competing for the limited amount of work in the area, but they were using many of our arrangements and playing up their association with the Riders. Then booking conflicts began as well.

I, of course, had a government contract with Sammy. He was my employee by the terms of his gaining entry into the country. I never called him on it though I easily could have. With a letter or a phone call I could have had him winging his way back to England. That was not my objective. I wanted only to hold the Riders and the Crusade together. Besides, I felt then, and still feel today, that Sammy was duped. He was innocent of any malice and just believed some outrageous falsehoods that were fed to him. Sammy was trying to make his living at playing jazz. As I have said before in these pages, to professional jazzmen, a gig is a gig.

Sinclair and Pulver were a different matter. Both had day gigs. What was the purpose in wrecking the band that had enabled them to meet and play with some of their musical idols? The only band they had recorded with? I could understand anyone taking an occasional gig now and then. But to compete with your own band for steady work? It made no sense to me then. It makes no sense to me now. The rift between the two factions widened. I didn't blame the ex-Riders who were hiring them. Once you're out of a band, go for it.

But there was more to it than that. Someone was sewing seeds of discontent, for reasons I did not know. Pulver and Rimington had gotten the impression that I was making a lot of money from Jazz Crusade which I kept secret from the band. Pulver was up front about it. He would leave notes in my mailbox explaining these allegations and then show up early for rehearsals to discuss them. He would pointedly ask me such things as how I could afford to own my own house if I was losing money on JC as I claimed. I pointed out to him that both my wife and I had good paying jobs, as he well knew. Then I'd ask him how he could afford his own house. This flustered him. Somehow that was okay. Art was too bright a person and too decent a man to come up with these ridiculous ideas himself. And he had much more to lose than gain by undermining the band.

Ill will permeated the band. Friendships built up over years came to their ends. Wisecracks and insults were being passed behind backs and to faces. I hoped against hope these guys would realize the importance of keeping the Riders together. Mouldy and Griff couldn't understand it any more than I could. Griff in particular became very bitter about the whole sordid mess. This fine band we had all worked so hard to put together was coming apart and I felt helpless to stop it.

25.   Big Jim's Little Six

Despite the band problems and the side fact that my marriage went belly up immediately following the Thomas/Penn tour, I looked forward to the upcoming July jaunt with my mentor Big Jim Robinson and my good friend Kid Sheik Cola. There was an added bonus. I had for some time corresponded with a Japanese banjo player named Junichi Kawai. He played in Japan's most respected traditional jazz band, the New Orleans Rascals, then known to us as the Original Osaka Jazz Band. The band was adroitly led by clarinetist Ryoichi Kawai. We had been greatly impressed when we heard their recordings. When Junichi informed me they were coming to America to tour, we immediately booked them for a concert in Connecticut to be shared by Robinson, Sheik and the Mouldy Five. It was the only concert appearance the Mouldy Five ever made.

The joint concert started our tour with Jim and Sheik. We would then go on to gigs at the Villa Rosa, the Rocking Horse and at the Candlewood Marina. We put one full day aside for recording at the Moose. Our Japanese friends were as thrilled at the prospect of playing on the same bill with Robinson and Sheik as we were to be billed with them. The concert was on Friday, July 29th. We had a great time getting to know each other before the gig. Mouldy, Griff and Sinclair had never met Sheik and, of course, none of us knew the Rascal members. Kimonos and Jazz Crusade records were exchanged as gifts.

The performance by the Rascals was outstanding. Their fine trombone player, Tsunetami "Tommy" Fukuda, was featured on a traditional Japanese folk melody named "Sukura, Sukura" that was so beautiful that I later copied his rendition and started featuring it with the Easy Riders, always mentioning him and the Rascals as our source. The crowd loved them. I had Mike record the concert for future issuance on Jazz Crusade. Unfortunately, it remains among the unissued material.

Maybe because of our band problems, or the stiff competition, the two intermission sets we played at the concert were total musical disasters. Even Jim seemed to have an off night. There were all sorts of foul-ups. Jim brought in "I'm Alone Because I Love You" in Ab instead of his usual Bb and had the band scuffling to find his key. Both Griff and Sinclair were blowing wrong chords all night long. My beat was choppy and indecisive. It was a mess. I didn't get enough decent material on tape to fill out one side of an album. I erased everything we did. Fortunately there was plenty of good material by the Rascals to fill an album and more. I did include on the final album cut the concerts grand finale jam session with the combined bands. This included three trombones as I joined Jim and Tsunetani on Bugle Boy March. It was quite a climax to the concert. I have not heard that track in over twenty years but it still sticks in my mind as one of the musical highlights of the Sixties Crusade.

We bid our Japanese friends sayonora as they headed for New Orleans and we continued on our tour. Sinclair did not continue with us. He had been called up for his active reserve training and left the day after the concert. With him off the tour Sammy became his old self again. We were all friendly for the rest of the tour and made some great jazz that improved day by day.

I have mentioned before that I thought Sheik was underrated. He was not a flashy stylist like Thomas or Percy Humphrey but he was a good solid lead man that you could always work your lines against. He started playing in the 1930's in New Orleans. After serving in the Army Air Force during WWII, he returned to lead his own band. He joined, and recorded with, the Eureka in the early 1950's. He was a popular draw at Preservation Hall, as much for his warm personality as his playing. I never met a person who didn't like Sheik or whom Sheik didn't like. He was always at the hall whether he was playing or not.

He was the same on this tour. He was always breaking everybody up with a joke or gag. The only time he wasn't laughing was when he was blowing. And if he could have figured out how to do both at the same time, he would have. By the time we reached the Moose Hall to do our recording session on Sunday, July 31st, Jim and Sheik had swept away any ill will that might have been kicking around and we were ready to cut some great records. If you had told me a couple of days before, after our pitiful first performance together, that we could put three top-notch albums in the can in a single seven hour recording session, I would have said you were nuts. But that's exactly what we did.

Sammy and I had discussed several times the idea of doing an album recreating the 1944/45 Lewis-Robinson American Music recordings with no trumpet. I knew that I had not come far enough along on my horn playing to be able to stay up with Sammy on a session like that on trombone. There was no doubt he could do it or that Mouldy and Griff were up to it. But I sure as hell could do it on drums. So when we booked Robinson I said,"Sam, let's do it." He was delighted.

My hope was to put a session in the can with Sheik and Jim and then try for a second one with just Jim and Sammy on horns. To my delight, we breezed through enough material for the Robinson/Sheik album within two hours. Mike had recorded so often at the Moose that he took his sound balance in about ten minutes. The band pumped right along with virtually no second takes. And what fun we were having! We did "Dippermouth Blues" and Jim just knocked everybody out with his solo choruses. Unexpectedly, he then threw a little tag on the end of the tune and everybody jumped on it like it was a rabbit coming out of its hole. Then we all broke up laughing while Jim yelled, "I'm sorry!" Fortunately Mike broke up too and forgot to turn off the tape machine so I was able to put the whole incident, laughter and all, on the album. Laughter after midnight; tears before dawn.

We recorded the dirge "What A Friend We Have In Jesus" with Sammy on Eb clarinet and Handy's bop tune "In the Gutter" with Robinson bopping away on the weird chords. I even talked Jim into recording his first ever vocal on "Bye and Bye." When he heard the playback, he laughed like hell, slapped his knee and pointed at the tape machine yelling, "That's me. Jim Robinson!"

When I was confident I had more than enough in the can for an album, we sprung the news to Jim about the trombone/clarinet session. We hadn't given him advance warning even though Sammy and I had long since come up with a list of tunes to do. I knew we would have to catch Jim in a happy mood to get him to take it on. When I broke him the news, he said, "Bill, you sho knows how to work an old man."

We read him our list. He asked about one number Sammy picked, the "Valley of Death." He didn't recall any such tune. Sammy assured him he would have no trouble with it. In fact he did. We had to do several takes on it to get even a marginally acceptable track. If I had had any extra material, it would not have made the album cut. To our surprise, Jim turned down one number: "Ice Cream," the tune he has become the most closely associated with. Sammy and I had reservations about putting it on the list in the first place because it was so overdone and because we knew it would be impossible to come close to that first great American Music version. We finally decided to put it on the list because its absence would be so obvious that we were afraid to NOT include it. Jim killed it dead with the amazing comment that he was, "too old to do that without a trumpet." He suggested that we do it with Sheik. We didn't do it at all.

It took about an hour longer to do the "1944 Revisited" album than the "Little Six" one. It was hard work too. The session showed me something that was to become very important a little later. The rhythm section wasn't hurting one bit without a piano. In fact, it was a lot cleaner, crisper sound. In terms of old-style New Orleans jazz, this was perhaps the mouldiest release Jazz Crusade ever produced.

It was about suppertime when we finished the session. The management of the Moose Hall brought in a supply of sandwiches and a pitcher of beer. We were having such a good time eating and drinking that no one even mentioned packing up. After we ate, Sammy said, "Let's play a few more."

Jim laughed and said, "You guys gonna play forever if you gets the chance."

Sheik started talking about some tunes he'd always wanted to record. Griff joined in, "It's okay with me. I came here to play."

I looked at Mouldy. He just nodded. He was ready. "Warm it up, Mike, we're gonna do a few more," I said. Mike threw the switch.

By this time of the evening, Moose members started wandering into the hall. They would listen to a tune or two and head into the bar. We played another couple of hours without even thinking about the tape machine. Whatever tune popped into one of our heads came out through the horns. It was one of those rarities, a jam session among friends. Sheik suggested "Dipsey Doodle," "Birth of the Blues" and "Angry." Mouldy called "Casimer's Whooping Blues." I threw in a slow "Down By the Riverside." We played till we wore each other out. We all just quit at the same time. Nobody said, "that's it." It was, as Yogi Berra might have put it, over when it was over. It was a day of jazz I will long cherish in memory. Sammy was back with us, if only briefly. I was playing with my idol and my friends. This was what it was all about.

The "Big Jim's Little Six" album I produced from this session was one of Jim's favorite albums. I gave him a box of 25 of them, most of which he quickly distributed to friends instead of selling them to Allan Jaffe for resale at Preservation Hall, which is what most of the musicians did with their complimentary copies. Every so often he would send me word that he needed more of them and I would ship him another box.

Sheik liked the session too and well he might. It is the essential and definitive Kid Sheik album. He was never better recorded or in better form. Rimington was also at the peak of his early period on this session. As you can tell, "Big Jim's Little Six" is one of the Jazz Crusade releases of which I am the most proud.

Instead of issuing volume two, I decided to sell the remaining Robinson/Sheik masters to George Buck to help finance another Kid Thomas and the Easy Riders Jazz Band session. Buck was delighted to get the album and issued it under the title "Sheik-Robinson New Orleans Stompers." I was glad he put Sheik's name up front.

ONE NIGHT ONLY
THE ORIGINAL OSAKA JAZZ BAND
DIRECT FROM JAPAN

The Osaka Jazz Band has worldwide recognition and will be on a nationwide tour, playing in New Orleans, Minneapolis, Los Angeles, Canada and MERIDEN, CONNECTICUT.

and

THE MOULDY FIVE with

SAMMY RIMINGTON, BILL BISSONNETTE, BILL SINCLAIR DICK GRIFFITH and DICK McCARTHY

Featuring from New Orleans

Jim Robinson - Trombone

Kid Shiek - Trumpet

Presented by: The Connecticut Traditional Jazz Club, Inc.

FRIDAY, JULY 29, 1966 - HOLIDAY MOTOR INN

Main Street, Meriden (Jct. Route 91)

8:30 p.m. - 12:30 a.m.

Advance Ticket Prices
$2.50 guests $1.00 C.T.J.C. members

Ticket Prices at Door
$3.00 guests $1.50 C.T.J.C. members

**New Orleans Rascals/Big Jim's Little 6 poster
Connecticut Traditional Jazz Club
July 1966**

26. Somewhere Over The Rainbow

How could it have happened? How could this band that had accomplished so much in such a short period of time disintegrate within a few months? Misunderstanding? Partly. Personalities? To a degree. Egos? Some think so. Outside forces? Families and "friends" played their roles. Lack of dedication? I think not. Deliberate malevolence? At least on the part of one bandsman I believe. Leadership? Guilty.

Once the calming effects of the Robinson/Sheik tour wore off and Sinclair and Pulver returned, the situation deteriorated rapidly. By the time Thomas arrived in late September, it was only the anticipation of his arrival that held things together. A jazz club concert featuring joint appearances by Thomas and the Riders and the Canadian Black Eagle Jazz Band helped to keep things in equilibrium. The Eagles were a really good band. We all got together at my house and had a party to equal the one we had with the Rascals. They brought along a few groupies, one of whom took me aside and asked if she could stay on and live with me. Just to show you how screwed up I was over the worsening state of band affairs, I said no. If she's reading this now, I want her to know I've changed my mind!

I don't recall taping the concert although, for the life of me now, I don't remember why I didn't. In any event, the concert was a good one. It was the last the Easy Riders in its most well known form performed for the CTJC.

We played a few more dates and ended up in the basement of a church in Wallingford where we had recorded the Mouldy Five. I had carefully selected the tunes I wanted to record. I definitely wanted to get Tom's unusual version of "Bells of St. Marys" on tape. Another favorite of mine was "Pagan Love Song." Tom wanted to record his vocal on "Tiger Rag." Rimington suggested "Cielito Lindo" and "Somewhere Over the Rainbow" and so on. There were ten tracks I wanted to cut.

It was a miracle we got through them all. Tom sensed immediately upon his arrival that something was wrong in the band. There was little small talk before the recording. How could there be? Hardly anybody in the band was talking to each other. What little discussion ensued was mainly in the form of complaints. Sinclair was unhappy that someone, none of the bandsmen, had rigged the piano with thumbtacks in the hammers. It must have previously been used by a ragtime pianist to get that tinny sound they loved so much. We pulled out those we could. Sammy didn't like the mike setup. Mike Fast moved them. Pulver and Mouldy were on a bandstand riser and neither of them liked it. Griff had trouble keeping his banjo in tune. Even Thomas complained that the room was too cold. I saved my gripes for the session.

As I stated previously, memories differ greatly among the participants as to how the final battle began. There is no doubt how it ended. The first clash came, surprisingly, between me and Thomas. We did a take on "Tiger Rag." Tom didn't do his now famous triple note out-chorus. I said I wanted to do it again and asked Tom to do the ending I liked so much. He didn't seem to know what I was talking about. I described it to him several times and suggested we just try the last two choruses again without recording. Once again he did something totally different. It was weird because Tom had done the ending I wanted every job of the tour up till then.

We took a break. During it, according to Mike Fast, Sammy walked over to him and started complaining about what a perfectionist I was trying to be. I should just record the stuff and edit out what I didn't like afterward. Sinclair remembers, he says, that he, Rimington and Pulver were united in their feeling that I should not be "bossing" Kid Thomas around. We began again with "Tiger" and Thomas blew through the ending just the way I wanted it.

Another incident happened on "Bugle Call Rag." Tom in his unorthodox manner, blew backup notes during the other members solo breaks but didn't play during the interludes between them. I thought it was neat but Sammy got upset by it. He tried to explain the normal sequence to Thomas with about as much success as I had with "Tiger." Tom said, "Oh yea, yea. I gotcha." Then did the same thing again. Sammy started to explain it again and Griff blew up. He told Sammy to back off and let Tom do it the way he wanted. The thing was out of control. If I had had any sense, I would have called a few quick throwaway tunes and gotten the session over with. But, I didn't and we all paid the price.

The climax came on "Somewhere Over the Rainbow" and it needn't have happened because we had already done the take on it that would end up on the "Love Songs of the Nile" album. I was doing another take just as a safety. The arrangement on the tune had Sammy bringing it in with a solo chorus. He began and on the very first measure I thought I heard him hit a squeaker, a common occurrence on clarinet. I called the take to a halt instantly. Sammy asked me why I stopped it. I told him it was because of the squeaker. He said he had hit no squeaker. I told him I had heard one and I didn't see any point in going all the way through the take just to throw it out later. That did it. A shouting match between Sammy and I soon brought everybody else in except for Thomas, who just sat staring at us, his jaw jutting out; and the sinister force, which watched quietly while savoring its evil handiwork. By the time it was over ten minutes later, the band was finished. We all packed up and went our separate ways never to play together as a band again.

I made a few flat-footed attempts to reconcile things through Sinclair. He was the last person I should have approached. We even used Bill, and possibly Sammy, a couple of more times over the next few months but it was over. I don't know how Sinclair, Rimington and Pulver felt about it. I know that Griffith, McCarthy and I were shifting between anger and despair on a daily basis.

Almost a year had passed since Sammy had joined the Easy Riders Jazz Band. In that short time we had played over a hundred gigs together. We had recorded with Kid Thomas, Jim Robinson, Capt. John Handy, Sammy Penn and Kid Sheik plus numerous unreleased sessions with the Riders and the Mouldy Five. We had toured with Billie and DeDe Pierce and played with the Eureka Brass Band. We also played with many of the New Orleans transplanted musicians living in New York. It was a lot of fun while it lasted. Now that the passage of time has softened the edges of the brutal ending, I occasionally hear from some of the participants recalling how wonderful it all was. Too bad they didn't think so at the time. But the moving finger writes. And having writ, moves on. And, as the tome concludes, nothing can change a word of it.

27. New Orleans – 1966

Two weeks after Thomas left for New Orleans, Griff and I followed. We hadn't planned the trip in advance but we needed something to lift our spirits. Nothing does that exactly like New Orleans. I felt I had to talk to Kid Thomas about the events that had transpired in his presence at the recording session. Griff was looking forward to meeting, and possibly taking a few banjo lessons from, Creole George Guesnon. We were both looking forward to seeing all of our musician friends again. We knew we were not going to give up on our music. We planned to arrange a new tour while we were there. One with a clarinet player and I knew just who that was going to be.

We rented a second floor apartment for a month fronting on Bourbon Street. It had a small balcony from which we could watch the tourist trade milling in the street below. Dixieland Hall, another kitty hall, was so close that all we had to do each evening to find out who was playing there was open the balcony doors and listen. I always liked New Orleans in the fall. October was not too hot and often even a little cool in the evenings.

On our first night I showed Griff around the halls. There were more than there were the previous year. There was one almost directly across the street from Preservation Hall on St. Peter Street and another new one on Bourbon back by Raymond Burke's shop. Even a few bars on Bourbon had black bands in them. It was a wonderful time to experience jazz in that town. Needless to say, the first musician we bumped into was Kid Sheik. We hadn't told anyone we were coming because we made our plans so quickly. He was amazed when he saw us. The Humphrey band was playing in Preservation Hall as we walked in. I went to the side door and looked in. Jim Robinson was blowing a solo when he spotted me. He stopped right in the middle of it and came over to greet us. He wrapped his arms around me and brought me into the hall to be greeted by the other bandsmen. All the while the music was chugging along.

The next day we headed for Tom's house. He welcomed us and invited us to stay for dinner. We talked for a couple of hours about what had happened. He was sad to hear that the band breakup appeared permanent. I asked for his candid opinion about what had happened and specifically what he thought of the complaints about my having bossed him around.

"Let me tell you somethin', Bill. You was the boss. What you think a bandleader is if he ain't no boss? Shoot, man, I knows who the boss is in my band. Me! And nobody best forget that no how. I come to Connecticut, I work for you. That's it."

I replied that I did know that but the point they were making was that Kid Thomas is not exactly your normal, everyday sideman and you didn't treat a star in the same way as your regular men.

"Why not?" Thomas replied. "You paying me good money when I'm up there. And then you making all them recordings and things. You better get what you want on those recordings. That's for sure. If I ain't giving you what you wants, what you gonna do but tell me? Nothin' else don't make no sense no how."

I was feeling better already.

"Let me tell you somethin' else too, Bill. You see them boys you got up there in Connecticut? Them boys got a lot to learn about life. When you working for a man, you does what that man tell you. You tries to make things easier for him not raise a ruckus every time you don't like somethin'. That's just life, Bill. Plain old facts of life, man. Ain't nobody gonna hire you if you over here making some kinda foolishness that don't fit in. No suh. Why you think my band's so good? Huh? Tell me that. Why you think? Cause I tells them what I wants. That's why. Nobody don't like it, shoot, they know what they can do and where they can do it, too."

Then he really surprised us both with a change of subject that jolted us straight back to reality. "Listen, why don't you boys play with me tonight down Preservation?"

Griff didn't hesitate. "Sure, man!"

I did. "What about Nelson?"

"He's off someplace with DeDe. I ain't called nobody yet."

We went back to the apartment to get ready. I had never played a paying gig in the hall before. It wasn't like in later years when the source of black musicians started drying up. There were few whites playing the halls then except to sit in for a number or two now and then. The few exceptions were top flight players like Paul Crawford on trombone who played with Punch regularly and clarinetist Raymond Burke. And you could only count Ray if you discounted the rumors about, "Raymond Burke's secret."

We arrived at the hall and set up. A few minutes before we started, Eddie Sommers came in, trombone case in hand. I looked at Tom and he looked at Eddie.

"What you doin' here, Sommers? You got the wrong night?" Thomas said.

"I got a call to come play with you all, Thomas," he replied.

"I didn't call nobody," Thomas said.

"It weren't from you Thomas."

What happened was that someone from the hall called Eddie knowing that Nelson was out of town. Tom was irritated. I told him not to worry about it. I would get as big a kick out of listening to Eddie as playing, I lied. But, thank God, he insisted on my playing. He went out into the carriageway and came back with another chair and waved Eddie into it beside me.

"Tonight we be using Kid Thomas' Brass Band!" he joked as he took his trumpet out of its case.

Sammy and Manny were delighted to see Griff and me sitting there. "Well alright, alright!" said Penn.

"Hello there, Mister Griff," Manny greeted. "This is just like being back in Connecticut."

The session went along fine. Eddie and I worked a lot of things together and we were having a lot of fun. As usual, the place was mobbed. Then I hoisteth myself on my own petard. I got a little cocky and asked Tom if we could do "I'm Alone Because I Love You." I had mastered the Robinson lead on it and I wanted to strut my stuff for Eddie and the audience. Tom told me to start it off, "like on the Redwing record." I jumped up and counted it off for the band. Here I was in Preservation Hall blowing Robinson's chorus with the Thomas band rhythm section bumping me along. And I played it nice. Just right. Nobody but Big Jim himself could have topped it.

I sat down and looked over at Eddie sitting next to me, his new artificial leg propped up on a chair. My smile must have looked just a little too smug because he picked up his trombone and blew me away. I have never heard anything so beautiful come out of the bell of a trombone before or since. I mean he would have had Robinson heading for the door after his chorus. The crowd went stark raving mad as he plopped his horn back on his lap. I looked sheepishly at Sammy Penn who was sitting there, hat and cigar cocked at rakish angles, smiling at me with a cheshire cat grin. When will I learn, I thought. You can't beat these guys. You just can't beat them.

The next day we headed for Guesnon's house. I had learned a lot about George and one of the main things I learned was that if you're looking for something from him, you damned well better show up with something for him. He had his own currency: cigarettes. I had a carton in hand when he came to the door.

"Hey, Bill. I heard you was in town over the grapevine. I figured you'd be over. Who's this cat?"

I introduced Griff and told George he was my banjo player. "He's interested in some lessons, George," I said as I held out the smokes.

"Let's see your banjo," George said. Griff produced the Vega Rimington had given him. "Ah! Very nice. Very nice." He took out a pick and played a few chords on it and then a single string run. Griff was VERY impressed.

Guesnon sat on the bed that was in his front room and Griff and I pulled up a couple of chairs. Before long Guesnon had us looking at his latest supply of pornographic aids including a new dildo he seemed particularly fond of. I had forgotten to forewarn Griff about this quirky habit of Guesnon's and Griff didn't know what to say. He just kept repeating, "Oh yes, good stuff, George. Very nice." I don't think Guesnon ever used any of this junk but he had a big box full of it to spring on his guests.

Finally George came around to the subject I knew was on his mind. "Did you listen to that tape I loaned you? How come I haven't heard from you about it?"

"Of course I did," I replicd. "I listened to it several times. I don't know what I can do with it, George. It's not the kind of thing I usually issue on my label." I had sent George copies of the three albums he had made for me in 1965 (and which he promptly sold to Allan Jaffe for resale at the hall). "How did you like the Jazzology Poll Winners, George?"

"All of them albums was good, Bill, but this album I did of my songs is the one you want to put out. It will make you even richer than you is now."

When did I get rich? Maybe it happened after I left Connecticut and Guesnon had heard about it before I did. It wouldn't have surprised me with his grapevine.

"George, you mentioned you had some other tapes. Tell me about them." He got angry that I mentioned them in front of somebody else, said he wouldn't discuss them and promptly began to do so. He said he had tapes that, if Louis Cottrell found out, would get him thrown out of the union. As usual he was exaggerating but it was obvious he did have something stashed away. He finally produced them from under a board in the flooring. I felt like I was looking into Whittaker Chamber's pumpkin or something.

But there they were: sessions with Kid Thomas, Kid Howard, Israel Gorman, Lewis James. Little groups, duos, trios, at most quartets. I asked him when they were recorded. Fifties. Sixties. What do they sound like? No! He had said too much already. He quickly put them back under the floor.

"Okay, George, you've got my attention. What's the deal?"

He replied, "I want you to buy that tape I loaned you. Then I want you to make an album out of it. It has to have the front cover just the way I want it. I'll give you a photograph to put on it. I have even written the notes for the back but you have to sign your name to them like you wrote them yourself. When you do all of that and I am satisfied with the record, you can come back and buy those other sessions I just showed you. And not only that but I'll do another recording for you too with my band which you can record here in New Orleans."

So that was the deal. Plain old George Guesnon state-of-the-art extortion. But, God, I liked this man for all of his faults. I asked him the price all of this was going to cost me. It was fairly reasonable if I could sell enough copies of his solo album to cover its production costs. This was questionable at best. He would not even let me hear the group sessions. He said he no longer had a tape recorder. He had gotten rid of it because Louis Cottrell was hot on his trail over the tapes. I made the deal. I was a sucker for Kid Thomas and Israel Gorman.

Griff went daily to Guesnon's for lessons. Every day he brought some little gift in addition to the few dollars George charged him. I learned later that Bill Sinclair and a banjo player friend heard about Griff's lessons and went to New Orleans to arrange some for the friend. Bill didn't know Guesnon and, I guess, thought he was just as friendly as the other musicians I introduced him to. Guesnon promptly slammed the door in their faces. I asked Sinclair years later, when he told me of the incident, if he had brought any cigarettes or gifts with him. He didn't know what I was talking about.

Griff and Guesnon, to my amazement, really hit it off. Guesnon would sometimes browbeat the hell out of Griff if he didn't like something he played but they became fast friends. By the time we left for home, Griff was chugging out Guesnon's famous "Rose Room" solo with no problem. They continued to correspond right up to Guesnon's death with George sending Griff chord charts and diagrams and things that only banjo players understand.

I put out George's solo album and left two blank album numbers after it in my next catalog that were supposed to be filled in later when I issued Guesnon's Secret Sessions and the other he promised by his band. I finally filled in one of the numbers with the Very Handy album after George's death. That left a mysterious missing album number in the Jazz Crusade catalogs. Over the years I have received many inquiries about it. I have kept the secret until now. JC-2012 was to be "Creole George Guesnon's Secret Sessions."

I invited Punch Miller to lead our next tour band. Next to King Oliver and Louis Armstrong, Punch had been the most famous New Orleans trumpeter to head North in the Twenties. For a while he gave Armstrong a hot run for his money. But personal problems and booze cut him down. I asked Albert Burbank to join the tour on clarinet along with old faithful Sammy Penn. We scheduled the tour for February 1967.

Griff and I had had a good trip. I had gotten closer to several musicians I hadn't known too well before including Alvin Alcorn, Alec Bigard and one of my favorite clarinetists, Paul "Polo" Barnes. They would all soon be on the way to Connecticut along with, you guessed it, Kid Thomas Valentine.

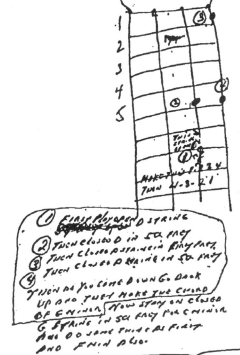

Letter from Creole George Guesnon to Dick Griffith
explaining Minor chords and arpeggio
October 1966

28. Transplants

Upon our return from New Orleans, Griff, Mouldy and I got together to plan our next moves in rebuilding the Easy Riders. We quickly discovered that the ex-Riders had been hard at work trying to steal our regular gigs. They succeeded only at the Rocking Horse. Losing that was almost a relief. A hundred mile round trip every Thursday evening for eight bucks a man was no great loss. We still had our good paying jobs at the Yankee Silversmith Inn and the Villa Rosa to build on.

We decided to go without a piano. Actually we preferred the rhythm section sound we attained on the Big Jim's Little Six album to the sound we had with piano. Drummers were, are, and always will be, a dime a dozen. We had several to choose between. Sammy was, of course, irreplaceable. He was, and remains today, in a class by himself among white clarinetists. We decided to split the clarinet chores between two local musicians. Our main man was Bill Connell. I had played with him in my teens and he was as dedicated to the New Orleans sound as I could hope for. The only problem with him was he had so many other interests that you just couldn't count on him to be available. As a back-up player, I chose young Paul Boehmke. Paul was first introduced to me by the son of a friend of my dad. He was so young when he first started with us that he needed a ride to the rehearsals and jobs because he was too young to drive. In 1967 when he became a semi-regular with the band, he was nineteen. He was an excellent player but not yet committed to the New Orleans style. But, that was a problem we had had many times before. I often brought in guest drummers such as Zutty Singleton and Freddie Moore. Just as frequently I would switch off on drums myself and feature trombone players like Jimmy Archey, J.C. Higginbotham or Vic Dickenson. We were not out of business.

The term we used to describe the many New Orleans style black players in New York was "transplants." Among them were some truly great jazzmen of legendary proportions. The four main ones we used were Archey, Zutty, Edmond Hall and Henry "Red" Allen.

Zutty Singleton was an extraordinary drummer. He was considered one of the best in New Orleans when he left in 1924 for St. Louis. He played in the bands of Louis Armstrong, Jimmie Noone, Fats Waller and many other renowned groups before settling in New York to become the house drummer at Jimmy Ryan's with first the Wilbur DeParis band and then with Tony Parenti. He was the drummer on many recordings now considered classics including those magnificent trio sessions with Omer Simeon and Sidney Bechet. I would often sit in on his drumset at Ryan's.

Zutty called everybody "face." This was usually preceded with a descriptive adjective so you knew who he was talking about. Jimmy Archey was "plungerface" because he used that mute so often. Parenti was "mustacheface" when addressed directly and "Hitlerface" behind his back, which Zutty said described both his appearance and his method of leading a band. I think Zutty had trouble remembering names and that was why he used this device. "Grifface" and "Mouldyface" loved it. I wasn't as pleased. My Big Bill became "Bigface."

Zutty played with us often. The time I remember most fondly was at a huge outdoor music festival in Waterbury, Connecticut. It was a Battle of the Bands in which we were pitted against a New York dixie band sponsored by Phil Becker's restaurant. Zutty stole the show and it was with the greatest pleasure that we wiped up the floor with the dixielanders after the hard time Becker had given me when he withheld payment on the Thomas tour.

Edmond Hall was everything you would expect in a New Orleans clarinetist: quiet, intelligent and soft spoken. But, God, the man blew a hot horn. We used him at least once a month on our regular gigs. He spent many years playing in New York and Chicago but it never changed his "down home" style. It affected us all when he died suddenly in January of 1967. He was another one I missed recording on Jazz Crusade. Of course he made hundreds of top-notch records during his long career. But one last New Orleans session with Kid Thomas and Zutty would have been wonderful to have.

We always had to slip Red Allen a few extra bucks to come play with us. Not a lot. Just enough so he felt special. I didn't mind. He was worth it. He had his pet name also. He called everybody he thought knew how to swing, "gate." Cute. It may even have been Red who put that slang expression into the jazz lexicon. Red left New Orleans in 1927. Before leaving he had played with at least two of the jazzmen who led the 1960's revival: George Lewis and Capt. John Handy. He left New Orleans to join King Oliver's band. He achieved great fame in his career and led an excellent big band in the 1930's. In the 1950's, he led a group at the world famous Metropole on Broadway. Many a Sunday afternoon I could be found there listening to his hot horn. He recorded with George Lewis in the period between the two revivals. When we played the opening at a new jazz spot in Hartford, we featured Red and the management booked us for the following three weeks. He reminded me of Papa Celestin in singing and playing style.

Jimmy Archey. What a trombone player! He made his mark with the legendary King Oliver Harlem recordings for Victor. Then he moved on to the Luis Russell band just as Red had. Archey was never short of work. He recorded hundreds of sides and I doubt he ever made a bad one. He could play any style but his great love was for the New Orleans idiom. I think he played with us mainly for the kicks. We couldn't always get him because he was so much in demand but whenever he could make it up to Connecticut he would. He introduced me to trumpeter Henry Goodwin who, although essentially a big band era jazzman, also enjoyed playing in the Riders. I will have more to say about him later because he was our regular trumpet player throughout most of 1967.

the

Easy Riders

SPECIAL GUEST FEB. 10th

are back!

JIMMY ARCHEY TROMBONE

AND THE **VILLA ROSA** HAS THEM!

EVERY FRIDAY, 9 P.M.–1 A.M.

First Session:
Friday, Feb. 10

Featuring Special
Guest Stars. First
Session: JACK FINE
on trumpet.

THE EASY RIDERS JAZZ BAND

Traditional Jazz

Yes, "The Riders" are back in the saddle again! Big Bill, Mouldy, Griff and the gang
will be featured every Friday night at their new home in Woodmont. That's The Villa
Rosa Restaurant, 141 Merwin Avenue, Woodmont (Milford). For directions on how to get
there and reservations call 878-1747. With your support, we'll soon be bringing up
all your favorites from New Orleans too! So Come On Down.

"The Easy Riders Are Back"
Villa Rosa flyer
February 1967

1967

deceased

HENRY "RED" ALLEN, trumpet

PETER BOCAGE, trumpet

EDMOND HALL, clarinet

LEWIS JAMES, clarinet, string bass

WILBERT TILLMAN, sousaphone

29. Punch And Judy

I guess it was appropriate that my next wife's name was Judy because I met her as I was arranging Punch Miller's first tour of Connecticut. Punch got his nickname because his sister's name was Judy. His father's last name was Burden but, as Punch hardly knew him, he used his mother's maiden name. His real first name was Ernest. So Ernest Burden became known as Punch Miller.

I hired Judy Spencer through a newspaper ad to be Jazz Crusade's secretary. The relationship soon degenerated into a marriage. She became friends with many of the New Orleans musicians but none closer than with Punch who promised to write a song about her but apparently never finished it. Judy becomes a central figure later in the Jazz Crusade story during the California period so I thought I would introduce you to the bride now and have that over with.

Arriving with Punch were Albert Burbank and Sammy Penn. This was one of Penn's few outings without Thomas. He had specifically asked me if I could bring him up sometime with another trumpet player. There was no ill will between Penn and Tom. Sammy just wanted to exert a little independence and to get a spotlight directed at him for a change that wasn't reflected off Tom.

It was a pleasure to welcome Albert into my home. I had often thought about the clandestine nature of our first meeting seven years earlier and it was high time I could openly treat him with the high esteem I felt for him.

We booked two concerts for the Connecticut Traditional Jazz Club in February with them. This was really only a mini-tour as the two CTJC concerts and my recording session on February 26th were all that we booked. The band was billed as Punch's Bunch with the Easy Riders. Burbank was afraid to stay away from his Bourbon Street gig any longer for fear somebody might jump his gig. After we booked the CTJC concerts, we discovered that Kid Sheik's Storyville Ramblers were coming through Connecticut on the same weekend. We briefly discussed postponing the Punch's Bunch tour with the club's governing board to enable us to take advantage of the Sheik opportunity. We had never cancelled a tour before and I was afraid we might hurt the musicians' feelings. The club graciously went out on a limb and booked both bands for the first concert. What a line-up: Punch Miller, trumpet; Albert Burbank, clarinet; Sammy Penn, drums; Kid Sheik, trumpet; Louis Nelson, trombone; Capt. John Handy, alto sax; Sing Miller, piano; Fred Minor, banjo; Chester Zardis, bass and Alec Bigard, drums. All for two bucks, folks. It would be a miracle if Mouldy, Griff and I were even noticed in such fast company.

One complication arose for our band. Mouldy's wife, Fran, as was her habit in those days, was about to give birth as the evening of the first concert arrived. She was so close that Mouldy wouldn't leave her. I called Bill Sinclair and asked if he could come in on piano for the two concerts so we would have a full rhythm section. He said he was going on a trip starting Saturday but he would help us out on the joint concert with Sheik on Friday. I was hopeful that maybe Fran would come through for us and have her baby before Saturday, freeing Mouldy for the second concert. If she didn't have it by Sunday, the recording session would also be in jeopardy.

The joint concert was a blast. It also gave me the opportunity to talk to Sing and Alecs about future ventures together. Sing was very anxious to record for Jazz Crusade. He had been a fringe player on the New Orleans scene. His background had been in big bands and his recent work was mostly lounge gigs. He was gaining recognition in the jazz field but he wanted to get more firmly established by cutting some records on jazz labels. There were many such fringe players we ignored in the Sixties that later generations of jazz fans would venerate because the Robinsons and Handys and Guesnons weren't around for direct comparison. But Sing was one who earned his recognition by working hard for it.

Because of the whopping success of the first concert, the second one was sparsely attended. Those who did attend were the lovers of the "Moose Hall Sound." Mouldy's baby still hadn't arrived but he agreed to play the Moose Hall concert with the understanding that he might have to leave in the middle of the concert if Fran called. Fran didn't let us down and we did the gig with a full band.

We were not as lucky the next day at the recording session. We left our equipment set up at the Moose after the Saturday night gig to save preparation time the next day for the recording. Sunday morning Mouldy called to tell me Fran was in labor and he wouldn't be able to come. He said if she had the baby, he would come down as soon as possible. It was either record without the string bass or cancel.

There was something special about this session that made me take the chance to go ahead. I mentioned Punch's early career briefly before. Permit me to go into a little more detail and relate some things Punch told me after the Friday night concert which made this recording session a must. Punch was Armstrong's closest rival in the 1920's. He recorded with every name band

and on every major record label. Armstrong was fortunate to have good business management and to keep his drinking under control. Punch had no such luck and, in the mix, was a woman who Punch would love all of his life. When they broke up, Punch's career went down the tubes. He ended up playing in circus bands and small road shows.

Among his closest friends when he was riding high was Jimmy Archey. I didn't know that when I casually mentioned to Punch that Archey frequently played with the Riders.

"You all knows Jimmy Archey? Why I ain't heard of that man in years. He was my buddy in the Twenties and Thirties. I sure would like to see that man again."

Saturday morning I called Archey. "Jim, I have a man here at my house who says he's an old friend of yours and wants to say hello." I passed the phone to Punch.

"Jimmy? Jimmy Archey? Why this is Punch Miller. . . What you mean dead? I ain't dead, man. Where'd you ever get an idea like that? I'm here in Connecticut with Bill. Burbank and Penn are with me. . . Hold on. Bill, where you all say we be playing tonight?. . . Jim, he says at the Moose Hall in Stamford. Yeah, the Moose. . . Wait I'll put him on. . ." I gave Jimmy directions.

That evening Jimmy showed up with Henry Goodwin. He and Punch talked away the breaks reminiscing about how hot the bands were in the old days. As they talked, I couldn't help thinking what it would be like for them to play together again after all those years. The more I thought about it, the more I realized that I was about to fire the trombone player I had off the recording session: me!

"Jimmy what are you doing tomorrow afternoon?"

"I got to play tomorrow night at nine in the evening at Jimmy Ryan's."

"I'm recording Punch here tomorrow at one in the afternoon. How would you like to do the recording gig?"

"Well that would be fine, Bill. Real fine."

It would be the only time I recorded one of the New York Transplants with a New Orleans band. Recording Archey would be an expensive thrill.

So. Here it was, Sunday morning and I couldn't very well phone Archey back to cancel the date both he and Punch were looking forward to with so much anticipation. When we arrived at the hall, I explained the situation to Griff. He was flabbergasted to hear that he and Sammy were to be the whole rhythm section. We delayed as long as we could, hoping for a call from Mouldy Dick. Then we started taking tracks. After an hour, we had about four numbers done. I was not very happy with the results but under the circumstances they were better than nothing. Then, in walked Mouldy Dick.

"It's a boy!"

Good old Fran! What a difference a bass player makes. Particularly a strong one like Mouldy. We breezed through the rest of the session and did remakes on the ones Mouldy had missed. I decided to do a big production number with Penn singing "I Believe I Can Make It By Myself." I told everyone to take as many solo choruses as they liked but nobody less than three. It turned out fine and Archey took one of the most astonishing trombone solos I have ever heard on record. He went on chorus after chorus blowing his renowned "talking plunger" style horn. I sat there and watched the man blow it and I've heard the solo a hundred times on tape. I still don't believe it. But, don't take my word for it. Let's hear from Jim Robinson. I played him the master tape. He sat, totally absorbed, listening intensely to Archey's solo. At its conclusion, Big Jim looked up, a slightly stunned expression on his face, and said, "Oh, shit. And he's such a little man, too!"

At the end of the session Burbank said, "Wait! There's one more song we have to record." He started playing Happy Birthday for Mouldy's new son, Kenneth. Everyone joined in. Mike Fast said, "Okay now let's make a take for the album." He flipped on the recorder and they played another chorus. I couldn't have left that off of the album if I wanted to. Mouldy would have killed me. But I was glad to have it. It was one small tribute to a jazzman who worked his butt off for his music all through the Sixties and to whom nobody ever bothered to say thanks.

Thanks, Mouldy Dick.

The Connecticut Traditional Jazz Club, Inc.

presents

DIRECT FROM NEW ORLEANS
A JAZZ SPECTACULAR

CONCERT #1

2 GREAT BANDS

KID SHEIK'S STORYVILLE RAMBLERS

FEATURING: LOUIS NELSON - TROMBONE   CAPT. JOHN HANDY - ALTO SAX
SING MILLER - PIANO   H. A. MINOR - BANJO
CHESTER ZARDIS - BASS   ALEC BIGARD - DRUMS

AND

PUNCH'S BUNCH with the EASY RIDERS

FEATURING: PUNCH MILLER - TRUMPET   ALBERT BURBANK - CLARINET
SAMMY PENN - DRUMS   BILL BISSONNETTE - TROMBONE
MOULDY DICK McCARTHY - BASS   DICK GRIFFITH - BANJO

Friday, Feb. 24, 8:30 P.M.–Holiday Inn, East Main Street at I-91, Meriden, Conn

CONCERT #2

PUNCH'S BUNCH with the EASY RIDERS

THE SAME GANG FOR AN ALL-OUT JAM SESSION

Saturday, Feb. 25, 8:30 P.M.-Moose Hall, Main Street, Stamford, Conn.

ADMISSION TO EACH CONCERT: CTJC MEMBERS - $1.50 Advance - $3.00 at door
Non-MEMBERS - $3.00 Advance - $3.50 at door

**Kid Sheik/Punch's Bunch Concerts
Connecticut Traditional Jazz Club
Februar 1967**

CONNECTICUT JAZZ NEWS

Published By: THE CONN. TRADITIONAL JAZZ CLUB, INC.

P. O. BOX 132 WETHERSFIELD, CONN.

TWIN - BILL JAZZ FESTIVAL

1. HOLIDAY INN • MERIDEN • FEBRUARY 26th • KID SHIEK and PUNCH'S BUNCH

2. MOOSE HALL • STAMFORD • FEBRUARY 25th • PUNCH'S BUNCH

13 —— TOP NEW ORLEANS JAZZMEN —— 13

KID SHIEK'S STORYVILLE RAMBLERS

GEORGE "KID SHIEK" COLA...TRUMPET
Plays first trumpet for the Eureka Brass Band. Has toured England and other parts of Europe with Kid Martyn's Ragtime Band.

CAPT. JOHN HANDY.........ALTO-SAX
John is well known to all C.T. J.C. followers, having played here with the December band and the Easy Riders.

LOUIS NELSON.............TROMBONE
A regular with Kid Thomas' Algiers Stompers for the past thirty years. Has toured Japan three times with George Lewis and played in Europe in 1966.

"SING" MILLER..............PIANO
Sing has confined most of his efforts to the New Orleans area with Kid Shiek's band and is considered by our Jack Guckin as "the hottest piano man in New Orleans".

FRED "M.A." MINOR...........BANJO
Played with the original Sid Desvigne group in New Orleans. Has recorded many times for Kid Shiek on Mono and Jazz Crusade records.

ALEX BIGARD................DRUMS
A real "old-school" drummer who played with the legendary Kid Rena's band. He is a brother of famed clarinetist, Barney Bigard.

CHESTER ZARDIS..............BASS
An artist who has played with many of the great groups including Kid Rena, Chris Kelly and the great Bunk Johnson.

PUNCH'S BUNCH AND THE EASY RIDERS

ERNEST "PUNCH" MILLER...TRUMPET
A leading figure on the New Orleans Jazz scene for the past thirty years. Punch has played New York and Chicago and has been to Japan with the George Lewis group.

ALBERT BURBANK..........CLARINET
Was a member of the first New Orleans jazz group to play in Conn. back in 1951. Has been featured with many band including Billie and DeDe Pierce.

BILL BISSONNETTE.........TROMBONE
In 1965 Bill won the "Best New Jazz Artist" division of the Jazzology poll. He is well known in Conn. and the leader of the Easy Riders.

SAMMY PENN..................DRUMS
Sammy is a regular member of the Kid Thomas Band and Punch's Bunch. He has played with the Easy Riders and on the Riverboat in Conn. and is always a welcome sight on the stand.

DICK "GRIFF" GRIFFITH.......BANJO
Griff has been regular banjoist with the Easy Riders for five years. Studied with Creole George Guesnon in New Orleans and has recorded many times for C.T.J.C. releases.

**RICHARD "MOULDY DICK" McCARTHY...
BASS**
A regular with the Easy Riders since their start in 1962. Has recorded with Big Jim's Little Six, the December band and is well known to C.T.J.C. fans.

30.   Thomas At The Moose

The musical success of the 1944 Revisited experiment by Robinson and Rimington enticed me into a similar experiment which proved to be equally successful. Just as that album presented Jim Robinson in a more frontal mode, I wondered if the same could be done with Kid Thomas. Tom was not a solo oriented musician. But what if I could record him in a small band context just as I had done with Jim? It was worth the shot.

The opportunity arose over the St. Patrick's Day weekend. The Yankee Silversmith asked me to put together a special concert for the holiday evening after the big New Haven parade in which we were invited to play on a float. What better Irishman could we get than Kid Thomas? We also scheduled him in on our Villa Rosa gig and planned a Moose Hall concert for Saturday, March 11th. By this time we were sponsoring more of our own events. The Connecticut Traditional Jazz Club governing board was slowly changing election by election. They were still presenting New Orleans concerts but the erosion to other types of jazz, which eventually led to its demise, had begun. In addition, they were drawn into the competition between our band and the ex-Riders. We had compiled an excellent mailing list of our own and could turn out a good-sized crowd for outstanding events like a Thomas visit.

It was a whirlwind three day tour. On the Moose Hall gig we used only five pieces. They were: Thomas, trumpet; Bill Connell, clarinet; Dick Griffith, banjo; Mouldy Dick McCarthy, bass and me on drums. Tom was a little leery of not having a trombone in the front line so we tried out the group the preceding night. If it hadn't worked out, I could have always called in Jimmy Archey or Freddie Moore and expanded the group for the recording. Thomas hit it off with Connell immediately, He compared him to Al Burbank in style. Tom said there would be no problem for the Saturday concert.

We hadn't done a lot of advertising for the concert and about a hundred of our most ardent fans turned out. The session was relaxed and I let Tom call the numbers as he desired. Though informal, it was an exciting session. Thomas loved the Moose. It gave the big sound we needed for such a little band. Thomas worked harder that night than I ever saw him work before or since. He called many tunes that surprised us such as "Marie," "I Want To

Be Happy" and "St. James Infirmary Blues." I thought he was particularly strong on "Put On Your Old Gray Bonnet" and "On A Cocoanut Island." The biggest surprise was "When the Saints Go Marching In." It mystified me that Tom called the tune so frequently. You would have thought he would have been long since sick of it. But this night he called it half way through the gig instead of saving it for the finale like he usually did. The thing raged. I don't think I have heard it played in such straight forward, hard-driving jazz style since the classic Bunk Johnson recording on American Music.

I was really pleased with this little session and put out as much as I could squeeze on the album. I have to admit there were a lot of fluffs on this album. But the spontaneity of the session made them inevitable. I never worried about minor gaffs on concert sessions anyway. You take the bad to get the good. It is still one of my favorite JC's and certainly my favorite of my drumming records.

The next afternoon we played the parade on the back of a flatbed truck. The Silversmith had hired some boys to run along beside the float and pass out leaflets promoting the concert afterward. At one point along the parade route, Thomas leaned way over to blow at the crowd and fell off the truck! He scampered back on, pulled a green holiday derby hat from his gimmick bag, slipped it onto his head and started yelling, "Look at me! I'm the Jolly Green Giant!" When Kid Thomas was in high spirits, he was a master showman. At the evening concert I brought in a drummer and went back on trombone. Thomas, Connell and I made a very mouldy front line. The next day, Thomas was gone again.

For the next year, this kind of quickie tour happened so often that I couldn't list them all. Every few weeks we would fly Tom, or Tom and Sammy, or just Sammy, or Tom, Sammy and Manny up for weekend mini-tours. Thomas must have played forty or fifty gigs with us in Connecticut between the summers of 1967/1968.

the

Easy Riders

And Look Who's With Them!

are back!

KID

THOMAS

Friday, March. 10th - 9 PM

VILLA ROSA RESTAURANT

141 Merwin Avenue, Woodmont, Connecticut
For reservations & directions call 878-1747

Saturday, March 11 - 9 PM

MOOSE HALL - Stamford

Main Street, Stamford, Connecticut. This
session will be recorded "live" during the
concert. Admission: $ 2.50 per person.

PRESENTED BY *Jazz Crusade*

Kid Thomas at Moose Hall flyer
a Jazz Crusade production
March 1967

KID THOMAS VALENTINE
on his
TRUMPET

YANKEE SILVERSMITH INN
SUNDAY, MARCH 13

FOLLOW

KID THOMAS

AND

THE EASY RIDERS

"AFTER THE PARADE"

TO

DINNER AND CONCERT

AT THE

YANKEE SILVERSMITH

Exit 66 Wilbur Cross Parkway
Wallingford
only 25 minutes drive

To help celebrate
Kid Thomas' return to Connecticut,
the Silversmith will include Rosé Wine
with the purchase of dinner upon
presentation of this card

THERE WILL BE

GREAT

MUSIC — FOOD — BEVERAGE

3 HOUR CONCERT — ADMISSION $2.00

St. Patrick's Day leaflet
Yankee Silversmith Inn
March 1967

31.   Alcorn, Barnes, Bigard

We hadn't planned to bring in another tour band until the summer but, by a stroke of good fortune, we were invited to play at a ritzy boat club in New Jersey that apparently had money to burn. So we decided to burn it on the altar of New Orleans jazz. They were having their big annual bash and wanted a Mardi Gras dance. They asked the price including a couple of musicians direct from New Orleans. I told them it would be pretty expensive with transportation costs and all. Actually, transportation in those days was very reasonable. A round trip night flight, New Orleans to New York, or vice versa, was $98.00 on Delta. I quoted them a hefty price that included my cost to do a separate recording. They accepted it immediately.

I called Alvin Alcorn, whom I had long admired from his Kid Ory days, and clarinetist Polo Barnes. I invited them up for a couple of concerts and a recording session. Five days were all Alvin could spare from his busy schedule. We booked them from March 31st through April 3rd. About a week before the tour, I decided the new drummer we were breaking in was not going to work out. I was not going to risk a bad tour so I called Alec Bigard who was delighted to receive the invitation to come with Alvin and Polo. I told him I was sending all of the plane tickets to Alvin and for him to tell Alvin and Polo that I had added him to the lineup. Our leaflets had already been printed and mailed so Alec came as a surprise to our audiences. He was upset about that because he wanted the flyer to flash around New Orleans to prove he had become a member of the Connecticut brigade.

Paul Barnes was the most literate and gentlemanly of the New Orleans musicians. Articulate, even urbane, it was a pleasure to converse with him. During the 1920's, he played with Celestin's Original Tuxedo Orchestra. He joined the King Oliver band at the same time as Red Allen and played with Bad Eye Joe off and on until 1935 when he returned to New Orleans. He also recorded with Jelly Roll Morton during that period. He lived in New York for awhile in the 1940's. Most of this early activity found him playing saxophone. He packed his sax away and played clarinet into the Sixties where he could be found playing at several of the kitty halls. Unfortunately, few of the Sixties Revival fans were knowledgeable in early jazz history and Polo was just another clarinet player to them. He did little recording. Those he made were outstanding including, and especially, the definitive and beautiful quartet album he did for Icon. His older brother, Emile, "Mile'," had become one of the legends of the revival period and Polo long stood in his shadow despite his more prolific early career.

Alvin Alcorn began in the big bands. He was in the third generation of New Orleans jazzmen. He toured and recorded with Don Albert in Texas. His association with Polo stemmed from a brief period in 1940 when he played trumpet in Paul's band. He joined the great Kid Ory Creole Jazz Band after Teddy Buckner, another big band player, left to form his own group in 1951. While with Ory, he was featured on some of the seminal traditional jazz recordings of the 1950's. He returned home to New Orleans in time to catch the beginnings of the Sixties Revival. He played infrequently at Preservation Hall. According to his own testimony, he was finally banished from the hall because he was accepting too much work at the other kitty halls, in particular Dixieland Hall. Alvin thought that Jaffe used him as an example to the other musicians of what could happen to them if they strayed too often.

Alec Bigard was the older brother of renowned clarinetist Barney Bigard of Ellington Jungle Band and Louis Armstrong All-Stars fame. Alec stands in that great and unique category of New Orleans "street" drummers which includes Paul and Louis Barbarin. He once played with the band that made the very first of the 1940's revival recordings, that of Kid Rena. He was a great friend of Kid Sheik and one of Creole George Guesnon's few close pals.

We started them off at the Villa Rosa. The following day we traveled by car to New Jersey. As we turned off of the Jersey Turnpike into the nearby hills, the change of scenery was dramatic. We exited from an industrial nightmare into a beautiful wooded countryside. It is tempting to call the place we played at a yacht club because it was so lavish. But, in fact, it fronted on a a lake too small for yachts. It was a tuxedoed, begowned, dancing crowd. We were treated like visiting royalty which is, of course, the way whorehouse jazz musicians should be treated all the time by everybody. I wouldn't experience anything like it again until we hit Southern California. We were put up overnight in various private homes. These were interesting three story houses, the upper floor of which were guest, or perhaps servant, quarters. We were invited to stay over for a second night and play again. I could have kicked myself for having already booked the band into the Silversmith.

The Silversmith concert was well attended and we used a photo from that concert on the cover of the album that resulted from the tour.

We recorded as usual at the Moose Hall with Mike Fast engineering. The numbers I selected to record were quite a departure from the type of material I normally recorded but they were well suited to this band. Polo, as promised, brought along his alto sax and used it on a few numbers each night.

He had been reluctant to bring it and he was even more dubious about recording with it. I wanted to have Jazz Crusade be the first to record him on sax since he put the horn aside in the Forties. He graciously acceded to my request and used it on part of the album. By the time I next recorded him in California, he was once again playing it on a regular basis. My little push was responsible for the return of a great saxman.

I was also a fan of Paul's singing so we started the session off with a vocal duet by him and Alcorn on "Bourbon St. Parade." With the exception of the vocal it was strictly an ensemble number. Right after the vocal we played an exceptionally soft chorus before exploding into the ride out chorus. After we made it, Polo asked me a question.

"Bill, on that soft chorus, you were playing a strange melody against me and Alvin that sounded familiar to me but I just can't call its name. What song is it from?"

Alvin said, "You know that's funny you mentioned that Polo because I was meaning to ask that same question. I know I been hearing that thing someplace."

I was surprised they recognized the melody and picked up on it. I thought I had slipped it past everyone. It was a melody written by that hot old jazz master Peter Ilyitch Tchaikovsky: the counterpoint french horn melody from the central part of "Marche Slav." You can't put anything over on these guys.

We did a real pretty "Blueberry Hill," a bluesy "Beale Street Blues" that Polo was lovely on and a raucous "Sheik of Araby" that had everybody gasping for breath at the end. On "Sheik," Alec, who was using my drumset, went to work on my tuned temple block set on a rhythm section chorus that was outstanding. The tune "went over the top" about midway through the out chorus and we had to slide into home to score. "Sheik" stands as a living monument to musical recklessness.

As the New Orleans guys were getting ready to board their flight home, I mentioned to Alvin that Griff, Mouldy, me and our families were coming to New Orleans in a few weeks. Alvin asked me what date we were coming in and our flight number. I told him the date but I didn't know the flight number. I asked him why he wanted it.

"Well, maybe I can pick you up at the airport. Be sure to call me tomorrow with the flight number and your arrival time."

I thanked him for the offer and promised I would call within the next few days with the information. He said, "No, call me tomorrow for sure. I have to make arrangements."

He had a surprise in store we would never forget.

from New Orleans:

PAUL "POLO" BARNES

ALVIN ALCORN

and the

THE EASY RIDERS JAZZ BAND

Traditional Jazz

DIRECT FROM NEW ORLEANS come two outstanding jazz musicians for their first appearances in Connecticut. Alvin Alcorn is well known to all traditional jazz as fans as the trumpeter with Kid Ory's Creole Jazz Band; a band that made some of the most significant jazz recordings of the 1950's. Paul "Polo" Barnes is a member of one of New Orleans' legendary "jazz families". He has appeared annually at "Disneyland" featured with "The Young Men From New Orleans". His alto playing is legend in New Orleans, He is known as the greatest alto player ever produced in New Orleans. Paul has not featured his sax work for many years but he has agreed to come out of retirement on this instrument for this one Connecticut tour. Only two concerts by this duo featured along with the Easy Riders Jazz Band are planned for this area:

Friday, March 31, 1967   The Villa Rosa Restaurant, 141 Merwin Avenue, Woodmont,Ct.
                          For reservations call (203) 878-1747. 9 PM - 1 AM.

Sunday, April 2, 1967   The Yankee Silversmith Inn, Route 5, Wallingford, ct.
                          for reservations call (203) 529-9305. 5 PM - 9 PM.

Alcorn/Barnes Flyer
Silversmith/Villa Rosa
March/April 1967

32. The Reception Brass Band

I guess in any career there comes that moment, that one supreme moment, that tops all the others. The moment you would choose if you could just relive one.

On Saturday, May 6, 1967, Mouldy Dick McCarthy, his wife, Fran, and two of their sons, Richie and Timmy, Dick Griffith and his wife, Sue, my future wife, Judy, and I flew to New Orleans. Mouldy Dick had been talking about going for years. He had listened to the tales Griff and I brought back from earlier trips. For someone as devoted to New Orleans jazz as he was, they must have been hard to believe. New Orleans: where, on any evening, and many afternoons, you could go to listen to three or four top jazz bands for a buck a pop. New Orleans: where you might bump into Slow Drag Pavageau or Chester Zardis strolling down the street. New Orleans: that's the way it was in 1967. Now he was finally on his way. The trip of a lifetime.

The day before we left I received another phone call from Alvin Alcorn. This was the third time I talked to him since he returned home from Connecticut. I had called him to give him our flight information. He called back a week later to reconfirm it. And now here he was again.

"It's Alvin, Bill. I just wanted to double-check that you all are coming tomorrow."

"We'll be there, Alvin. Are you still going to be able to pick us up? You know there are going to be eight of us in all counting the kids. We can grab a couple of cabs in if it's any bother."

"That's why I called, Bill. I had a job come up for tomorrow afternoon so I will not be able to meet you, but I've made arrangements to have you picked up anyhow."

"That's really nice of you, Alvin. How will I recognize them? Do I know them?"

"You'll know them when you see them. I'll be playing in Dixieland Hall tomorrow night. Maybe I'll see you there once you're settled in."

"We'll stop in for sure, Alvin. See you tomorrow."

As our jet entered New Orleans airspace, I started wondering how I would find the people Alvin was sending. Perhaps it was Leonard and Sonny. Well, we would know in a few minutes. The plane touched down.

It was a beautiful day, as May is everywhere in America. Griff and I were excited to be back but the others were ecstatic with anticipation. We grabbed the carry-ons and emerged into the long corridor that led to the terminal and baggage area.

Mouldy said, " I hope everybody's not out of town on tours. I came to hear some jazz."

He didn't wait long to hear some jazz or find out who was in town. As we started down the corridor, the huge doors at the far end swung open and jazz music filled the air. We stopped dead in our tracks. There was no mistaking that sound. It was a New Orleans brass band.

Griff yelled, "They must be seeing somebody off!"

I suddenly realized what Alvin had been up to. "Or MEETING somebody," I yelled back as I heard a trombone riff that could only be my man, Big Jim Robinson.

The band marched up the corridor. It was the brass band you dream about in your fantasies. Lined up two by two as they came up the hallway, they were led by Jim Robinson and Shoboy Thomas on trombones. Next came Punch Miller and Kid Sheik followed by Kid Thomas and Manny Paul.

"Jecesus," muttered Griff. Mouldy had dropped his bag to the floor and just stood gaping. Behind Tom and Manny marched Polo Barnes and Sammy Penn. Finally, taking up the rear were Alec Bigard on snare drum and Chester Jones slamming the Onward Brass Band's bass drum!

Following behind was a massive second line that must have included every tourist arriving and departing New Orleans that afternoon. . . all coming to see who the bigshots were that commanded this sort of reception. We were the bigshots: three young white musicians from, of all places, Connecticut with their wives and kids in tow. Being welcomed to the city where jazz was born by the greatest New Orleans brass band ever assembled.

Most of the players were decked out in their brass band regalia, white shirts and brass band caps, except for Thomas who had on a pullover shirt. He, Paul and Penn wore their regular hats.

On they came. The other passengers who were debarking with us all stopped as well, put down their bags and started to applaud. First for the band and then for us! They didn't know who the hell we were but they knew we were SOMEBODY. The strains of "Just A Little While to Stay Here" grew louder and louder. They finally reached us and abruptly stopped playing and gathered around all laughing and shouting greetings at once. We were all hugging and exchanging handshakes as the crowd stared and our women looked on dumbstruck. I could imagine their thoughts. No wonder these guys are always sneaking off to New Orleans if this is the way the party BEGINS. Even Mouldy's kids were struck silent for the first time in their young lives. What kind of bigshot is dad anyway?

After exchanging greetings, we walked out into the main concourse with the band blazing away behind us. Hundreds of people crowded the entrance to the terminal trying to catch a glimpse of the "celebrities." And out we walked, Griff waving to the crowd as if he was Secretary of State or maybe the first President to carry his own banjo case. One woman ran over to Sammy Penn and yelled, "Who are they?"

"They's very important cats, Lady," he grinned.

Outside of the terminal, we threw all of our luggage into the back of a pickup truck Alvin had supplied and we split up into the various musicians cars for the ride into the city. I was deep in thought as we drove in, thinking about the airport greeting. It was so incredible. Here were ten of the most famous New Orleans jazz musicians in the world and they each broke into their daily schedules to come out and welcome us to their city. These men we respected and admired so much were here to show their love and respect for us. Was this what it was finally all about? Love and respect? I hoped so because those were the things that could make all the headaches and heartaches worthwhile.

Judy broke my reverie, "Why didn't you tell me about the airport thing?"

"Because I didn't know. Alvin must have set it all up and then he wasn't even able to come enjoy it."

I thought about the snapshots Sue Griffith took at the airport of the band. God, I hope they'll come out. Nobody will ever believe this otherwise. And Alvin wasn't in the picture, the guy who set it up. That wasn't fair. I wondered what our fans would think when they saw those photos. And not just them. What is some jazz historian in the year 2020 going to think when he trips across it? He'll probably spend the rest of his life investigating what great event brought about the gathering together of the greatest brass band in history. He will be surprised to finally have to write, "The reason this unique band was assembled was to meet Bill Bissonnette, Dick Griffith and Dick McCarthy on their arrival for a two week vacation in New Orleans." Then another thought crossed my mind.

Where the hell was Mike Fast when I really needed him.

33. New Orleans – 1967

Word of the airport reception swept through the ranks of the New Orleans musicians. As we went from kitty hall to kitty hall to listen to the music, jazzmen came up to us to apologize for not having been there to greet us.

"I'm sorry I wasn't at the airport, man. Nobody told me about it or I woulda bin there fo' sure."

"I couldn't get no ride out there, Bill, or you would have for sure seen me."

"I had to work and couldn't get away."

We heard it over and over again. The airport extravaganza had become a major event. Not being there was missing opening night at the Met. If everybody had shown up who said they wished they had, it would have topped Johnny Casimer's funeral.

At Dixieland Hall I thanked Alvin Alcorn for his thoughtfulness in arranging our reception, He too apologized for missing it. Of all the musicians who played at the airport only Shoboy had not been to Connecticut. And, unfortunately, he never did come.

I had rented rooms for this visit to New Orleans from Allan Jaffe instead of Larry Borenstein who provided them in previous years. We were in a beautiful old Quarter building with all of our rooms fronting on a common courtyard. Griff and I spent the first couple of days showing Mouldy and the families the tourist sights: the French Market, Jackson Square and St. Louis Cemetery #2 (where, believe it or not, I usually stopped to hex a few of my antagonists by putting a note and coin on the grave of Marie Laveau, the voodoo queen. It probably doesn't work of course but, hey, what the hell, if I could sock it to 'em for a dime it was worth a shot. Right?). In the evenings we could always be found in one of the kitty halls.

On our second evening in town, just as we had assembled to head out to grab something to eat before hitting the jazz halls, there came a knock at my door. It was Allan Jaffe looking for Mouldy Dick.

"Hi," he said, "I just got a call from Chester Zardis. He said he wasn't feeling well and won't be able to play tonight. I know it's short notice but I was wondering if Mouldy would mind playing in his place tonight with Billie and DeDe."

Would he mind? My God. Dick said he would be happy to "help out" and Jaffe left. Mouldy turned to us nonchalantly and said, "I guess I won't be able to make the rounds tonight. Damn it, I have to work." Then he broke out laughing.

His second night in New Orleans and there he stood between Billie Pierce and Cie Frazier. Just behind George Lewis, Dede Pierce and Louis Nelson. He didn't LOOK scared. He didn't SEEM intimidated. He told me afterward he was terrified through the first set. By the second, he was wailing. At the end of the night, he was one smug little bastard.

The next afternoon we held a free-for-all jam session in the hall with other visiting jazzmen. In addition to Griff, Mouldy and myself, we had Orange Kellin on clarinet, Lars Edegran on piano and Clive Wilson on trumpet. I don't recall who played drums. It was a lot of fun and we opened the doors so tourists and jazz fans could wander in and out.

Polo Barnes invited Judy and me to dinner at his home one evening. He met us in front of Preservation Hall and suggested we take the bus to his house. As we waited for the bus, Polo turned to us and asked if we might feel more comfortable entering and sitting separately. He assured us that he would understand and take no offense. He didn't want to be a source of any embarrassment to us. It was Judy's first brush with "the old ways." She was shocked at the suggestion. We would sit together, she said. When the bus arrived Polo stepped on first and promptly walked to the back, passing many empty seats, to sit just behind the white pole that used to segregate the races. He needn't have done so. Those rules had fallen under the weight of the 1964 Civil Rights Act. But not for Polo. And not for many other elderly blacks who were unable to adapt to the new freedom. I sat next to Polo and Judy sat right across the aisle from us. An old black woman who was sitting a few rows in front of Judy got up and moved to a row behind her. That's the way it used to be. Another younger black couple stayed in their seats a few rows in front of us. That's the way it is.

I had grown accustomed to the older blacks habit of deference. I closed my eyes to it knowing that it only caused confusion and fear among them to try to change. Let them alone. These new things were for the next generation to savor. It would have anguished Polo Barnes to attempt to take his birthright now after all these years.

Judy was even more alarmed to see the reaction of Polo's wife to our visit to her home. Obviously she knew we were coming and she had cooked a great meal for us too. But, once we arrived, she froze with terror. Polo tried to calm her by talking about how he had stayed with me in Connecticut and what good friends we were. She repeatedly got up from the table on the pretext of having something to do in the kitchen. She then stayed there until Paul called her back in. Finally, after one long absence, Judy got up and went into the kitchen to find Polo's wife sitting there shucking peas. Judy offered to help and was rebuffed. She then tried repeatedly to start a friendly conversation to no avail. It was no use.

As we walked back to the bus, Polo apologized for her behavior. He said she couldn't get used to the changes that were taking place. She was frightened and suspicious of all white people he told us. Unlike him, he said, she just couldn't accept the new freedoms they had won. After going to great lengths to explain his wife's fears, he climbed into the bus and once again headed straight for the back.

One afternoon, Mouldy stayed with the wife and kids to do some sightseeing while Griff and I headed for George Guesnon's house. As we arrived, Guesnon was heading out the door with his banjo case in hand.

"Hey, how you cats doing?" he said. "C'mon, I'll sneak you into a gig with me." At that moment Harold DeJan pulled up in his car. We all jumped in. The gig was a union sponsored benefit at New Orleans Charity Hospital. I remember that Ernie Cagnolatti, Jim Robinson's trumpet man, was playing the job but I don't recall the others. I do remember that there was no trombone player or drummer. I remember that because they were my instruments and I could have sat in on either if I had had an axe there. By the time the job was over, Griff and I had to head right back to meet the others for dinner. Griff made his arrangements with Creole George to begin his daily lessons again and I told George I would be over the next day to talk some business.

In the period since I had last been to New Orleans, I had released the Guesnon solo album "Echoes From New Orleans" almost exactly to George's specifications. I deleted two or three sentences from the liner notes he wrote, in my name, because they were just so outlandishly self-laudatory that I couldn't put my name to them. I also used an eye-catching red to highlight the front cover instead of the blue George wanted. All of the songs were arranged exactly as he wished and the front cover prominently featured the photo of him he gave me. He could have no complaints about this production.

Wrong. Creole George Guesnon could complain about anything. As soon as I walked through the door of his house, he was jabbing his finger at the red cover.

"What's the matter with the color, George? I think it adds a lot of class to the jacket."

"Class!" he bellowed. "Class!? It looks like a Goddamn whorehouse! I told you blue. BLUE!"

"Hold on George. . ."

"Hold on shit! And what about the way you ruined the liner notes? You promised you would put the notes on just the way I gave them to you. And you threw half of them out."

"Half of them?" I responded, "I took out three sentences George. They were just too much George. Nobody would believe that I would write stuff like that. C'mon, George, be reasonable."

"Well, let me think about it some more. Now get out of here so I can give Griff his lesson. Come back tomorrow for sure. And bring money."

It sounded worse than it was. The bottom line was "bring money." That meant the deal was still on. I would just have to suffer the slings and arrows of an outrageous Guesnon and the tapes were mine.

I figured I would outsmart George and bring Judy along the next day in the expectation that he would keep his temper under control in the presence of a lady. Wrong again. He wouldn't even let us into the house. He stepped out on the front porch and went into a harangue that lasted over an hour. Never once did he invite us in. He told us how everyone was abusing him. He said he had stopped playing at Preservation Hall and he was not going to record ever again. He might just quit playing altogether. I interjected that Manny Sayles would be delighted to hear that. He might even win the next Jazzology Poll if Guesnon quit. George was not amused. He was sick and tired of everybody, "getting rich off of me while I live in goddamned poverty." He said he was particularly disappointed in me because of the way the album was produced but he graciously told Judy that that was probably only because I was, "young and stupid," and not malicious like the others. I appreciated the caveat. He then said he was prepared to forgive me and permit me to buy, "the tapes we talked about." He said that eyeing Judy like she might be Louis Cottrell's Mata Hari. However, the third session we discussed, that of a new recording by his band, was out as he refused to record again.

Spleened out, he finally asked, "Do you have the money?" I counted it out. He went into the house and returned with the little box from under the slat in the floor. He handed it to me and pocketed the money. I didn't dare open the box in front of him for fear he might think I was checking to make sure the tapes were really there and I would then have to listen to another hour on how I mistrusted him. George was waiting for it too. He seemed disappointed I didn't check the box. We talked for a few more minutes until Griff arrived for his lesson. I thanked Guesnon for the tapes and Judy and I left. It was the last time I ever saw Creole George Guesnon but we would talk once more during one of the most bizarre events I was a party to in the 1960's.

I didn't hear the tapes until we got back home. The sound wasn't great. I didn't expect it to be. But it was adequate for a home taping and here were Thomas and Israel, Howard and James playing some rough and primitive music of historical importance. I planned to issue it but never got to it. It survives, I trust, somewhere deep within the vaults, or perhaps cardboard boxes, of the Jazzology/GHB archives.

34. Your Brother's Suspenders

In June we picked up the best steady job we ever had in Connecticut. The price we had to pay was giving up our other steady gigs. This job was full time, four days a week. It was at a new place that opened on Fairfield Beach called Your Brother's Suspenders. We played Thursday, Friday and Saturday evenings and Sunday afternoon. It wasn't a big place, seating perhaps seventy customers, but it became so popular during the Summer months that several hundred people would pass through the doors on any given day. In order to keep the crowds turning over through the course of the night, we played the gig in "shows" instead of sets. The only difference was we did three long sets instead of four shorter ones. In this way the management could say the first show is over and hustle the people out to let in another group from the long lines that were waiting outside. The only problem was, once the people were seated, they wouldn't leave at the end of the show. We came up with a little trick to clear the room that used to break Sammy Penn up every time we did it. If the line of people outside was getting too long, the manager of the place would signal me at the end of a set. We would swing into the "Saints" and start marching around the room inviting everybody to join the second line behind us. Once they were all up and following us, the manager would throw open the back door of the place and we would march out into the rear parking lot with the whole throng gaily chasing us. Once we were out, the manager would slam the rear door shut and open the front. In would pour a new crowd. We would then take our break and watch the displaced fans trying to get back in. This worked for awhile but one night they had a near riot about it and the manager had to call the cops. We never tried it again.

At this time, the regulars in the band were Griff, Mouldy Dick, Paul Boehmke on clarinet and tenor, drummer Meade Passoretti and myself. Technically we didn't have a regular trumpet man but, for all practical purposes, Henry Goodwin from New York was playing steady with the band. He played every Friday and Saturday with us. We didn't use a trumpet player on Thursdays and Sundays except when we flew Kid Thomas or Punch Miller in, which was just about once a month. Sometimes we would bring Sammy Penn in if he was itching for a trip and, occasionally, Manny Paul too. The gig lasted well into the fall when the tourist trade slacked off at the beach.

The Suspenders was a crazy place that pumped out more beer per minute than any place I had ever seen. The crowds were mostly young college students barely old enough to drink. The place always smelled of pot. It was the Sixties middle class pseudo-counter-culture at play. It became known as such a hot jazz spot that even Bill Sinclair would drop in once in awhile. We thought he did it to hear Thomas and the others. Then Thomas tipped us off that he was really there to try to book him and the others while they were in town, at our expense. Fortunately there was no piano in the place so we didn't have to extend him the courtesy of inviting him to sit in.

Thomas got a big charge out of the Suspenders and he could be found climbing up on the bar or out in the audience with his wig on almost every night he was there. The college kids loved him and he would plop back into his seat after one of his tricks and yell, "Kicks, man, Kicks!" One evening when Penn was there, Thomas was playing really hot. Tom kicked off "Just A Closer Walk With Thee" on the one and three beat for a fast tempo romp. Penn thought the half time kick was in 4:4 and came in at an almost dirge-like tempo. Mouldy and Griff took their pickup from Penn. Tom tried to pick the tempo up for the lively crowd. He wanted to get away on the tune but Sammy just kept plodding along at the tempo he had set. Tom kept signaling Penn to pick it up to no avail. Finally Thomas took his horn down and glared at Penn over his shoulder. Sammy gave him his broadest, toothless smile and said, "You stay right where I got you, Thomas!" At the break Thomas dragged Sammy over to me and started ranting about what Penn had done. Sammy, by this time feeling no pain, told him, "Now look here, Thomas, you know when we comes to Connecticut, I be working for Bill, not you. Now listen, Bill, didn't you think that was a good tempo for that little thing?" I just shrugged my shoulders at Thomas.

"Shoot man, shoot!" Thomas sputtered and spent the rest of the evening in his "jutting jaw" mode.

On several other occasions, Tom and Sammy were offered joints by fans or players. Sammy tried one once and sailed off into heaven for the rest of the gig. Thomas always got pissed when offered one and the offers soon stopped.

The bandstand was raised about three feet off the floor and had a low railing around it, upon which Mouldy usually sat while he whipped his string bass. McCarthy was a tough man on a bass. Three times during the Sixties he had to have the neck of his instrument reglued and pinned because he was literally tearing the thing apart as he played. He could be even tougher on a bottle of Scotch. This one night as we were jamming away, I was pumping brass with my eyes closed as I often do. Suddenly I couldn't hear the string bass which was unusual because Mouldy stood right behind me on the bandstand. I opened my eyes and there was Mouldy standing in FRONT of me.

"How the hell did you get down there, Mould?"

"I fell over the railing," he replied casually as if falling off a bandstand was a common event. In the Riders it was.

In the middle of the summer, we came across a local trumpeter who was the best we ever had in the Riders. Hank Nadig was the son of a magazine publisher who published a jazz column I wrote and was a fan of the band. Let me tell you Hank played some powerful Kid Thomas style trumpet. He was so good that even when Thomas came up we let him play second horn. He stayed with us until I left Connecticut for California. I never recorded him and that is a shame. I believe he later moved to Massachusetts.

35. Last Connecticut Recordings

In September, the Suspenders gig was winding down. Mouldy Dick was now sharing the string bass chores with a newcomer to the band. I met Jim Tutunjian on a Fourth of July parade float. Mouldy was unable to make the gig because of ever more frequent family obligations. Mouldy had five kids by now and asked that we cut back his band activities. Boehmke recommended Tut to me for the job. They had been high school classmates. Tut was only nineteen and was just starting out on upright bass but he had been playing Fender for several years with local pop and country bands. As the summer progressed, Mouldy became less and less available. We began using Tut at the Suspenders. I was happy at the prospect of helping break new, young talent into our music. I had turned thirty on February 5th. My birthday was two days after Kid Thomas' birthday.

While the Suspenders money still flowed, I wanted to do one more tour with Tom, Sammy and Manny Paul. The opportunity came when one of our fans planned her wedding. She was to become Mrs. Barbara Greene and she wanted Kid Thomas to play at her wedding reception. It was a Jewish wedding and her fiance seemed to want a more traditional affair but Barbara wanted Kid Thomas and that was that. The extra money we would get for blowing the wedding reception would buy a recording session. We flew the three jazzmen up.

Many eyebrows shot up as our strange entourage walked onto the stage to set up for the wedding gig. We had gone all out (for us) and worn suits for the gig but I think the guests expected matching tuxedos. And I also doubt they expected to see characters like Thomas, Paul and Penn. We closed the stage curtain and set up. Barbara came backstage, looking beautiful in her wedding gown, to greet us and to tell us not to worry about a thing. They'll love us, she said. I was leery and pointed out again that our wedding band repertoire wasn't very extensive. She laughed and said, "You're what I want. Just play for me and the hell with the rest of them."

The curtain parted and there we stood face to face with a couple hundred wedding guests expecting to hear the "Girl From Ipanena." So what tune did Thomas call as an opener to catch our Jewish audience's attention? The "Sheik of Araby!" And not only that but for the first time ever, he sang it!! When it was over and we looked out at the stunned wedding party, Griff leaned over to Boehmke and said, "I got five bucks that says he calls "Hindustan" next." Boehmke broke up laughing.

Tom called it.

There's another story I must tell you about that day. As I mentioned, we were all dressed up in our best suits for the wedding gig. The band assembled at my house before leaving for the job and Sammy started pestering Griff for a photo of the two of them together. He wanted, he said, a photo of Griff handing him some sheet music. We were in a hurry and Griff tried to put him off saying they could do it the next day. Sammy persisted. He had to have it while they were both dressed in suits. It was all very mysterious and urgent so we stopped everything while Sue Griffith took the photo of Sammy and Griff standing in my backyard with the sheet of paper being passed between them. In the picture Sammy is smiling at the camera while Griff is smiling at Sammy. A very formal pose. Griff finally found out what it was all about months later from Manny Paul.

"You know what Penn did with that photo Griff? He took that thing to New Orleans and spread it all over town that it was a picture of him with the mayor of Bridgeport presenting him with the keys to the city!"

Our last Connecticut recording session was made during the week of September 10th or 17th. None of us remembers the exact date. The sessions have not yet been issued although they are some of the finest Kid Thomas on tape.

We recorded these last sessions at the Moose Hall. We did two distinct sessions. The first was for an album I was planning to call Dance Hall Days. The personnel for this session was Kid Thomas Valentine, trumpet; Bill Connell, clarinet; Manny Paul, tenor sax; Dick Griffith, banjo; Jim Tutunjian, string bass and Sammy Penn on drums. Tom and Manny were to pick all of the selections which were to reflect what it sounded like back in the dance halls of New Orleans where blacks played for blacks for dancing. It was a remarkable session. The tempos were restrained and the tune selection out of the ordinary for a New Orleans band. They recorded "Pennies From Heaven," "Rum and Coca Cola" and "The Object of My Affection." They did a very slow rendition of "Hello Dolly." The hottest thing they blew was "Babyface." They also recorded "I'm Forever Blowing Bubbles" with a hilarious vocal by Penn which was, I'm sure, not meant to be funny but he had been hitting the bottle and he got his words slurred and mixed up.

I joined them for the second session which also had some interesting material. Included were "Lonesome Road" and "See See Rider Blues." But the highpoint of the session was a tune suggested by Tom that none of us had ever heard before. It was a country tune called "The Rose of Old San Antone" and it was one lovely number. Mike engineered these sessions as usual and it would be the last he would do for me until I returned to jazz in the mid-1980's when I brought him in from Baltimore to engineer my first recording session of the new age.

It was certainly fitting that I used Thomas and Manny on this final Connecticut recording session. They had been featured on my first guest star album just three and a half years earlier. It's amazing, in retrospect, to think of how many recordings we made during that short period. It's even more amazing that so many of them were good ones. Even classic ones in a few instances. A phase had ended. The only original members of the Riders remaining were Griff and I. We had the makings of a good new band in Nadig, Boehmke and Tutunjian but I thought we needed a rest. More than that I needed a change of scenery. I thought about moving to New Orleans (and probably should have) but I didn't think the daily competition of Jim Robinson and Louis Nelson was conducive to making a name for myself. I may be dumb but I ain't stupid. I started thinking about California.

Sammy Penn and the "Mayor of Bridgeport"
Griffith Jazz Crusade Memorabilia
1967

Front Cover
Jazz Crusade Catalog
1967

36.   Intermission

Let's take a break. For most followers of Jazz Crusade in the Sixties, the story seemed to end here. No new records were released after I left Connecticut and, to those not personally involved, Jazz Crusade appeared to disappear from the face of the planet. As you will see, this was not the case in fact and one of the purposes of this book is to clarify this final phase of the Crusade and to let you know that some marvelous Jazz Crusade recordings you never heard about are still to be released.

As you now know, George H. Buck Jr. bought my record company in the early 1970's and a few of the unissued sessions have already been released including those with Punch Miller in California and the Eureka Brass Band. Still to come, I assume, are two California sessions: one with Kid Thomas, Capt. John Handy, Sammy Penn and a guest appearance by, then virtually unknown, Carol Leigh; and another Earthquake McGoon "live" session with Alvin Alcorn, Polo Barnes, Alec Bigard and Sing Miller. There is also an album combining the best vocals of Sing Miller accompanied by the Punch Miller and Alvin Alcorn bands. From Connecticut there are still the final two Kid Thomas sessions. Plus a wealth of early Riders material with Sammy Rimington which probably will never be released. Many of the original Jazz Crusade albums I released have been re-issued. I hope most of the balance will be sometime in the future. And George has told me that at least some of the more popular ones will be released on compact disc.

I like to break clean. Ask any of my three ex-wives, they'll confirm it. After the events I am about to relate concerning the final year and a half of the Jazz Crusade, my love of jazz was superseded and overruled by personal considerations that need not be delineated here but which were important enough to keep me distracted from jazz events during the Seventies and early Eighties. By divine intercession, I saw, and spoke to, both Jim Robinson and Kid Thomas shortly before their deaths; events I will relate a little later. But, I often reflected on the Crusade days, spurred to do so by mail from jazz enthusiasts that, somehow, continued to be forwarded for years afterward. For awhile I read them but finally, as I drifted away and my interest waned, I simply threw them out unopened. Sometime during that period, I was visited at my home by Girard Guichardon, a French jazz fan, and some of his friends. I spoke to them awhile, gave them a few leftover Jazz Crusade albums and sent them on their way. I mention this to open a subject for discussion. And that subject is the non-playing jazz supporter.

New Orleans jazz is active today not only through the efforts of those musicians who choose to play it. The players have a vested interest. They want you to come out and listen to their musical accomplishments. There is no such thing as a performing artist free of ego. There are musicians, usually amateur, in the good sense of the word: those who play not for a living but for their art, whose non-performing contributions have exceeded their musical contributions. I may be in this category myself so I do not intend this as a put-down of their musical talents. One of these that comes to mind is Hannes Anrig, an excellent mouldy Swiss trumpeter, who started and continues to manage, the fabulous Ascona Festa New Orleans festival in Switzerland. Another is Tom Schilp of Germany, a great drummer who promotes jazz incessantly along with his friends Hans-Werner Grunewald and Adolf Klapproth. There is Junichi Kawaii of Japan who I mentioned earlier. And in Connecticut, Pete Campbell, a trumpeter who I think will finally agree with me that we never agreed on anything, but who kept the Connecticut Traditional Jazz Club going for years virtually single-handedly in its later period. But, as I said, these are musicians and we should expect them to do their share and more.

But what to make of those who do not play and do so much heavy lifting? Finally I'm to the point. Jazz continues because they love it. I'm not talking about the fans, as much as we need them. What do you make of George H. Buck Jr., who built a hobby into the world's largest jazz record label? And Jack Guckin, referred to so often in these pages, who ceaselessly worked for the success of the Crusade? And Rocky Clark, who started every jazzmen who ever played traditional jazz in Connecticut before the Sixties on their way? And Leslie Johnson out there in Minneapolis who publishes THE traditional jazz journal, "The Mississippi Rag?" And the historians: Alden Ashforth, Sam Charters, Dick Allen and the rest. The record producers: Grayson "Ken" Mills, Sonny Faggart, Leonard Brackett and Tom Bethell to name just a few. And people who do their work on a local level. Marshall Peterson, who did all of the work for the Santa Rosa jazz club in the Sixties. And abroad. I have mentioned Girard Guichardon from Macon who has worked tirelessly for jazz. In Lyon, France there is Rene Chalandon who makes "Jazzogie," a jazz club, function and who has started many an excellent young jazz musician, like France's best lady drummer Marie

"Zuttyfacc" Dandrieux, on the road to jazzville. And in Belgium, Jackie DeRidder who has a small nightspot called "Ragtime" and who started a jazz festival in Ninove. And the writers who promote jazz through the written word: Gene Miller in Connecticut, Marcel Joly in Belgium, Jean-Pierre Daubresse in Paris, Paige Van Vorst here in the U.S.A., Friedrich Hachenberg in Germany. And the photographers, such as those who took the photos included herein: Dr. Edward Lawless of San Francisco, Donald Moore of Maine and Andrew Wittenborn of New York. What do we make of such people?

You say you never heard of most of these people? Why am I wasting your time with this stuff? Somewhere in this book I have to say a few things that don't relate to a straight history of the Crusade. But, these people do relate. . . and hundreds, perhaps thousands, of others I haven't named. These people make the wheels of jazz go round. And it's time you heard a few of the names that do this. These folk will probably never have books about them, or recordings of them, to flash to their progeny to show what they did in the Great War because they were the first sergeants and second lieutenants who never get written up like the generals or, for that matter, the dog-faced privates. I wanted to mention them and thank them for their contributions. There were others I have surely failed to mention but they are just as important and there are legions I never knew who did nothing directly for me but whom you ought to thank the next time you see them.

There is one among them whom you can easily spot because he is a giant and towers above all the rest. He is Bill Russell to whom we all, everyone of us who ever listened, enthralled, to a New Orleans jazz record, owes his homage. He is perhaps the one who needs a book written about him, if it hasn't already been written. I wish I was good enough at this to do it.

Finally an appraisal of jazz, albeit short. As you probably realize it is dead. We cavort with ghosts. Jazz died roughly about the time Duke Ellington did. There has been nothing recorded in decades that has added anything new to the genre. Growth is life. Life is growth. I'm not saying, of course, there is no good jazz to be heard today. There certainly is, in all species of jazz. But it is all nostalgic. Nothing new. How good you are today seems to depend on how well you recreate, not how well you create. This is tragic but useful information to have. Innovation, that marvelous clay from which Armstrong, Morton, Oliver, Waller, Noone, Beiderbecke, Henderson, Moten, Ellington, Hawkins, Lunceford, Parker, Bunk, Lewis, Thomas, Davis and a very few others were sculpted, has dried up.

In our field, perhaps it was unfortunate Ken Mills selected the name Preservation Hall for his venture. Because all we have been doing ever since is trying to preserve the music exactly as it was without any form of conservative evolution. Some musicians broke through the wall: Kid Thomas and Capt.

John Handy added much that was new and exciting and we benefited from it. With Jazz Crusade, I actively tried experimentation with the form and occasionally succeeded. In the Eighties I tried it again with a band designed to sound the way Morton or Noone might have sounded if they had lived and grew within the idiom. It failed. Innovative musicians require innovative audiences. Perhaps it is just as well. Perhaps Allan Jaffe was right so many years ago when he said the music should die with the musicians. Sort of like burying the catapult bearers along with the Pharaoh. We can still hear it the way it was, lightened considerably by the skin tone of its practitioners. And that's the answer, of course. Young blacks didn't follow the foot tracks laid down by giants. We whites can barely play this damn music, never mind innovate with it. What Ken Mills once told me about the black musicians, that they don't improvise, they "variate," applies more to us white imitators. The blacks he spoke of did improvise at one time and continued to do so until they hit on the perfect improvisation. But once they found it, like the Robinson "Ice Cream" solos or Lewis' "Burgundy St. Blues," they were smart enough to realize they had reached it and essentially stuck with it while still "variating" all over the place. So, dead jazz will continue to live(!) and that's a good thing seeing there will apparently be nothing new to come our way.

Let's get on with the final Crusade.

1968

deceased

GEORGE LEWIS, clarinet

CREOLE GEORGE GUESNON, banjo

37.   Guesnon's Farewell

During the first half of 1968, I brought no New Orleans musicians north. I was busy planning my move to California. There is little to report about this period except for one bizarre incident.

It happened late at night, around midnight if my memory serves me well. I was in my den doing some paperwork when the phone rang. I picked it up and heard an hysterical voice shouting on the other end.

"Bill! Bill Bissonnette! This is Guesnon." The voice was panting, out of breath. "I'm dying!"

"George, calm down." My mind was reeling. "Tell me what's happened. Are you alright?"

"I'm dying! Creole George Guesnon is dying and nobody gives a shit! Nobody gives a shit!"

I could hear the terror in his voice and he was gasping. "George get to the hospital. Quick! Who have you called?"

"I ain't called nobody but you. Nobody cares that George Guesnon's dying here. You got to help me, Bill. Help me!"

This was unbelievable. Here I was in Connecticut, fifteen hundred miles away, and he's calling me to help him. I told him to hang up the phone and I would get him help. He ranted on and I yelled into the phone, "Hang up goddamn it and I'll get you help!"

The phone went dead and I sat there wondering what to do. Judy heard me yelling from the bedroom and came into the den. I told her what happened. "You better do something quick," she said. I picked up the receiver and called Preservation Hall. I didn't recognize the voice that answered. I insisted that they get Allan Jaffe to the phone immediately. It was urgent. Allan came to the phone.

"Allan, this is Bill Bissonnette. I just got a call from George Guesnon and I think he's really sick. He might have had a heart attack or something. He's hysterical and can't seem to catch his breath. I think you better get an ambulance over to his house right away. I didn't know who else to call."

"I'll go myself. Thanks for calling." The next day Allan called to say George was in the hospital and they were taking tests. By the time I returned to New Orleans, on the way to California, George Guesnon was dead.

The Photo Artistry of

Ed Lawless

1. Capt. John Handy	9. Alvin Alcorn
2. Sammy Penn	10. Alec Bigard
3. Punch Miller	11. Barry Martyn
4. Paul "Polo" Barnes	12. Judy Bissonnette,
5. Kid Thomas Valentine	Sing Miller
6. Kid Thomas Valentine	13. Gargan Ball Band
7. Sing Miller	14. Alcorn, Barnes, Bigard
8. George "Pops" Foster	15. Lu Watters

Ed's fascination with jazz photography began with an interest in the music itself, in 1951. Since then, Ed has taken thousands of jazz photos around the world including Japan, Australia and Germany. He is well-known throughout California, where he is frequently in attendance at California's many jazz festivals, snapping away with his Nikon and Rolleiflex cameras. His photos have appeared on over 40 record album covers and in innumerable jazz publications including The Mississippi Rag and The Second Line. He is a member of the New Orleans Jazz Club of Northern California and the Jazz Photographers Association . He does all of his own darkroom lab work.

A surgeon by profession, Ed and his wife currently reside in San Francisco.

Capt. John Handy

Sammy Penn

Punch Miller

Paul "Polo" Barnes

Kid Thomas Valentine

Kid Thomas Valentine

Sing Miller

George "Pops" Foster

Alvin Alcorn

Alec Bigard

Barry Martyn

Judy Bissonnette, Sing Miller

Gargan Ball Band: Bill Bissonnette, Jim Tutunjian, Sammy Penn,
Cyril Bennett, Capt.John Handy, Dick Griffith, Kid Thomas

Earthquake McGoon's: Big Bill Bissonnette, Alec Bigard,
Sing Miller, Alvin Alcorn, Polo Barnes, Jim Tutunjian

Lu Watters

38. Heading West

California was going to be one hell of a gamble. Every cent I had was on the line. I sold my home and everything in it.

The only New Orleans style band in the state was the Kid Ory band in Los Angeles. Ory was, and is, one of my musical idols. Big Jim and Kid Ory stand at the summit of jazz trombonists. You really have to work at finding a truly classic New Orleans jazz recording that one or the other is not on. There are many trombonists in jazz I admire: Albert Warner, Louis Nelson, Geechie Fields, Tricky Sam Nanton, Jack Teagarden, Jimmy Archey, Eddie Sommers, Thamon Hayes, DePriest Wheeler, John Thomas, Bill Mathews and Bobby Thomas to name only a few. But Jim and Ory eclipse them all. I had hoped to meet Ory while in California but, by the time I got to L.A., he had moved to Hawaii and I never met him.

Another trombone man ruled the roost in San Francisco. Turk Murphy was a product of one of the most influential white bands in the history of jazz. It was the Yerba Buena Jazz band led by Lu Watters. In the 1940's, the Watters band made a series of recordings loosely based on the 1920's recordings of some of the great black bands, especially that of King Oliver. Interestingly, the sound they came up with did not so much capture the early sound as it did create a new sound which in itself would be copied by innumerable later bands. They even recorded a session with Bunk Johnson which merely highlighted the differences between the two styles. After the break-up of the Watters band, Murphy came to national fame in his own right playing the Watters style with a looser rhythm. He had his own jazz nightspot, financed by Pete Clute, his pianist, in San Francisco named Earthquake McGoon's. It was a place I would get to know very well, but Murphy and I were not destined to become friends.

In 1968 I left Connecticut for the West Coast. With me were my wife, Judy, and Jim Tutunjian, who had by that time replaced Mouldy Dick in the Easy Riders. Jim was ready for a change of scenery and when I mentioned the California experiment he jumped at the chance to come along. We turned the trip into an adventure and toured the U.S.A. on the way out. I wanted to stop in New Orleans, only a THOUSAND miles out of our way, to see how the musicians there would react to an invitation to play in California. I then wanted to visit friends in San Antonio, Texas, including Jim Cullum Jr. We would then travel through Las Vegas and on up the West Coast to San Francisco where I planned to base the Crusade.

We pulled a small house trailer which we planned to sleep in to save on expenses but it proved too uncomfortable for the three of us so Judy and I stayed in small motels and Tut had the trailer to himself. Larry Borenstein booked us rooms in New Orleans. Billie and Dede were on the road but just about everyone else was in town. The Thomas band was playing at Preservation Hall the night we arrived. I told Tom about the California plans and indicated that he was the first musician I wanted to bring out for a tour.

"Well, I always said I was on my way to Hollywood. Looks like this time I'm really going. Just call me when you needs me, man."

Sammy Penn's face lit up with that great toothless grin when I told him. He said, "Just make sure Thomas don't get there in front of me, Bill."

I assured him they would be coming together, along with Handy, on the first trip. "If I can't make it there with you three lunatics, all is lost."

I saw Cap a few days later and he was overjoyed with the prospect as he had family in Los Angeles and was looking forward to seeing them again. Fantastic. Here I was going to San Francisco to find work and all these guys talked about was going to Hollywood and Los Angeles. It was useless to explain the long distance between the two cities to them. I would just have to come up with some work in Southern California for them.

I also talked to Sheik (who never did make it out there), Robinson, Punch, Sing, Alec, Alvin and Polo about early trips out. They all thought it was great. We stayed in New Orleans a month before moving on to Texas.

I love San Antonio. It is the most livable city in America. While there we stayed with the fellow who had been my landlord while I was stationed there in the service. After several days of sightseeing, we finally ended up one night sitting in the Landing, where Jim Cullum's band held forth. I am not a big fan of dixieland, as is well known, but this band was just a bitch-and-a-half group. It's hard to believe all the good stuff that comes out of Jim's horn in a four hour gig. My friend Harvey Kindervater was still playing drums with the band. He was playing better than ever. We all hugged and laughed and I turned down a gracious offer to sit in. I can't play that white stuff no matter how well it's done.

We made short work of Las Vegas and headed for San Francisco. Jimmy Tut had left us in New Orleans and took a bus direct into San Francisco. We met him there. We rented a nice big house in Novato, a town outside of San Francisco across the Golden Gate Bridge in Marin County. It had four good sized bedrooms and the garage had been converted into a small efficiency apartment where we set up our office and where Tut decided to sleep.

California had an immediate and unexpected effect on Tut. Now if you knew Jimmy at that time you would not have thought him to be the domestic gentleman gardening type. Therefore, I was surprised when soon after settling in, I spotted him with a hoe out in the backyard digging out and planting a garden. Everyday he went out and did his weeding and watering. Soon sprouts appeared. They grew taller and taller until I could contain my curiosity no longer.

I said to him, "Tut, what are you growing out there and when do we get to eat it?"

He replied, "You don't eat that, Bill."

"You don't? Then what do you do with it?"

"You smoke it," he replied.

Before leaving Connecticut, I had done the artwork on several brochures to advertise our booking service. The only thing I left out were the address and telephone number, to be filled in when we had established them. Within a week of our arrival, we were ready to start promoting the California Jazz Crusade. The most important thing was to establish personal contact with the local jazz scene and the media. Another question would be how we would be received by the San Francisco Local of the American Federation of Musicians. The one thing all A.F. of M. Locals seem to have in common is their antipathy towards outsiders coming into their jurisdictions. I found this to be even more true in California.

I had a list of most of the major jazz societies in California which I had culled from various publications. I contacted the president of the club nearest to us, which was in Santa Rosa. He invited me to their next concert.

Bob Fargo, the first Easy Riders trumpet man, had moved to San Rafael in Marin County several years earlier. I looked him up and he offered to take us around to the Frisco jazz spots. We stopped in to hear the Murphy band at McGoon's and then traveled down to a small nightspot on the docks to hear a girl singer I had heard on a private jazz club recording a few years earlier. I had been really impressed with her on the record and thought we might be able to do something with her on Jazz Crusade. We arrived fairly late in the evening and listened to a mediocre set by the band. There was no singer with the band. At closing, we asked the waitress, who was sweeping up, if she knew a singer named Carol Leigh. We explained that we had heard she was singing at the club. The waitress asked why we wanted to find her. I said I was a fan of her records and wanted to meet her in person.

She smiled and said, "You just have. I'm Carol Leigh."

I invited her to sit with us and told her of my plans. She was cordial but skeptical. She told us she would be singing at the Santa Rosa concert we planned to attend. I said we would see her there.

The music at that concert was average with two exceptions. The first was Carol's performance which was outstanding. The audience didn't seem to appreciate, understand, or, for that matter, even pay attention to, the quality of the singing to which they were being treated. The second exception was a performance so great everyone in the place snapped to attention. When Pops Foster stepped onto a bandstand, he was impossible to ignore. He received a well deserved standing ovation for his one set. I should be tarred and feathered for not recording him with any of the groups I brought out.

At the conclusion of the concert, they held the traditional open jam session. I suggested to Tut that he go up. He replied, "After that bass player?" I hadn't brought my trombone but there were two drum sets on the stage. One had already been occupied by a guy who hadn't played on the concert. I jumped on the other. By the time we were through the first number, the other drummer and I had taken each other's measure and both liked what we heard. He was a more modern drummer than me. . . but then who isn't? After the session he came over and introduced himself. His name was Armi Passorell. We became instant friends which was most fortunate for me as he was the secretary of the Santa Rosa Local. Without his future help, the California Crusade would have been stillborn.

In talking to various people at the concert, I picked up useful pieces of information about the local scene. Several people told me that they thought Turk Murphy was going to be a very unhappy man when he got wind of my booking activities and would probably work through the San Francisco Local to thwart me. Not knowing Turk, I had no way of evaluating this information so I chose to ignore it. I was also given the home address of Lu Watters but I was warned that he had absolutely no interest in jazz and that he did not welcome guests at his home. Still I planned to look him up.

Several days later I made an appointment to meet with the governing board of the New Orleans Jazz Club of Northern California, the official name of the Santa Rosa group, to present a proposal. It was an interesting, if familiar, meeting. I had been through this many times in Connecticut and it never changes. Half of the board never heard of Kid Thomas, Sammy Penn or Capt. John Handy. The rest were mainly interested in hearing the price. When I submitted my quote, the shock wave silenced the room. They would never pay "that kind of money" for a concert. I had anticipated this and had a counter-proposal ready.

"Let me make you another offer I think you will like better. I'll do this concert for you for nothing but the gate receipts at the concert. You keep $150.00 to cover your expenses but we get all the rest."

Even this raised some objections because the club would not make a profit if the concert was a success. I told them they couldn't have it both ways. If they were unwilling to risk a loss, they shouldn't complain about not making a profit. I pointed out the prestige the club would gain by being the first to bring these New Orleans stars to Northern California. I didn't expect to get a firm commitment at that meeting but I did. They asked me to step outside so they could discuss it and, a half hour later, it was booked. My first booking in California and it didn't guarantee me a cent. Wonderful. Now I had to come up with enough other work to cover expenses.

When we did our first mailing of brochures, I sent one to Earthquake McGoon's on a hunch. It was just as well to let Turk know what we were planning rather than have him learn about it through back-channels. I certainly didn't expect to hear from him and I didn't. I heard from Pete Clute, Murphy's partner in McGoon's, instead. And the news was marvelous. Clute welcomed me to California and told me that Turk's band was going on the road for a month. Usually when they did this, they hired local musicians to fill in at the club. But my flyer caught his attention and he wanted to know if I would be interested in doing a month, five nights a week, at McGoon's with Thomas, Penn and Handy. He would make all of the arrangements with the union so there would be no problems with them. There was one problem he said. He could only afford to pay scale for the gig. The gig was five hours a night so scale included an hour of overtime. It was pretty good money and still left two days a week open for other bookings. The only question in my mind was how the New Orleans men would react to the long hours. When I mentioned this to Clute, he explained that banjoist Clancy Hayes played and sang solo during intermissions and he would do a full half hour. So each of our sets would only be a half hour also. That sounded good to me and I booked the gig. Our days off would be Sunday and Monday. Fortunately, the Santa Rosa concert was scheduled for a Sunday.

The Frisco Local gave us trouble after all. Clute called back a week later and said that the Local objected to the fact that there were no Local members at all on the gig. I had, in fact, hired one Local man for the job. He was a displaced British pianist named Cyril Bennett. I had heard him at one of the local clubs and liked his clean, swinging, Fats Waller style. But the Local wanted at least three of their members on the gig or they would not permit us to do it. I went down to the union hall to see if I could straighten things out. Now anybody who knows me will tell you that diplomacy is not my strong suit. By the time I left the hall, I had had shouting matches with everyone from the president on down. I would use Frisco guys if I wanted the gig. Period.

I called my new friend Armi. I told him what was going on and asked if he could help me. He invited me up to the Santa Rosa union hall where he, as I mentioned before, was Local secretary. I went up and described in detail my rebuff at the Frisco union hall.

"What bullshit," he cried. "Those guys in Frisco can be real busters when they want to be."

He asked me what Local I belonged to and I told him that Tut and I were in the Bridgeport, Connecticut Local. He said that was no help out here.

"Well, you're both in the Santa Rosa Local now," he said. "I'll fill out the necessary papers."

He then picked up his phone and dialed the secretary of the San Francisco Local and advised him that I was now in the Santa Rosa Local and he was formally requesting permission for my band to play at Earthquake McGoon's as a courtesy to his adjoining Local. They didn't like it one bit but Armi was a tough little secretary and they relented.

"I don't know how to thank you, Armi," I said. "You really saved my ass."

"I'll tell you how you're gonna thank me, Bill," he replied. "A couple of times a year our Local sponsors concerts at the local colleges in my jurisdiction. Usually I get a few of the dixie guys together and we blow the gig. But, this year these kids are going to get a real treat and hear some real New Orleans jazz from your band including your men from New Orleans. And for scale too!"

I laughed. "We'll be happy to do it for you, buddy, and it will be good for your soul and your chops to hear Sammy Penn on drums. Maybe you'll learn a little bit about jazz drumming!"

Several things were breaking for us now. A jazz club in Los Angeles responded to our mailing and booked a concert featuring our New Orleans band along with, of all groups, the Firehouse Five Plus Two. We also booked a date at the University of California at Santa Barbara. But the clincher was a megabucks gig in Palm Springs for the American Cancer Society. This event (you call them events when they pay this kind of bread) was to be hosted by actor William Gargan and to feature, along with us, the noted Irish tenor and radio star Dennis Day. The cream of Palm Springs society would be attending. Our classy brochure sold this job and paid for itself in the process.

Although this would be the highest paying gig I ever booked and a highpoint of the whole 1960's Crusade, plans were being laid clandestinely which would put the gig in serious jeopardy and threaten the very survival of the California Crusade. But I was within reach of two brass rings: Handy would get to see his family and Kid Thomas was "on his way to Hollywood."

California Brochure
Jazz Crusade
1968

Mon., Dec. 9, 1968 ☆ S.F. Examiner—Page 37

A Jazz Crusade That Means Business

By PHILIP ELWOOD

Most jazz fans are crusaders of a sort (as their friends will readily testify) and New Orleans jazz fans tend toward the fanatical.

But Big Bill Bissonnette' has carried his enthusiasm for traditional New Orleans music far beyond the average addict's involvement.

Bissonnette has moved his Jazz Crusade Inc., from Connecticut to California and by early 1969 will have begun his first venture in the state.

Jazz Crusade is an interesting combination of musicians and production ideas. Its basic purpose is to present New Orleans jazz and jazzmen in concert and on records to as many people as possible.

DYING OUT

"In a few years some of the New Orleans originals will be left," Bissonnette said, "but as long as they're alive and playing I want to work with them, record them, and present them to the public.

"When they're gone I'll go back to my office job; at least I'll have done what I wanted to do for a few years of my life."

Six years ago Bissonnette, a tailgate trombonist, got his Jazz Crusaders band going in Bridgeport. "We played the standard stuff and tried to capture the real New Orleans sound that we heard on records," he recalled.

It was after trips to New Orleans that the Crusaders became a Crusade. "Practically none of the old timers are working in New Orleans." he noted, "and the two places that present authentic jazz can't hire anyone steady."

IMPORTS

"New Orleans uses jazz as a Chamber of Commerce come-on but Negro musicians, young or old, get almost no benefit from the tourist trade."

The Jazz Crusade then began importing selected older musicians to Connecticut to play with their band In much the same way that Bunk Johnson, in 1943, was brought from Louisiana to San Francisco to play with local traditional jazzmen.

"Our crowds got bigger and bigger," continued Bissonnette, "so we brought more musicians up north, and recorded them more frequently."

GREAT CAPT. JOHN HANDY
New Orleans music coming

Jazz Crusade records now have about 30 LPs available.

TOUR SET

Such greats from the past as Kid Thomas Valentine, Punch Miller, Capt. John Handy, Albert Burbank and many more played in New England with the Crusaders.

"We came to California because there are lots more people, more colleges, and a history of traditional jazz activity out here. We have already set a tour for February, and a number of dates are booked.

"It seems, so far, to be the younger people who are interested in our concert package."

The California Jazz Crusade will include dances, clubs, concerts, and even masses, played by Captain Handy, an alto saxophonist, Kid Thomas on trumpet, and Sammy Penn on drums.

A START

San Franciscan Cyril Bennett will play piano, Bissonnette the trombone, and one of the Connecticut originals, Dick Griffith, will be on banjo.

"Eventually we'll have even more of the best New Orleans men with us, but this is a good start," commented Bissonnette.

"It isn't just that I want to get a lot of gigs for the band and let people out here enjoy the music," he concluded, "it's also that I get a tremendous kick out of playing this music myself. And it's not many of us that really have fun while we're working."

**Philip Elwood Article
San Francisco Examiner
9 Dec 1968**

1969

deceased

PAUL BARBARIN, drums

GEORGE "POPS" FOSTER, string bass

NOONE JOHNSON, bazooka

ALCIDE "SLOW DRAG" PAVAGEAU, string bass

SAMMY PENN, drums

JOE WATKINS, drums

39.   First California Tour

Kid Thomas, Sammy Penn and Capt. John Handy arrived in San Francisco at The end of January. Dick Griffith had arrived a day earlier. It was important to me to have Griff on this tour. His family commitments precluded any permanent move to California. I was hopeful a successful beginning for the Crusade might start him thinking about joining us at a later date. He agreed to come out for this first tour to test the water.

We started with the New Orleans Jazz Club of Northern California concert. As we were doing it on speculation and our sole income from it would be gate receipts, I worked diligently in promoting it. Because of the McGoon's gig, and a few others I brought in, my expenses were covered for the entire tour. The Santa Rosa concert would be clear profit. I visited the two leading jazz critics in the bay area, Philip Elwood of the San Francisco Examiner and Russ Wilson of the Oakland Tribune. Elwood was known to be sympathetic to the traditional jazz cause. Wilson had been less so. Both gave us extensive positive articles before the concert and the club went all out with its publicity also. The result was a turnout that was larger than any the club had ever had.

As we started to set up, I noticed there were no chairs on the bandstand. I asked Marshall if he could find us some. He seemed surprised at the request and asked me what I wanted them for. For the band to sit on I replied.

"You sit while you play?" he said with astonishment. "I've never heard of that before. I don't know how the crowd will react to that." He rounded up the chairs.

The concert was a blow-out. The audience response was fantastic. Pops Foster was in the audience to see his old friends from New Orleans and he joined us for a set. Thomas whipped out his baby bonnet for "Milk Cow Blues" and brought the house down. There was another surprise guest in the audience. You could have blown me over with a puff when Fred Vigorito appeared in front of me. He was stationed in the area with the service and happened to see an article about the concert in the newspaper.

The club threw a private party for the band and selected club members after the gig and many local musicians showed up including my new friend

Armi.

"How'd you like Penn?" I asked him.

"Well, I certainly never heard anyone like him before!" he replied.

There was a small bandstand set up and a jam session started shaping up. Before long Handy was up on stage wailing away on one of his solo marathons to the cheers of all of us. Soon Griff, Sammy and Thomas were in on it too. I had business to attend to and Marshall and I moved to the quietist corner we could find and he counted out an impressive amount of cash. It was an auspicious beginning indeed.

We opened at McGoon's the following Tuesday. The club was perfectly laid out for the presentation of jazz. There was a raised stage from which the musicians looked out over the heads of the dancers on a small, sunken dance floor directly in front of it. There were tables for two around the floor's perimeter and a long wooden bar extended the length of the room on the wall opposite the bandstand. It too was on a raised section and we could look directly across at a mirror which stretched the length of the bar. Above this was a balcony which encircled the room and ended just short of the stage on both sides. The acoustics were that of a small concert hall, or, to be more precise, a music hall, which is what the place originally was. The bandstand was dominated by Pete Clute's baby grand piano. On either side of the piano were risers for the rhythm section. This still left a good ten foot depth for the front line. The microphone arrangement was so well thought out that, when we recorded, we simply put the recording mikes next to the house ones.

Pete Clute greeted us on our first night and showed us the dressing room and the backstage alleyway that led to a curtained entrance, center-stage, rear. He introduced us to Clancy Hayes who was getting ready for his first set by downing a few drinks. The routine, as explained to me, was that Clancy would signal me as he started his last number and the band would enter while he was playing and join him on the ride-out choruses. At the end of the number he would take his bows and depart. We were then on for the next half hour.

Clancy was, to my mind, the white banjo player stereotype. A jovial, extrovert who loves to sing-a-long as he plays. Everybody's buddy on stage, yet very depressed when sitting alone at the bar between sets drowning his sorrow with drink after drink. He didn't seem to have the slightest interest in jazz for its own sake. Jazz was merely the vehicle that permitted him to get out in front of the audience. He was not a great banjo player but, my, what a beautiful singing voice the man had. Tut seemed to hit it off with Clancy but Griff and he looked at banjo playing from totally different perspectives. The few times we talked, he reminisced about the good old days when he would gig for comedian Jackie Gleason, along with trumpeter Bobby Hackett, performing for "The Great One" aboard his private train on cross country trips. Hayes spoke often about Bing Crosby, with whom he had once recorded, and who was apparently his role model.

I asked him about the time in the 1940's when he played with Bunk Johnson. Bunk had done some recordings with the Yerba Buena Jazz Band of which Clancy was a member. He shrugged them, and Bunk, off as being insignificant. To Clancy, Bunk was just an old Southern black who couldn't play very well and who didn't even know many of the old jazz tunes the Watters band specialized in. He confirmed an oft repeated anecdote concerning Bunk and the Yerba Buena's drummer. Bunk criticized the drummer's two-beat foot and tried to show him New Orleans time by sitting down at the set and playing a few Baby Dodds style riffs. Incensed by his remarks, the drummer told Bunk in no uncertain terms that he didn't know what he was talking about and he didn't need any help from some old "has-been." Clancy ended up playing drums on the recording. It's too bad George Lewis hadn't been there. He would have loved it!

We ended up not using a piano on the first McGoon's gig. For some reason Pete Clute did not want Cyril on the job. I don't know if it was the extra money or just that he didn't want any local guys playing in their absence. Whatever it was, Cyril was not to play. He did play with us on our other concert dates and on the recording we did with this group.

Pete offered to put some of the musicians up in the old seafarer's hotel above the club. Not having seen it, I mentioned it to the bandsmen. Griff had been staying in the trailer which was parked in our driveway. Tom and Handy were sharing a room in our house and they were ready for some privacy. We looked at the rooms in the hotel. They were straight out of Charles Dickens. Each was about the size of a one man prison cell and, to further the analogy, they were furnished with a narrow bed, a tiny table and a single bare light bulb hanging down from the high ceilings. They were decrepit but clean. There was one small bathroom at the end of the hallway with just a sink and toilet. To my surprise, Thomas and Griff decided to stay there.

One morning Griff phoned me from the hotel. "Bill, is Thomas with you?"

"Of course not," I replied. "Isn't he with you at the hotel?"

"Not here. I went into his room just now and he's not there."

I thought for a moment. "He's probably gone out for a walk, Griff."

"I don't think so. I would have heard him pass my room. Besides, I'm sure he would have invited me along. You know something? I didn't see him after the gig last night either."

Now I was starting to get worried. It was not like Thomas to just go wandering off. I asked Griff to look around the neighborhood while I got ready to drive down.

As I was dressing, Griff called back. "I found him. He's locked in the club."

"What?"

"As I walked past the club looking for him, I heard this banging on the door from inside. I called out and Tom answered. He said, 'Griff, get me out of this place.' He sounds really pissed, Bill."

I couldn't help laughing. "I'll bet he's pissed! I'll call Pete's wife to go down and let him out. See you tonight." As I hung up, I couldn't help wondering what kind of day poor Griff had ahead once the fire-breathing Kid Thomas Valentine was turned loose.

Thomas was still steaming when I arrived at the club with Sammy and Cap. I asked him how it happened. It seems he was hungry after the gig and went into the club's kitchen to make himself a sandwich. No one noticed he was missing and they locked up.

"Where did you sleep, Tom?" I asked.

"Where'd you thought I slept, man? On the bandstand."

Tom saw no humor in this episode and we all tried to stifle our smiles... except Penn, who broke up laughing every time he looked at Thomas that night.

"Just play your damn drums, Penn. Just play your damn drums!" Thomas barked.

Sadie showed up that night for the first time. Sadie was an elderly black woman who would make Sweet Emma look like a beauty queen. In addition, she was a very loud lady. And, best of all, she was on the make with Handy from the moment she laid eyes on him. To further complicate things, she made a few passing glances at Penn who immediately fell in love. So here's the situation: she's chasing Handy and Penn's chasing her. And Thomas is disgusted with the whole thing on top of his night sleeping on the bandstand. This was not a happy night of jazz.

Something very curious was happening every night at Earthquake McGoon's and it took us several days to figure it out. Clancy would go on to an almost empty house. He would call us up and, by the time we got on stage, the place would be swarming with people. We would play our set to the screaming crowd and, as we took our bows, the whole audience would get up and walk out. Clancy would go back on to his empty house and, a half hour later, the thing would happen again. Now I couldn't believe that either we were so popular, or Clancy was so unpopular, that these fans would keep coming and going set by set. Finally Turk's wife told me what was happening. Every hour a tourist bus would stop outside and the tourists would come in for their one assigned drink and to listen to one set by the band. Then they would all pile back into the bus and head for their next stop, probably some topless or gay bar. Some jazz fans! It's no wonder we were playing the

"Saints" three or four times a night by the request of the audience.

Wandering in and out of this scene was Turk Murphy. We had been introduced on our first evening at the club but it was perfunctory. He came in again on the second night, sat at the far end of the bar and never bothered to meet our New Orleans guests. I stopped by on a break and tried to start up a conversation. It didn't work and I never tried again. None of this is to put the man down. He was an important trombone player and, I am told, a real nice guy. All I'm saying is that you couldn't prove it by me. The following week his band went on the road and I didn't see him again.

One day Sammy was acting strangely. He seemed tired, almost lifeless. He didn't come out of his room all day and hardly touched a drink. I asked him if he wanted me to get a substitute on drums for the evening's gig. He told me he was okay and would do the job. He played a listless job. After it, the band went out to breakfast at our favorite all-night cafeteria as usual. I was concerned that the five hour a night gig was too much for Sammy. As we were eating, Thomas suddenly turned on Sammy.

"What's the matter with you, man? You couldn't even keep the time tonight. You been doing too much drinking, man. That's what I think."

A chill went through the air. Sammy just looked at him. Then he said, "I'm sorry, Thomas. But if you was moving pianos all night like I was, you'd be tired, too."

Tom's mouth dropped open. "What you talking about, Penn? Moving pianos? Where were you moving pianos all night?"

I was flabbergasted. We didn't even have a piano in the house at that time. "What are you talking about, Sam?" I asked.

"Well, Bill, I had this dream last night that I was hauling pianos upstairs and downstairs all night. And when I woke up this morning, I was so tired man I could hardly move from all that lifting. You can't work like that all night and still play good drums."

What do you say to that? I mean, what do you say?

The Traditional Session

Published By

New Orleans Jazz Club of Northern California

P.O. BOX 2312
Santa Rosa, California 95405

Volume 4, Number 8   February 7, 1969

KID THOMAS VALENTINE
First California appearance will be at the New Orleans Jazz Club Session, February 16, 1969
at 3:00 P.M., Flamingo Hotel, Santa Rosa, California.

Newsletter Cover
New Orleans Jazz Club of Northern California
February 1969

40. Trouble In Paradise

As I mentioned earlier, I had booked a megabucks gig with the American Cancer Society in the Palm Springs area. Each year they sponsored a celebrity ball as a fund raiser. They were looking for a novel theme just when our Jazz Crusade flyer came bouncing in amongst the mail. Jinx Ray, the chairlady of the event listed it along with a few other ideas at a committee meeting and it was agreed to contact us about it. After one telephone call, I had her sold on the idea and she quickly got it approved. They were going to have a Bourbon Street Ball. The contracts were signed and we were all looking forward to it as the highpoint of our swing through Southern California.

Then it started to unravel. As required by union regulations, I filed a copy of the contract with the Los Angeles Local of the A.F. of M. In the past, they had provided all of the musicians for the annual ball and they didn't like being cut out. Someone from the Local called Jinx wanting to know why she was bringing in an outside band for the event. She told them they wanted to try something different this year and thought New Orleans jazz would be a novel idea. The Local man told her that they could provide a "dixie" band as good as any (undoubtably true). Jinx said the whole idea was to have musicians direct from New Orleans. He said the Local would not approve the contract unless half of the players in the band were members of the L. A. union.

She called me to explain the situation. She said that money was not the problem. They didn't mind paying for four more musicians. She even hired a dance combo from the Local but that didn't satisfy them. We MUST use four local musicians. I could hardly believe my ears. We were all members in good standing with the A.F. of M. and they were trying to screw us everywhere we went. I told her they could not supply men who could play our type of jazz but, if they wanted to send out four guys to sit on the sidelines and not play, and she didn't object to paying them from funds other than ours, I couldn't care less. She said she would check with them again and get back to me.

In the meantime, we were playing college concerts on our days off. We did Armi's benefit gig also. We were booked onto a local television talk show. The featured guest on the program was comedienne Imogene Coca. When the New Orleans men heard she was to be on the show, they became very excited. Kid Thomas said he was going to get her autograph to flash around New Orleans to prove he'd met her. A more unpleasant woman I have yet to meet. She snubbed the members of the band and complained that we were taking too big a slice of the time. As a result, we had one of our numbers cut from the schedule. By the time the show was over, Thomas decided to forego the autograph.

Jinx Ray called me back in a state bordering on hysteria. The Palm Springs job was off she told me.

"What do you mean off?" I asked. "We have a contract and my men are looking forward to the job."

"Well, it's just impossible under the circumstances."

I asked her what circumstances she was referring to. She became very evasive and I had to really push her for an explanation. When she gave it, I didn't blame her for wanting to cancel the gig. The Local man had called her back and told her that he had "investigated" the New Orleans musicians and he was sorry to inform her that they were a bunch of senile drunks who could barely still play their instruments. Her affair would be a total disaster if she brought in these dregs.

I was fuming. "Look, this guy is telling you a pack of lies. I don't blame you for being upset but, I'm telling you right now, we are showing up for this gig and that's that. If you don't want us to play, just put our money in my hand and we'll leave. But..we..are..coming. If you want to be fair, you'll let us play when we get there. If your crowd is not pleased with our performance, you just say so and I will donate our entire fee to the American Cancer Society."

Her voice was shaky, "I just don't know what to do. I believe you but I have a committee here that is up in arms about what the union said."

I said, "We've been playing up here everyday with no problems. Why don't you call Philip Elwood or Russ Wilson, the local newspaper jazz critics, and ask them what they think about the band?"

She replied that she didn't know what she was going to do. I felt sorry for her plight but it was none of my doing so she could just frost it as far as I was concerned. I called Armi and asked if he could help. It was one thing to confront the adjoining San Francisco Local, where he had some clout, he said, but L.A. was a world unto itself and one of the most powerful Locals in America because of their control of the whole movie industry's music. He could do nothing but sympathize.

We continued working at McGoon's and started to work on our first California recording session. I always prefer "studio" sessions to "live" ones. There is a certain charm and excitement to a concert recording, but, if you want good jazz, you should take the time to do it right without worrying about pleasing a crowd, which tends to react to visuals as much as to the music. I decided to cut the album at Earthquake McGoon's on a Monday night. I wanted to feature Carol Leigh on a few of the numbers. I really felt this girl had a great future in jazz if people would just start listening to her. Now, with the happy hindsight of over a generation, it is obvious my hunch was right. She has become the premier hot jazz vocalist of her era. Unfortunately, Jazz Crusade had nothing to do with it. The few numbers I did with her were never released. She did it by herself; a combination of persistence and amazing talent that the world couldn't forever ignore.

I wanted this to be a special recording session and we worked very hard to make it so. The band numbers took hours to get just the way I wanted them and the results were superb; perhaps the best of any Jazz Crusade album. The session took so long we just didn't get to the numbers with Carol. The recording engineer suggested we do the remaining two tracks with Carol at his studio. I agreed and set a date for the second session after we got back from Southern California.

Jinx called again. Her attitude had completely changed. "Everything's okay now, Bill, and I want to apologize for any problems I caused you."

"What's happened?"

"Well," she began, "after I spoke with you, I asked Mr. Gargan if he could arrange for one of his friends in San Francisco to drop in at Earthquake McGoon's to hear your band. So he phoned Ben Blue and asked him to do it. He did and phoned Mr. Gargan yesterday to say he had never had so much fun listening to a band in his life. So, please come and forget everything that's happened. I called that man at the union and told him we were going ahead exactly as originally planned.

"But, and I hate to throw another monkey wrench into the works, there is one other problem. I've found out that Dennis Day hates jazz and he has been complaining to everyone about having a jazz band on the same program with him. I didn't want to mention it with everything else that's been going on, but I thought you should just be aware of it. He is a gentleman and I'm sure there will be no problem at the ball. See you next week!"

So we were back on and Thomas would still get to Hollywood. Ben Blue, one of the foremost comedians of stage and screen, had managed to walk into McGoon's, check out our band and leave without being recognized. That was a shame because I would have loved to get his reaction to Sammy Penn.

41.   Sammy's Secret

As I have described to you, the relationship between Kid Thomas and Sammy Penn was multi-faceted. They were close friends. They were musical peers. But, most of all, it was a leader/sideman arrangement. Which meant, to the old-time jazzmen of New Orleans, that Thomas was Penn's benefactor and protector and Penn was Tom's subordinate in matters musical. In short, Sammy was the bad little kid trying to get away with stuff and Tom was his nanny. Occasionally Sam would put one over on Tom. This one I'm about to tell you about was the best of all.

Judy and I decided to throw a little surprise birthday party for Tom. Nothing big, just the band members and a few friends. It turned out that they included my birthday too so it was a double surprise. It's not the party I'm going to tell you about though. It was one of the events leading up to it that gave Sammy his chance for a little fun.

Thomas had evidently caught on to the fact that something was going on behind his back. He didn't know what and he decided to find out by giving Penn the Third Degree.

Here's how I found out about it. I walked into the living room and Thomas was sitting alone in an easy chair. His lower jaw was jutting out as it did when he was angry. I asked him if everything was okay and he replied, "Shoot, man, of course everything's okay. Why wouldn't everything be okay, man?" The way he said it proved everything was not okay. He was boiling and didn't want to talk about it. I walked into Sammy's room to find him lying on the bed chuckling to himself. I asked him what was so funny. He related to me this conversation he had with Thomas a few minutes earlier:

Thomas: "Listen Penn, I knows something's going on behind my back. I walks into the room and everybody suddenly clams up. I sees you and Bill whispering behind me and even Handy and Judy and Griff. What's going on, man?"

Penn: "There ain't nothin' going on Thomas. You must be imaginating things, man."

Thomas: " I ain't imaginating nothing, man. I knows there's something going on and I wants to know what it is right now."

Penn: "Well, listen, Thomas, I ain't supposed to say nothing an' Bill and Judy gonna get mad if I do. So don't ask me no questions 'cause I can't tell you nothing."

Thomas: "Listen Sammy, nobody gonna know if you tells me. I sure ain't gonna tell 'em you told me."

Penn: "How do I know that? Are you sure you can keep a secret, Thomas?"

Thomas: "Sure, I can keep a secret, man."

Penn: "Well, so can I."

With that he walked away.

42. Thomas Goes to Hollywood

Our four weeks at McGoon's were drawing to a close and we were getting ready to head south. Sadie was still showing up every night at the club and Handy was getting nervous about her amorous advances. The only thing that was saving him from her clutches was that, every time Sadie started cozying up to him, Sammy Penn would rush over and start horning in, trying to get her attention. It was a lucky thing for me that she didn't take a liking to Sammy or I would have really had my hands full. Cap was relieved when we left the club. He thought his problem with Sadie was at an end. He was wrong. Sammy told her he and Handy were coming back out to Frisco shortly and she should be looking for them.

Judy went to the club almost every night we played. Usually she would sit with various couples who had become fans of the band. There was an elderly lawyer and his wife who came a couple of times a week. They were wonderful dancers and, no matter how hot the music got, they would be on the floor doing a fast foxtrot. There was also an astronomer who came frequently. One of my interests is cosmology. I would sometimes sit with him on my break and he would try to talk jazz while I was pumping him for the latest information on quasars and neutrinos.

We had two days off before we headed out on tour. On one of those afternoons we were all watching a news program on television. It always surprised me how diligently the New Orleans men followed current events. The newscaster was talking about the new house President Nixon had just purchased in San Clemente. When he announced the $1,500,000 price tag of the estate, Handy jumped out of his chair and said, "What?! That man's only been President a month and he stole that much already?!"

Judy decided against taking the southern tour with us. She had picked up a good job and didn't want to jeopardize it. She had managed to gain the trust and affection of the New Orleans musicians and they were sorry she couldn't come. We took two cars. Tut and Griff rode together in Tut's car and Tom, Cap, Sammy and Cyril rode with me in my station wagon. We headed down the beautiful coastal road that runs the length of California. We wanted to stop at San Simeon to see the Hearst mansion. As we passed Monterey, I noticed a small sign which said something about road work ahead. I didn't pay it much mind and we drove on for many miles. There was no traffic on the road at all in either direction which was surprising for California. Suddenly the road ended at a barricade. We got out to look. The road had slid into the ocean. We could see across to where it picked up again but there was a void between. So, that's what the sign was telling me. We lost several hours returning to Monterey and getting back down to where we had been on the alternate route. We still had plenty of time to make the first gig but we were all dead tired when we pulled onto the campus of the University of California at Santa Barbara.

As we walked through the Student Center lobby, I started to sense that we might have a problem here. The walls were covered with anti-war, anti-American and obscene posters. Here was the radical counter-culture in spades. We met the student who had booked the band and he led us to the cafeteria which had been re-arranged into an auditorium for our performance. Several hundred seats had been arranged in rows in front of the low bandstand risers and tables were set up around the periphery. There was a nice spinet piano on the bandstand. The concert was scheduled for 8:00 p.m. We had a couple of hours to kill so we went for dinner and returned to set up. Some students were already there milling about.

Thomas took me aside and said, "Look at all those hippies, Bill. This gonna be some kinda trouble tonight."

I told him not to worry. "They'll love this music , Tom. You should do on that stage tonight what you always do and we'll be just fine."

In that I was right. The concert was a smash success and Thomas put on one of his greatest shows, baby bonnet and all. But Sammy was the real hit. He chomped on his cigar, eyed all of the girls and sang his heart out on "Girl of My Dreams" and "Saints." During the intermission many of the students came up to talk and get autographs. Several of them had been to Preservation Hall and one said she had even seen Sammy there.

After the concert, as we started to break down the equipment, I noticed Sammy hadn't started packing up his drums. I looked around and spotted him talking to a group of black students. As I walked over to get him, I noticed that he was not flashing that famous grin. In fact, he looked like he was arguing with one of the students. I said hello to everyone and reminded Sammy that it was time to leave. He said he would be right over. He looked angry so I quietly asked him if there was a problems.

"Oh don't worry about a thing, Bill. I just have to straighten these boys out and I'll be there," he said.

I went back to the bandstand and packed his set up for him and put it in the car. Sammy was still in heated discussion with the students. What was going on? I called across the room to him that we were pulling out. He waved, made one more comment to the student who seemed to be the spokesman for the group, and ran over and jumped into the front seat beside me. As we pulled away he started to laugh.

"Bill, man," he said. "You know what those boys were saying? They was spouting stuff that you white boys were exploiting me and Thomas and Handy. I asked them what this 'exploiting' mean. You know what that means, Bill? That means you trying to take advantage of us. That's what that supposed to mean. I said, 'You all talking about Bill?' They said that's right, that's who they talking about." Sam turned to Thomas and Handy in the back seat and continued, "They said, we shouldn't ought to be playing with Bill because all the white man doing is exploiting us all. That's what the man said, Yessir, that's what he said."

I asked Sammy what he said to them.

He laughed again. "Why I told that boy that you was blacker than he was!"

We stayed the night in a motel. The next morning broke sunny and warm. This sure wasn't the way Connecticut was in March. On the road, we started up a steep incline that went on for miles. When we finally went over the top we ran straight into. . . a snowstorm! It was incredible. One minute we were in sunny Southern California, the next we were in the equivalent of a Connecticut "Nor'Easter." Cars were skidding all over the road. Many were in snowbanks along the side. I pulled over and got out to see how Jimmy and Griff were doing behind us. Griff rolled down the window and yelled, "Jeeesus, welcome home to Connecticut!" We drove for a mile or two in this blizzard and then down a dramatic, sweeping incline that was like a roller coaster ride. By the time we got to the bottom, it was in the Seventies again and the sun was shining. Our cars dripped melting snow for an hour.

Then came the climax of a career. I knew this would put Kid Thomas in high spirits as soon as I spotted it. "Tom, look up there." Spread across the hills in the distance were the big block letters Tom Valentine had talked about all of these years: H O L L Y W O O D.

"I always said I'd get here and I did," Thomas whispered almost to himself. Sammy nodded with quiet admiration. And I smiled to myself. For once, I had been able to fulfill one little dream for this man who had fulfilled so many of mine.

43.   Firehouse Five Plus Thomas

We drove straight to the theater where we were to play our concert with the Firehouse Five Plus Two for Jazz Incorporated of California. We unloaded our equipment and set up on the huge stage of the Wilshire Ebell Theater. We moved the piano into position and lined up the chairs across the stage. A fellow from the club who booked us helped with the work. We then went to get something to eat. When we returned, the Firehouse gang was just starting to set up. We watched as they took all of the chairs down, pushed the piano to the opposite end of the stage and started to move Sammy's drumset off to the side. Sammy didn't like that so I approached their drummer and asked why they were re-arranging everything. He told me that was the way they always set up. I replied that the way we had it was the way we always set up. They continued moving the drums. I asked the emcee whether there had been some change in the schedule as we understood we were going to be performing first and, therefore, the stage should be set for us. He asked if we couldn't play using the arrangement the Firehouse Five favored. Well, of course we could and, I supposed, they could have played using our set-up. But they wouldn't. So neither would we. Now if you think this is pettiness, you are, of course, right. But even Crusaders have their petty moments you know and this was going to be mine. And it's a safe bet that grown men who dress in red shirts and fire hats are going to have their petty moments and this was going to be theirs. So I insisted that the stage arrangement be returned to the way we had it. If they wanted to change it, they could do so during the intermission. So off went their drumset and back came the piano. I must admit I didn't feel as stupid about it then as I do sitting here writing about it now.

Then we asked for our chairs back. I guess that did it. California jazz fans apparently can just not take musicians sitting down while they work. It must have something to do with the California work ethic. I mean I never suggested for a minute that the audience must stand while they listen, did I? It wasn't as if I had asked if we could play with our flies open, was it? It was. Officials of the jazz club were summoned and a brouhaha was in the offing.

"Oh no, I ain't gonna stand up while I play," huffed Handy. Thomas was just as adamant. Sammy just puffed on his cigar through it all. He was going to sit no matter how it came out. Even in California they haven't figured out how a drummer can kick a bass drum and hi-hat at the same time while standing. When they do, rest assured his drum stool will be banished. Finally they relented and brought back our chairs. We overheard a few asides about the "old men."

As if all this wasn't bad enough, we got whupped in the concert. The Firehousers put out our blaze in short order. They played a brilliant set in their outrageous style, sirens wailing, bells clanging, and the crowd loved it. And, if I can get away with saying it to you New Orleans fans, so did I. I don't know if what they did had anything to do with jazz, but it was pure, sparkling entertainment of the highest order.

There were two highpoints to the concert and they were both "Tiger Rag!" We didn't coordinate numbers with the Firehousers and an interesting situation developed. George Probert, my favorite soprano sax player, Bechet notwithstanding, was playing the concert with the Firehouse Five. I had been corresponding with him about recording an album with some of the New Orleans guys. He wrote that he was a great fan of Capt. John Handy and would love to play with him sometime. I wrote back informing him that Handy would be coming to L.A. with us and perhaps we could all get together then. At the time of this correspondence, neither of us knew that Probert would be on the same bill with us at the Wilshire Ebell concert. When George and I met at the theater before the concert, I invited him to sit in with us for a number at the close of our set. He was hesitant because he didn't know how the other members of the Firehouse Five would react. But, the lure of playing with Handy was too much for him and he agreed.

As our set drew to a close, I invited Probert onto the stage, telling the audience of his long-held desire to play with Cap. He came out and shook Cap's hand and I announced to the crowd that we would finish up with "Tiger Rag." George made a strange face and ran over to me. He whispered, "I don't think I'd better play on this number."

I couldn't believe this great reed man would have trouble on "Tiger" so I said, "Sure you can," and kicked it off. He stepped back next to Handy. It was a great romp and the crowd went wild as Cap and George played chase choruses.

During the intermission, as the Firehousers were moving all the instruments around again, George came over to me and said, "I'm really sorry about not wanting to do that number with you."

"It turned out great, George," I replied. "Why didn't you want to do it?"

"It wasn't that I didn't want to," he said. "It's just that I have two of my best clarinet students here and for a month we've been rehearsing a special, three chorus long, trio on "Tiger Rag" with the Firehouse Five especially for this concert."

They did indeed do it again and it brought the house down again.

After the concert all of the musicians and club board members went for dinner to a place that had a fine traditional jazz group. After the party, as we were walking back to our hotel, we passed a nightspot that featured balalaika music. The door to the club swung open just as we were going by and the music poured out. Griff listened for a minute and then said, "Let's go in. The music's great." For the next two hours, Kid Thomas, John Handy and Sammy Penn, those masters of New Orleans jazz, had a ball listening to the music of the Near East.

The following day we had off and we all went to Cap's family's house for dinner. As we drove there, we passed street after street of cozy one family houses. Then we hit a block or two where the houses were all burned out. I asked Cap if he knew what happened to cause such a disaster.

"Don't you know where you at, Bill? This is Watts."

Los Angeles Concert flyer
Jazz Incorporated of California
March 1969

Playbill Cover
Jazz Incorporated of California Concert
March 3, 1969

Programme
Jazz Incorporated of California
March 3, 1969

44.   At The Jazz Band Ball

The next day we drove to Palm Springs and the Indian Wells Country Club where we would be playing for the American Cancer Society Celebrity Ball. Palm Springs, and its suburb Palm Desert, were exactly as I imagined they would be. Small and very classy shops, opened by appointment only, lined the main drag of the town. The country club was magnificent.

It was early afternoon when we arrived. No slip ups on this gig, thank you. We were met by Jinx Ray. Even Sammy Penn was on his best, most sober, behavior. He gave a swooping bow when introduced and said, "So pleased to meet you, ma'am." She explained our schedule and the entertainment program to us. We would eat at the country club in a separate dining room reserved for entertainers. Right after dinner we would play a single one hour set as the featured performers. Following that, the dance band would accompany Dennis Day for several numbers. If requested, we would return for a second short set. The dance band would then take over the rest of the evening and we would be finished. I would be introduced to William Gargan before the performance.

For those of you who may be unfamiliar with William Gargan's career, he was a noted film actor during the 30's and 40's. He then went into television and had one of the earliest hit series, Martin Kane Private Eye. His acting career came to its end when he developed throat cancer. The cancer was excised by an operation through which he lost the use of his voice box. He had a silver diaphragm implant in the front of his throat through which he was able to speak by the contraction of his stomach muscles. It is no insult to his memory, but only to clarify, to mention that this was the method used by the man who was the voice of "Popeye, the Sailor Man" and that was how Gargan sounded when he spoke.

Jinx reminded me about Dennis Day's aversion to jazz and suggested that we simply avoid him. She then led us to the motel where we would be staying. There were four double rooms for us. I bunked in with Kid Thomas. Tom had been sullen ever since our detour in Monterey. Although sometimes moody, he was always the professional on the stand. He insisted on starting on time and, once the music began, he was the boss. He was the leader at all times. Now, for reasons unknown to me, things were getting to him. As soon as we were left alone in the room, he unloaded it all on me.

"Bill, I'm going home to New Orleans."

I replied, "Well the tour will be over in a few days, Tom, and you'll be on your way."

"No, man, I mean I'm going now."

At first I thought he was kidding and I laughed and said, "How are you going to do that?"

"Easy, Bill. I'm gonna pick up that phone and call a taxi to take me into Los Angeles and then I'm gonna catch the first train for home today. I don't like all this foolishness that's been going on, man. Driving all over the damn place. Getting lost. Hippies. Bands with sirens and whistles. I'm just going home to Algiers right now."

I never saw Tom like this, but I knew I had a serious problem on my hands. I tried reasoning with him but his mind was made up. I was in big trouble if I didn't do something quick. He was lifting the phone from its cradle when I remembered the things he told me in his home in Algiers after the Riders break-up about leadership. This was the Big Gig. I was not going to have it slip through my fingers now.

"Look Thomas," I said, "I'm the leader on this gig. You agreed to play it and you damn well are going to play it and that's that. If you want me to drive you to the railroad station after the job and put you on a train, I will do that. But you're blowing this job first Tom and I don't want to hear another word about it."

He glared at me. I glared back. Not many people had talked to Kid Thomas like this. Certainly I never had. I didn't know what else to do to save the gig. Neither of us spoke for a long moment.

Then I said, "I'm going to take a nap. I can't tie you to the chair so I'll trust you to do what's right." I laid down and pretended to immediately doze off. Thomas stalked the floor like a tiger. Finally, he walked out the door. I opened my eyes and saw his trumpet case on the chair. He's not on his way home without that, I thought. Then I slept for an hour.

I awoke at dusk and stepped outside. Tom was sitting alone by the pool. I asked, "Everything alright Tom?"

"Yea, man. Sure. Same old soupbone."

We rounded up the others and drove to the country club. We sat down to eat serviced by several waiters. When the main course was served, Sammy said, "My, my, look at these sweet little chickens."

Cyril said, "Those aren't chicken, Sam. They are squab."

"Look like chickens to me, Puff," Sammy replied. (Sammy couldn't pronounce Cyril's name and kept calling him "Cereal" until Griff scolded him by saying, "It's not Cereal, Sam. Puffed wheat is cereal." From that moment on Cyril was "Puff" to Sammy.)

Handy had already filled his mouth when Tut said, "Squab is pigeon, Sam." Handy started spitting his food back onto the plate.

"Say what?" he exclaimed. "I ain't eating no damn pigeon. No, sir, I ain't. Is you kidding, Tut?"

Tut said he was not and Handy turned to Thomas who was munching away on a leg. "Thomas, you gonna keep eating that bird now that you knows what it is?"

"I done ate a lot worser stuff than this, Handy," munched Thomas.

Jinx came in and invited me into the guest dining room to meet Gargan. As we approached the head table, I recognized Dennis Day sitting about halfway down it. He didn't look up. I broke away from Jinx and went directly across the table from where he sat and said, in a loud voice to attract attention, "Mr. Day, my name is Bill Bissonnette. I lead the jazz band that is performing here tonight and I just wanted to tell you what an honor it is to be playing on the same bill with you. I've been a fan of yours for years."

He looked up as I extended my hand to him across the table. He hesitated for just an instant as all eyes turned toward him. Then he stood up, clasped my hand and said, "Well, I can assure you we are all looking forward to hearing your band."

"And I can assure you that we will do our best to entertain you, sir," I replied.

Jinx almost passed out at the audacity of my move but, as the smiles broke out around the table, I could sense the relief she was feeling. I exchanged greetings with Gargan and returned to my band. I guess if I can give Kid Thomas a little hell, I can certainly give Dennis Day a little heaven. I also felt a little more confident that we would be getting paid after all. And I must say, to his credit, Dennis Day had real class in the way he handled it. I'm sure he forgot the whole thing by the next day. But I will remember it for a long, long time.

So, up we went to play our set: all eleven of us. Seven mouldy jazzmen in our best Sunday suits and four of the L.A. Local's Finest all frilled out in their matching tuxedos. They went to sit on the sidelines and play with their valves while we blew the windows out with one of the best sets we ever put together. Even Dennis Day joined the standing ovation.

After the set, I went outside for a smoke. As I stood there in the darkness, puffing away, I heard a curious cartoon voice speak to me.

"I..used..to..smoke..three..packs..a..day. You..play..a..nice..horn. Are..you..really..going..to..finish..that..cigarette?"

I turned to face William Gargan looking at me from the doorway.

When Dennis Day finished his songs, Jinx came over and said, "Everybody would love to hear you all again. Would you do a few more numbers for us?

We went back onstage and played for two hours straight. The crowd danced, applauded and even did a sing-a-long with Sammy Penn leading them. Even the L.A. musicians were cheering at the end of a long, happy night.

As we were packing up, Jinx came over one last time and said, "Bill, it was just wonderful. Mr. Gargan asked me to tell you that, if there is ever anything he can do to help you, just let him know. He has many good contacts." I assured her I would take him up on that offer.

We returned to San Francisco after doing one last job in L.A. It was another television talk show gig. This time the guests included pop vocalists Ed Ames, once of the Ames Brothers, and Rosalind Kind, whose only claim to fame was that she was Barbra Streisand's younger sister. As a finale for the show, Ames and Kind attempted to sing the "Saints" with us. Both got hopelessly lost on the tune and a marvelous close-up shot of the two of them on the studio monitor showed them staring at each other in desperation as their voices trailed off. Suddenly, a growling vocal voice snatched it away from them and onto the TV monitor popped a full head shot of a grinning Sammy Penn singing away. He polished off the tune with a big grin and slapped his stogey in his mouth as the screen faded to credits. The director ran over to him when the cameras went off and thanked him for the save as the two pop stars looked on in disbelieve. Superstar Penn hardly talked to us minor back-up musicians all the way home. But every few miles he would start singing "Saints" and we would all tell him to shut up.

We finished up a few jobs in the Frisco area and finally went back into the studio to record the two numbers with Carol Leigh. She picked a great old number made famous by Mae West: "I Wonder Where My Easy Rider's Gone?" I asked her to do "Make Me A Pallet On the Floor," first recorded as "Atlanta Blues" by Sara Martin with the Clarence Williams Orchestra in 1923. We worked late into the night making the two tracks. We finally got outstanding performances by everyone. Handy was just about drooling during a magnificent chorus on "Pallet" when Carol sings, "Make it, baby," repetitively behind Tom's dirty plunger-mute chorus. To my chagrin, I discovered, when I played the tapes after the New Orleans men left, that the recorded sound, while acceptable, was inferior to the tracks we recorded at McGoon's. What a heartbreaker. But still they were a wonderful addition to the album because they feature Carol in an unfamiliar New Orleans jazz setting.

Before Sammy left for home, he said there was one piece of business he had to attend to. He had promised his family he would bring home some San Francisco Bay crabs. I told him I didn't think they would let him take them on the plane. He said he didn't care. He would mail them home! We went down to Fisherman's Wharf in the city and Sammy picked out the two biggest crabs he could find. When we got home, he walked across the street to the supermarket and got a big cardboard box and some wrapping paper. He wrapped the crabs and asked me to take him to the post office.

I said, "Sam, you better not tell them what's in that box and we better hurry or they're going to be able to smell what's in it!"

"Don't worry about nothin'. I used to work for the post office. I know how to handle those guys."

I insisted that he send them airmail and off flew Sammy's crabs. Sammy, Tom and Cap followed them the next day.

"BOURBON STREET BALL"

Sixth Annual Benefit of the
William Gurgan Cancer Fund
for the
American Cancer Society

Indian Wells Country Club
Palm Desert, California

Saturday, March Eighth

Bourbon Street Ball Programme Cover
American Cancer Society
March 1969

The blues were reborn at Bill Gargan's Bourbon Street Ball at Indian Wells Country Club, where Easy Riders Jazz Band, comprised of famed New Orleans musicians, wailed away. Event benefits American Cancer Society.

Photo Reproduction
American Cancer Society Concert
March 1969

45. Lu Watters

I had put Lu Watters' address aside during the first California tour. Now that I had a little free time, I decided to meet this enigmatic man who had started his own jazz revival in the 1940's and then walked away from it at its peak, leaving a legacy which continues to grow even now almost half a century later. I didn't understand how someone so dedicated to his music could have done such a seemingly contradictory thing. In a way, Ken Colyer, whom I also admired, did the same thing in England, although he at least continued to play jazz after leaving his own band. I didn't understand him either. If I thought those two events to be aberrations, what would I have thought if I had known then that I would do precisely the same thing within six months?

Among white musicians, Lu Watters stands as one of the great legendary figures of traditional jazz alongside Bix Beiderbecke, Eddie Condon and, today, Sammy Rimington. He had made only one recording since his retirement, and that only because it helped an environmental cause he believed in enough to dig his axe out and play for a single event. Fortunately, there is a wealth of recorded material from his creative period and he has, from time to time, made his charts (for this was not a footloose style like the Sixties New Orleans Revival model) available to young emulators such as the Bay City Jazz Band.

He lived in Cotati, out by Bodega Bay, the small inlet made famous as the location for the shooting of Alfred Hitchcock's masterpiece: "The Birds." He lived there, they told me, in a small home surrounded by piles of his beloved rocks. He was a geologist. I was also told he did not have a listed phone so one day Tut and I went looking for his house. It was isolated but not difficult to find. We parked at the end of the drive and walked to the house. I knocked several times before an attractive, though unkempt, woman opened the door.

"Is this the home of Lu Watters," I asked.

"Yes, it is. What do you want?"

"I'm a jazz musician from New Orleans," I lied. "I would like to meet Lu. I've been told I would be turned away but I had to try all the same."

She went inside for a minute and then returned to let us in. Watters was sitting behind a long rock-strewn table. On it was an ashtray full of ash.

Tut immediately recognized it as pot. We introduced ourselves and Tut offered him some leaf. I told him we were playing at Earthquake McGoon's with New Orleans black musicians and described the Crusade to him. He seemed interested in hearing about some of the New Orleans players, particularly those whose histories went back into the Twenties like Polo Barnes and Punch Miller. We discussed his early days in jazz, passing several hours in this manner.

He mentioned that there was still some very fine unissued material by the Yerba Buena band. He said either clarinetist Bob Helm or Turk Murphy had the tapes. I told him I would be interested in releasing them on Jazz Crusade. He replied that he had no control over them. I asked if he would ever consider recording again. To my surprise, he said he might on one condition. He was a fan of Albert Nicholas. He would seriously consider recording if I could arrange a session with Nicholas on clarinet. The thought of a recording with Watters, Nicholas and myself in the frontline with a New Orleans rhythm section was tantalizing indeed.

He also confided that he could use some money and that he might like to act as a booking agent for the Crusade bands. He thought he might still have some useful contacts. We decided to discuss it further at our next meeting. I wanted him to hear one of our groups before deciding to represent us. I invited him to come to a concert we were scheduled to play in Sunnyvale for Marshall Peterson's club with Alvin Alcorn and Polo Barnes. He said he made it a point to avoid jazz events and particularly jazz clubs. I prodded him a little and he agreed to consider it. I left him a couple of tickets. I visited Lu many times over the next few months and he and his woman often came to our house to visit. One thing that struck me funny was that his home was situated directly on the San Andreas Fault. Not near it. Right on the fault line. I guess if you're into geology that's a great place to live but his girlfriend talked about it constantly. I think that's why she came with him to visit so often. . . just in case. I am convinced that if the Jazz Crusade had continued, Lu Watters would have made a comeback in jazz.

46.   Alvin, Polo, Alecs & Sing

By June I was ready for the next tour. Once again, the Murphy band was going on the road, this time for a nationwide two month tour. Pete had been pleased with our first run at the club and asked if I could fill the two months at McGoon's. However, he wanted, if possible, to split the gig into two one month segments, each featuring a different New Orleans contingent. He didn't care who I booked, he just wanted some variety over the period.

I worked it out by setting the tour up in such a way that all of the outside jobs with the first band would precede the McGoon's run and all those of the second group would come after. This gave us almost four months of uninterrupted work. And I mean steady, every day of the week work. We had an occasional day off, but we more than made up for those by doing several double-headers such as a college concert in the afternoon before the five hour club date at night.

Judy had returned to Connecticut for a visit with her family. Well, if you want to know the truth, our marriage was in trouble and she went home to think things out. She didn't like California one bit and wanted to move back to Connecticut. I must admit, I wasn't crazy about the place either, but everything I had was on the line and returning home would mean beginning again from scratch. I felt I had to see it through, win or lose. In addition, now that I'm spilling my guts to you anyway, I would have to say there are some things that I am good at. . . but being a husband is not one of them. Fortunately, she returned before the last two tours; just in time to save my ass during the worst incident of my jazz career and to spend a happy, interesting afternoon with me getting pregnant. I will tell you more about the former, even though the latter was much more fun.

All of our gigs were in the Bay area. Once again we started off with a concert for the New Orleans Jazz Club of Northern California. This time they took the band on a contract instead of speculation. I mentioned to Marshall that Lu Watters might show up at the concert and, if he did, I wanted any drink tabs he ran up charged to me.

He laughed and said, "That will be the day when he shows up. We've been trying to get him to a concert for years. But rest assured, if he shows up, the club will pick up all charges."

A nice crowd showed up but not as many as at the Thomas concert. About midway through the second set there was a commotion in the back of the room. I was announcing the next number at that moment and looked up to see Lu Watters entering. People who recognized him started rising from their chairs to applaud. Many didn't recognize him of course because of his reclusiveness. I announced, simply, "Ladies and gentlemen, Lu Watters." Then the whole room exploded with applause as everyone got to their feet. It was a wholly deserved tribute to a jazz icon.

We played about ten jobs leading up to the McGoon's run. Polo was playing superbly. I had convinced him once again to bring his alto sax along. He had obviously been doing some wood-shedding with it. It was finally on the long, daily gigs at McGoon's that he got his sax chops back. He continued to play it, off and on, for the rest of his days. His style stood in total contrast to Handy's. Just as good, I think, but delicate and mellow like his clarinet work. Fortunately, it is all on tape. I decided to change audio engineers after the Carol Leigh session and got a couple of guys who did a great job of wiring McGoon's unobtrusively. Their recorders were located in the balcony where they could look down without being in anyone's way. This was important because the final Jazz Crusade recordings were going to be "live" on the job.

Alvin was playing very well and I suggested to him that we start introducing some of those wonderful Kid Ory arrangements he played in the Fifties into our repertoire. He thought that was a good idea and we held an afternoon rehearsal to show them to the other guys.

This would be the first time I ever worked with Sing Miller. I always enjoyed his playing and I thought his singing would go over well at the club. I booked him for the full four month run with both bands to keep some continuity. Because he was going to be around so long, I let him have first pick of our bedrooms at home so he could settle in for the long haul. He had done little traveling in his career so this was a big event for him. Of course he later became a regular in one of the Preservation Hall bands and eventually traversed the globe.

Then there was my buddy Alec. Alec Bigard (or Alecs, or Alex: every discography spells his name differently. He signed his contracts with me "Alecs" but we usually called him Alec or Al. Got that?) was the older brother of one of the most famous New Orleans clarinetists who ever lived. But, unlike Barney, Alec stayed home, a local musician. However, being a local musician in New Orleans is not the same as being a local musician anywhere else in the world. Alec didn't go anywhere and made few recordings. Many of the musicians and record producers shied away from him. Their complaint with Alec was that, every so often he would just go berserk and overpower a band with his volume. Nobody could figure out why he did it or could predict when he would do it. So he scared promoter, producer and musician alike.

But I knew the secret, so Alec didn't scare me a bit. The other producers were surprised when I brought Alec to Connecticut and when I got the best recording of him anyone ever had. It was Capt. John Handy who tipped me off to the solution of the loudness problem with Bigard. Handy was one of his best friends and it hurt John that Alec, "never went no place like the rest of us." When Handy asked me why I never brought Alec, I explained the situation to him.

"That's not the problem, Bill," he said. "The real problem is that Alec don't think to get batteries for that hearing aid of his when they start running down. So he plays louder and louder until he finally can't hear nothin' at all. Then he finally gets hisself some batteries and he's okay again."

Thereafter, bringing Bigard on trips was no problem at all. The minute he would step off the plane, I'd hand him two new batteries for his hearing aid and say, "Put these in right now, Al."

I enjoyed the musical contrasts we had in this band. Alecs, Jimmy Tut and I were hot, "black" players. Alvin, Polo and Sing were more, uh, Creole. We had an excellent repertoire. Good things like "Ting-A-Ling," "Yearning," "Maryland My Maryland" and other, more off-beat, tunes. It's not often that I can think back and say this tune or that tune was exceptional. You remember good nights, not individual songs. But this band had one number that was just a living bitch. It was the old parade tune "It Feels So Good." If we had done it parade style, it would have been just another throw away tune I'm sure. But Sing got the brilliant idea to do it as a slow boogie woogie which he would open with a piano chorus. Polo played alto on it while Alvin and I buried our horns in our plunger mutes. It was almost Ellingtonian in concept. It always brought down the house and Sing would laugh and stand up to take a bow every time we finished it. Nobody in the audience knew why the hell he was taking the bow. But we did. It was his arrangement.

One evening, as I was starting to announce the next number, a voice in the crowd yelled out, "'Ice Cream!' 'Ice Cream!' Play 'Ice Cream!'" The voice sounded familiar so I looked around the darkened room to see if I could spot the person who was requesting it. Sing spotted him first and said, "Over there, Bill. Look who's here!" Sitting at a corner table were Jim Robinson and Cie Frazier. It was Jim doing the yelling. I knew the Preservation Hall band was in town and had been sorry that cross-bookings wouldn't give us the chance to see them. Their gig finished up earlier than ours so here they were cheering with the crowd. I introduced them over the P.A. and they received a nice hand. Then I sat back down and called "Ice Cream!" Polo looked at me and grinned. On my solo I blew Jim's famous December Band chorus. Then I looked over at him and held out my horn as he had done to me so many times. He held up his hands, just as I had always done, and yelled, "Oh, no. Oh, no!" He broke up laughing and slapped his knee. I sat down, closed my eyes and said a little prayer, "Thank you, Lord, for not letting him take the horn."

47. Judy In Disguise (with glasses)

After we got home on the final night of the tour, the band assembled in Alvin's bedroom for their payoff. I always paid my musicians in cash; counted out to each of them in the presence of the others so that nobody would ever get the idea that they were being paid more or less than the rest. This had been a well booked tour and there was a lot of money involved. I was happy about it because I was about to pay the men more than I had ever been able to pay before. But, my happiness was short lived and, because of a misunderstanding, I was about to go through the worst incident of the entire Sixties Crusade.

As I completed counting out the money, Alvin said, "Is that all?"

I thought he meant was that the end of the tour. I said, "That's it, Alvin. The tour's over."

"I mean, is that all the money we get?"

I was bewildered. I had, as always, mailed each man a letter verifying the number and type of jobs we would play and the amount of money they would be paid. I said, "That's the amount you agreed to, Alvin."

Sing Miller chimed in, "What about the extra recording money?"

"What extra recording money?" I had included in their letter contracts that we would be recording one night at Earthquake McGoon's. I also stated that if any additional recording sessions were booked, they would be paid extra for them. Alvin apparently thought that meant that they would be paid extra for the McGoon's recording. I asked for a contract and read the recording clause to them again to insure that no mistake had been made when it was typed. It was as I have just described. But, they would have none of it.

"That letter says we will get extra pay for recording," Alvin said again.

"I just read it to you Alvin," I replied. " What's going on here?"

Polo and Alec sat quietly as the exchange heated up. I turned to Polo and asked, "Paul, did you understand that we were recording one night at the club as part of the deal?"

"Everything's fine with me, Bill," he said. "I knew we were going to make a record. I tried to tell Alvin that when he first brought it up to us."

"How about you, Alec?" I asked.

"I didn't think nothing about it until Alvin and Sing started talking about it and saying we should be getting extra. You know the way I feel, Bill. I just wants what everybody else gets."

During my whole career in jazz I had always worked close to the bone financially. This was not a music that commanded big bucks. Anybody who has done it knows you have to work hard to sell this music commercially. Everybody likes it. Nobody wants to pay for it. I had never taken more out of it than my expenses, and often not even those. What I wanted were the recordings that I felt were all important to the future of the music after these musicians were gone. Never before had a single New Orleans musician ever complained to me about payment. I paid equally and fairly and they never had to take daily expense money out of their pocket.

Now, here were Alvin Alcorn and Sing Miller essentially accusing me of ripping them off. My mind was reeling. "How much more do you want, Alvin?"

"Well, we recorded a whole night so we should get another five hundred dollars apiece," he said.

Two thousand dollars. In cash. Right now. It boggled my mind. And Alvin Alcorn was the vice-president of the black Local in New Orleans. He was a man to be reckoned with but I didn't know how. Coming up with two thousand dollars in cash before they left the next day was impossible. Perhaps I could offer to destroy the tapes. No. Not that. But, what? They all stared at me waiting.

Just as the tension reached its peak, Judy strode into the room. She had heard the loud, intense debate from the next room. She was liked and respected by all of the musicians, particularly Sing. But now she was breathing fire.

She walked up to Alvin and Sing, who were standing side by side, and said, "Alvin. Sing. I don't believe what I just heard! You know that Bill has devoted his life to you and your damn music. There's a lot better things we could be doing with our lives than this and you both ought to be ashamed of yourselves doing this to us after accepting our hospitality for the last two months. We don't have two thousand dollars to give you so you are not getting it today. But I give you my word you'll get every cent if it takes us a year to raise it."

She looked at Alvin, "I typed those contracts, Alvin, and I know what they say. They say you were to do that recording at the club as part of the deal and don't try to tell me differently. If you don't understand the contract, you better sit down and read it again until you do. We'll pay you the money you want, but I'll tell you something right now, you'll never come out here or anywhere for Bill again because I won't let you in my house!"

She turned to Sing. "And you. You can pack your bags tonight, Sing, because you're not going to pull this again with the next band that's coming in.

You're going home."

Alvin's face turned bright red and Sing's eyes were bulging. Polo and Alec started shaking their heads sadly as they looked at them. I was so stunned that I just stood staring at my wife.

Alvin spoke first, stammering, "Now, Miss Judy, don't get upset. We just made a mistake understanding the contract."

Sing turned on Alvin, "We? You the one who said we should get more money!"

Judy responded, "You said it too, Sing. I heard you say it."

"Well, but I never brought it up. Alvin brought it up."

"That's right. You didn't bring it up. You backed it up," she said icily.

They were both in full rout now. Alvin and Sing, in a race with each other to see who could get in the clear first.

"Listen, Miss Judy, we're satisfied with what we got and we made a good recording too. We don't want more money. Okay?" It was coming out of both their mouths in a duet. She turned on her heels and walked out of the room.

As soon as she left, Polo said quietly, "See what you all have done? I told you that you were lucky to be here with Bill. Now you gone and ruined it for sure."

Alec was too upset to speak. He just sat there looking into space. Alvin and Sing continued apologizing to me in loud voices that they hoped would carry into the next room.

I was so confused that I was still trying to convince the men that I wasn't trying to cheat them.

"We never meant nothing against you, man," Alvin said. "It was just a misunderstanding, Bill."

Sing interjected, "But we got it now, man. It's all over and I'm satisfied with everything."

Alvin, finally grasping the situation, said, "I want to come back again if it's okay with Miss Judy."

"Me, too!" said Sing.

Later in the night, about 5:00 a.m., Sing came into the living room where I was sitting watching a movie and calming down. He sat beside me on the couch and said, "I don't wants to go home now, man. I wants to stay and play with Punch. I ain't gonna cause no trouble, Bill. You can count on that."

Later that day, before we left for the airport to put them on their flight and pick up the new band, Alvin and Sing, separately, asked Judy if they could talk to her alone. I never asked her, or them, what was said. Sing stayed on so I guess he did some fast talking, but she never treated him the same again. For the first time, Judy didn't go to the airport. She said she had to clean up the rooms so Punch, Handy and Penn could settle right in when they arrived.

I can't conclude this chapter without adding two remarks. First: This was a genuine misunderstanding. I had to relate it because it was an important event in the history of the Jazz Crusade. Alvin and Sing were two of my closest friends. I hope I haven't reflected poorly on them. It happened but it was an abomination. It was unlike anything else that happened during those years. And, you, the reader, may even wonder what the big deal is. It's not unusual to have a business misunderstanding. But, to me, it was more. I had spent seven years, young years, cultivating my relationships within a group of artists unique in human history. Too strong? Think about it. Are you a jazz fan? Would it exist, in any form, without this group which includes their predecessors? I was inside and, for a moment, thinking I would be kicked out. Because of a misunderstanding. And then a cute little somebody walked in and shocked us all back to our senses. Which brings me to my second remark:

Now you know why I knocked her up.

Poster
Earthquake McGoon's
July 1969

30—S.F. Examiner ☆ Wed., July 2, 1969

Jazz Crusaders Have That Swin

By Philip Elwood

You like New Orleans swing?

Yes, I said swing . . . not jazz, not the stuff most people think of — thump-thump, two-beat, ricky-tick jive.

What I mean is the subtle-shuffle New Orleans swing rhythm which we associate with Bunk Johnson and Kid Ory, Sid Bechet and Louis Armstrong.

And the band that opened last night at Earthquake McGoon's. Call it the Jazz Crusaders band. Whatever, it's got that swing.

Runaway star of the Crusaders group is trumpeter Alvin Alcorn, an old friend for many of us from the Kid Ory days of the early 1950s.

Alcorn, who recorded extensively with Ory (and Don Albert in the '30s) is the sweetest t r u m p e t e r alive from the old jazz school. He can drive a band hard on up-tempos, but his real forte is beauty on the blues and ballads. Warm, round, tones and effortless shifts in range and technique.

Clarinetist P a u l Barnes sits left of Alcorn on the McGoon's stage, as he sat when he played with Joe Oliver's last bands nearly 40 years ago. Another pretty player, Barnes is a New Orleans dance band veteran, not one of the hard-toned marching bandsmen.

Drummer Alex Bigard,

older brother of clarinetist Barney Bigard is a rudiment perfectionist — neat, swinging, competent. And pianist Jim Miller is strong as a vocalist (good voice, attractive phrasing) and steady in the ensembles.

Bill Bissonette and Jim Tutunjian, trombone and bass, complete the band — neither have the rhythmic relaxation which identifies the old timers.

This Crusaders group is a dance band. A minimum of solo spectaculars and an emphasis on a variety of tunes. The New Orleans guys are about 60 (Barnes is older) and professionals. None are third-rate accidentals who s o m e t i m e s pass as New Orleans jazzmen.

And A l c o r n, alone, is worth hearing.

**Philip Elwood article
San Francisco Examiner
2 July 1969**

WORLD OF JAZZ

Sextet's Debut Well Received

By RUSS WILSON
Tribune Jazz Writer

Four sprightly New Orleans jazz veterans, assisted by a pair of Bay Area instrumentalists, made an auspicious debut at Earthquake McGoon's last night.

The sextet will be at the San Francisco club for three weeks, and if the welcome it received from the opening night listeners is an omen the engagement should be as happy as the band's music.

For trumpeter Alvin Acorn, whose warm-toned, sensitive playing was a highlight of the night's offerings, the occasion marked his second visit to this area. The 57-year-old musician played with trombonist Kid Ory's band at the Hangover club 13 years ago.

Clarinetist Paul Barnes, who doubles on the alto saxophone; pianist James Miller, and drummer Alex Bigard are making their first appearance here.

As associates they have trombonist Bill Bissonnette and bassist Jim Tutunjian, who moved their Jazz Crusade operation from Connecticut to Marin county last year.

Once it got to grooving, the band performed with a light but sure touch that was both sprightly and joyful.

Barnes, a onetime associate of King Oliver and "Papa" Celestin, has a rather light tone but plays with a singing, melodic delicacy that is delightful.

Besides providing tasteful comping and occasional solos, pianist Miller also sings now and then. His voice is melodic and pleasing.

Drummer Bigard, whose younger brother is clarinetist Barney B. fills his role with unobtrusive strength.

Bissonnette's raucous trombone provides a contrast to the lyricism of the two other horns; he is at his best on plunger mute interludes. His stylized honky-tonk vocals found favor with the listeners.

Tutunjian's slap-style playing furnished a strong beat.

Russ Wilson article
Oakland Tribune
2 July 1969

48. The Last Crusade

Sing came along for the ride to the airport to help make the band switch. I think he was afraid to be left alone with Judy after the morning hubbub. We were going to pick up Punch Miller, Capt. John Handy and Sammy Penn for the next tour. I didn't know it at that instant, but this would be the last Crusade tour. The last Jazz Crusade recording session. The last few times I would play my horn for many years.

A few days before the end of the last tour, a fellow came into Earthquake McGoon's. He was having a great time and ordered a round of drinks for the band. We all went and sat with him on the break. During the conversation, he mentioned that he worked for the airline on which this band was flying home and the new band was coming in. He asked me if I knew the flight numbers of the two flights. I gave them to him. When we arrived at the service counter to drop the luggage, the woman behind the counter took one look at the tickets and said, "Oh, Messrs. Alcorn, Barnes and Bigard, we are so happy to have you with us on this flight. Could you wait just one minute?" She then dialed a number on her telephone and said, "The gentlemen from New Orleans you spoke to me about have arrived. Yes sir. Right away, sir." She came around the counter and asked us to follow her, leaving a line of customers indignantly waiting unattended, and led us down the hall toward the boarding area. She stopped and opened an unmarked door on the side wall and said, "Right this way, gentlemen."

We stepped into a beautiful little air-conditioned lounge furnished with comfortable easy chairs and a beverage and snack bar attended by two hostesses. She then said, " The flight with the other gentlemen coming in from New Orleans will be landing in just a few minutes and we will escort them here to join you. Please make yourselves comfortable." Then she left.

We didn't know what in hell was going on. A few minutes later, in came Handy, Punch and Sammy. They had been escorted off of the plane ahead of everybody else and brought here. As we greeted each other, a hostess asked everyone if we would care for drinks. Sammy's eyes lit up and he said, "Oh yes, ma'am. I surely could go for that." We all sat down and began talking about how wonderful the airlines had suddenly become with this new service. Then in walked the fellow we met at Earthquake McGoon's.

The hostesses rushed to him to take his drink order and tend to his needs. Whenever they addressed him it was, "Yes, sir. No sir. Sir. Sir. Sir." He told us again how much he enjoyed himself at the club. He asked if our check-in at the service desk was handled alright. "Yes, sir." No problems on the flight in from New Orleans? "No, sir. Sir. Sir. Sir." Now we were doing it too!

When it came close to the time for the flight out, I mentioned that we better get to the gate. Sir said there was no hurry; someone would come to escort Alvin, Polo and Alec to the plane. We had another round with our buddy Sir, before they had to leave. Then he bid us goodbye and disappeared out a back door. I never found out what this man did for the airline but he sure knew how to treat mouldy jazz musicians. Yes, Sir.

Sammy jumped into the front seat with me for the drive home. "Say, man," he said, "you all remember those crabs I sent home when I was here?"

"Sure. How'd they make out. Did you get them?"

"Oh, I got them fine, Bill, but they went bad before we could eat them."

"That's too bad, Sam. I knew you were looking forward to them."

"Oh no, man, it worked out just fine. I took them crabs down to Charity Hospital in New Orleans to a doctor friend of mine and had him shoot them full of formaldehyde so's they wouldn't rot away. Then I mounted them on a piece of wood along with some rope and seashells. They're hanging in my living room right now and, oh, don't they look beautiful!"

That evening Pete Clute, Bob Helm and Lu Watters dropped by for a small welcoming party. Helm mentioned the great stand of redwood trees in nearby Mill Valley. All of the New Orleans men seemed really interested in what he was saying and we decided to drive over to see the forest the next day. The drive was along a hair-raising, cliffs-edge road but it was worth the trip. All of us were enthralled with the mighty, ancient trees. We stayed several hours walking among them. Sing started singing one of the songs he frequently did in the club called "Who Threw the Whiskey In the Well." He said the trees reminded him of it because there is a line in it that tells of a drunken preacher who was, "higher than a Georgia Pine." That night Sing did the number and changed the words to "California Pine." Nobody in the audience understood his little joke.

Punch Miller was one of my dearest friends. I would sit for hours listening to him tell stories about the Roaring Twenties. He was one of the cats who made it roar. He had a marvelous way with a story, interjecting little musical interludes as he went along. A story would remind him of a song and he would start singing it. A song would remind him of a story and he would start telling it. On and on. Never boring. Every so often he would stop just long enough to take an insulin needle out of his case and jab it into his leg. Once he hummed a familiar melody and I asked him the name. He said it was called "Isabella," after the queen. I had heard it before as "Rip 'Em Up, Joe," a piece Percy Humphrey often did. Punch said he had recorded it at the height of his career in the Twenties and had a big hit with it. "If Percy got that tune, he got it from me."

Pete Clute thought up a publicity gimmick to get a little press coverage for the band's opening at the club. A press release was sent out that Punch Miller was going to be presented with a trumpet that had belonged to Louis Armstrong. The band was to go down to the club early for the press event. Punch was to accept the horn in front of the club and then we were to march up Clay Street in brass band fashion for the television news cameras. Of course it was doubtful that Louis Armstrong had ever been within a thousand miles of the old junk trumpet and we were to return the horn to the club after the press left. It was all strictly hype. I carefully explained all of this to Punch. "Yea, man. I gotcha man. I plays this trumpet and then gives it back to the club."

The press and the band showed up. The hoax was perpetrated. When the mock presentation was made, Punch went into a soliloquy about how he was as big as Armstrong but Louis had gotten all the breaks and Punch had gotten none and, and, and. . . all on camera. Finally, we did the little parade and that was that. When it was over, we went into the club to get ready for the gig. I was taking my axe out of its case when Punch came running over, yelling, "Bill, Bill, you know what just happened? That man who gave me Louis' trumpet just come over and grabbed it back!" I explained the whole thing again about it just being a publicity stunt and that it wasn't Armstrong's horn. Punch plopped dejectedly into his chair next to me and said, "Oh, man, and I was going to bring it home to New Orleans and show it to everybody."

We had very good press on this tour. Among those who saw a feature article on John Handy was John Handy. No, that's not a misprint. Those of you who are familiar with the more modern jazz styles will know that there is another well-known John Handy. Not only that, his instrument is the alto sax. The "modern" John Handy showed up at the club one night to hear the "traditional" John Handy. He wore his trademark fur hat. He introduced himself to Cap who, to my surprise, was not only familiar with him but started to discuss some of his recordings with him. The two Handys were at least a generation apart in age as well as style. After our first set the younger Handy ran up to Cap and said, "Damn, man, you sure blow some horn."

"Oh yas. Deed I do," replied Cap. He invited Handy the Younger to sit in with us and he gladly accepted. He went to his car for his tool and was soon blowing along on several of the strangest sounding numbers any of the rest of us ever played. But it was a good sounding duo: John Handy and John Handy.

John Handy, the other John Handy, wasn't the only celebrity that showed up that night. There were two others. One was newscaster Bernard Kalb, who frequently dropped in when we were playing. He, of course, later went on to the Reagan State Department. The other big timer who showed up was. . . Sadie! We heard her before we saw her. When she let out her first yell, Cap looked over at me and said, "Oh no!" Sammy's eyes blazed as he popped a fresh cigar in his mouth. This was going to be some tour.

I mentioned earlier that there was a lawyer who frequented the club with his wife. Although I had never seen him outside of the club, we became friends. I always enjoyed spending breaks with him. I had thought about going into the law but music had gotten in the way. He had followed my plans for the Crusade closely and knew that we might have to terminate the Crusade because our money was slowly running out. One evening at the club, he asked me if I could stop by his office the following afternoon. I asked if he was planning to sue me. He said he wasn't but there was something important he wanted to speak to me about.

I was impressed with his office. It was larger than the dance floor at McGoon's. He was the senior partner in the firm. We small-talked for a few minutes and then he came to the point.

"There is a state law in California that permits a law firm to take in apprentices even though they have not attended law school. If, after five years, they can pass the bar exam, they can then practice law in California."

I replied, "That's a great law. But what's it got to do with Jazz Crusade? You gonna make a corporate lawyer out of Sammy Penn?"

He laughed and said, "No, I'm going to make a lawyer out of you. I admire what you are doing for jazz and I'd like to see you stay in San Francisco. If you'll agree, I will take you into the firm as an apprentice. You can still do your jazz work on weekends. It will be tough but I'm confident you can do it."

I was dumbfounded. I just didn't know what to say. I eventually turned down the offer because another, even more important, event soon changed everything for me. There are few decisions I have regretted more. And I have to tell you something really stupid. As I sit here at this typewriter, for the life of me, I cannot recall this marvelous man's name. But I shall always remember him and the offer he made me. It's got nothing to do with jazz I know but I just wanted to share it with you.

The gig at McGoon's was going very well. Sing was a changed man after his run-in with Judy. Punch was just full of good tunes. Handy was playing more relaxed than I've ever heard him. Sammy was drinking heavily but playing well despite it. I decided to hold off until the very last night of the tour for our recording to polish some of the new numbers Punch was laying on us. I'm glad I did because it turned out to be one of my favorite Jazz Crusade sessions.

One night, after the gig, we were preparing to leave when I noticed Handy wasn't with us. "Where's John," I asked. "I don't want him getting locked in like Thomas was."

Sammy smiled and said, "He's backstage."

"What's he doing there?"

"He's hiding," said Sing.

"Hiding? Hiding from what?"

Sing said, "You better ask him, man. I don't know nothing."

I went back into the club looking for Handy. "Cap? Where are you? Come on, we're leaving."

"Bill! That you man? I'se here behind the stage."

"Well come on. We're leaving."

"I can't come out, man. Sadie's after me. She say she taking me home wit her tonight no matter what, man. If I comes outta here, she gonna get me for sure. She's waiting down by the corner!"

I went back outside and asked Sing to check out the corner. He said, "No. No. Not me, man. I ain't goin' nowhere's near that old woman."

Sammy came running over. "I'll go, Bill!"

"The hell you will Penn. I got enough trouble without you chasing your dick all the way to Sadie's house. You stay right here."

I went back into the club and prodded Cap to come out. We formed a flying wedge around him and whisked him into the car Tut had brought around and we made our getaway.

It didn't look like we would be able to continue the Crusade beyond the one year trial period Judy and I had agreed upon. We were making good money on the tours. The problem was the dry spells between tours. The bills kept rolling in whether we were playing or not. In addition, the main ingredient in our profit margin was the steady work we had been getting at McGoon's. Obviously, I could not run a business that depended on the comings and goings of the Murphy band to show a profit. What we needed was a Club Hangover type of place that could provide steady work for us. None developed.

Then Judy provided the clincher. "I'm pregnant." It was a totally unexpected development that would have stopped the California Crusade by itself. I was delighted with the news but I knew she would want to have her baby at home in Connecticut. And that was a reasonable request I would not deny. She did what she said she would do and stuck it out for almost a year. We had had our problems, and worse were still to come, but she watched without reproach as I spent off our resources trying to promote this music I loved so much. Now it was her turn to do her thing and mine to go along. I told her we were going home right after the tour.

She said, "You can still play there, you know." I knew better. New Orleans jazz was not a hobby with me. I was a crusader not a dilettante. It was time to literally face the music.

But there was still some fun to be had. We had two more weeks at McGoon's and several concert gigs coming up. I didn't tell the band about my decision to retire from the music scene. We did tell them about the baby. They were as excited as I was. Four prospective honorary grandfathers all laughing and congratulating us.

I have a little story to tell you about Punch which, if he was alive, he would surely object to my telling because it would embarrass him no end. Punch's memory would frequently fail him on little daily matters. He would, for example, forget where he put his eyeglasses and search all over the house for them until someone reminded him they were pushed up onto his forehead. That sort of forgetfulness. But he had one forgetful habit that topped all the rest. At the club he would go to the Men's Room just before each set and invariably forgot to zipper his fly when he was through. As we entered the stage, I would always stand to the side of the entrance and announce what our first song was going to be to the band as they went on. And so it went:

"'Joe Avery's Piece,' Sing."
"'Joe Avery's Piece,' Tut."
"'Joe Avery's Piece,' Cap."
"'Joe Avery's Piece,' Punch. Your fly's open."

Punch would look down and say, "Gosh darn, I done forgot that thing again!"

Sadie must have given up on Cap. We didn't see her again until our closing night. And she didn't pester anyone even then. In a way I'm glad she made it for our last appearance because she can be heard occasionally yelling in the background of the recording we cut that evening. It was hearing her on those albums that made me think of including her antics in this narrative.

It all came together that night even in the process of all coming apart. I alone knew it was to be my swan song. The last recording. Probably the last time I would play. One last glorious evening. And we had great fun because it was also the last night for McGoon's and the band was ready to celebrate. I didn't realize how fortunate it was to record that night until I heard the resulting albums upon their release seventeen years later. All of the magic is still there if you listen.

I have always maintained that the only thing that is important in jazz is recordings. There is no way to describe jazz in words. It is indefinable. Many have tried. None have succeeded. But play a single record, from any style, and it all lays out in front of you if you have the ears to hear. The music speaks for itself. That's why I have not attempted to describe it in this book. Listen and you will know. So it lives as long as the recordings survive. Not one second longer. If you think Punch Miller is really dead, I suggest you put on the recording we made that night at McGoon's. Does that sound like a dead man to you? As his music lives, so does he. I had a little joke I used to announce from the bandstand when we were about to play "Perdido St. Blues," which I think makes my point. I would say, "Johnny Dodds was going to sit in with us on this number tonight but at the moment he's dead." It wasn't a very funny joke but it is true that he is dead only "at the moment." He springs back to life the instant you put that remarkable recording of his on your turntable and that acid tone cuts the air. Not a ghost. No ghost blows blues like that. The man lives.

I don't know how many recordings Sammy, Punch or Handy made after this one. Not many I'm sure. It is their last will and testament. Listen to it and find out what they left you from their estate. It is very valuable stuff.

Poster
Earthquake McGoon's
August 1969

Old jazz stars perform at restaurant

Punch Miller, an old-time jazz trumpet player from New Orleans' Preservation Hall, will headline a four-hour jazz program to be held Sunday afternoon at the Bold Knight Restaurant in Sunnyvale.

Other top names scheduled to appear include Capt. John Handy, alto sax; Sammy Penn, drummer, and Sing Miller, piano.

The program, to be held from 3 to 7 p.m. is presented by the New Orleans Jazz Club of Northern California, headed by S. Marshall Peterson of Santa Rosa.

Punch Miller, also known as Kid Punch, now 71, was one of the leaders of the New Orleans trumpet style during the years 1919 to 1927.

Kings of that style at the time also included Buddy Petit, Chris Kelly, Sam Morgan and Kid Rena, but Miller is the last of those still alive and playing. Miller was known for his fast fingering, and with Mutt Carey, he worked out the fast riff passages that has become the third strain in "Tiger ...".

After World War I, Miller returned to New Orleans and joined Kid Ory's band, replacing a youngster named Louis Armstrong. Later, he rejoined Carey's band and still later formed his own group. In 1927 he went North and for many years played and re-

corded with such musicians as Jelly Roll Morton, Sidney Bechet, Si Oliver and Tiny Parham.

After the Depression he traveled constantly with carnivals, circuses and tent shows. In 1956 tired of wandering, he stayed in New Orleans, scrounging for what work he could find.

In 1959, he nearly died from a serious illness, but a year later he was back in good health and playing with vigor. He cut the now famous Icon long-playing jazz album, which also featured Capt. Handy. Three years later, he toured Japan with George Lewis and his Preservation Hall Band. Miller is known for his scat style vocals and for several original old tunes — "I've Been Mistreated," "Punch Miller Blues" and "Bongo Bongo."

Capt. Handy is a veteran of the Sam Morgan, Tut Johnson, Chris Kelly, Kid Rena and Kid Howard bands, and has led his own Louisiana Shakers for more than 30 years.

Penn is the regular drummer with Kid Thomas Valentine's band and appears with him several times a week at Preservation Hall. Sing Miller has performed at both Preservation Hall and Dixieland Hall.

Filling out the band at Sunday's concert will be Bill Bissonnette and Jim Tutunjian.

Capt. John Handy

Newspaper article
Palo Alto Times
8 August 1969

49.   Now Is The Hour

The JAZZ CRUSADE was winding down. The last of the New Orleans musicians were back home. Tut decided to stay on in California with his new wife. He even got a day gig.

During our last few days in Novato, Judy and I arranged for the pickup of our rented furniture and packed our bags for the long drive home. I called an old boss of mine in Connecticut and quickly got a nice job offer. We sold the trailer. No point dragging that thing back.

On the very day we left, a letter arrived from Jinx Ray, the woman who had arranged the Palm Springs concert for William Gargan. It read:

"Although I will be in touch with you later to see if we can't work out something for ACS next spring, I suggest you write to Mr. Peter Maheu at the Frontier Hotel in Las Vegas and tell him that you played for the Annual Gargan Ball in Palm Springs. Tell him you feel sure that Mr. Gargan will give you an excellent endorsement. This might open the door for you in any one of the Howard Hughes hotels because Mr. Mayheu and his father are the two people involved in operating this phase of the Hughes Empire. Keep us posted on how you get along. Mr. Gargan sends his regards."

It came too late.

I backed the car out of the driveway and headed east, over the Golden Gate Bridge, and on to Connecticut. This time there was no side trip to New Orleans.

It was the end of the Jazz Crusade.

1970 - - - - -

deceased

EMILE "MILE'" BARNES, clarinet (1970)

OCTAVE CROSBY, piano (1971)

CAPT. JOHN HANDY, alto sax, clarinet (1971)

EARL HUMPHREY, trombone (1971)

ERNEST "PUNCH" MILLER, trumpet, vocalist (1971)

SYLVESTER HANDY, string bass (1972)

ANDREW MORGAN, sax, clarinet (1972)

TONY PARENTI, clarinet (1972)

ALBERT NICHOLAS, clarinet (1973)

DEDE PIERCE, trumpet (1973)

BILLIE PIERCE, piano, vocalist (1974)

ARTHUR "ZUTTY" SINGLETON, drums (1975)

ALBERT BURBANK, clarinet (1976)

NATHAN "BIG JIM CROW" ROBINSON, trombone (1976)

EDDIE SOMMERS, trombone (1977)

ALEC BIGARD, drums (1978)

LOUIS "PRES" COTTRELL, clarinet (1978)

PAUL "POLO" BARNES, clarinet, alto sax (1981)

ALLAN JAFFE, helicon (1986)

RAYMOND BURKE, clarinet (1986)

EMANUEL SAYLES, banjo (1987)

"KID THOMAS" VALENTINE, trumpet, slapstick (1987)

50.   Coda

Farewells.

Over the course of the next few years, the only contact I had with jazz was to hear reports of the deaths of my friends.

First, and one of the toughest, was Sammy Penn, only two months after my retirement. Sammy used to talk about death quite frequently. He was not afraid of it. To him it was the Sweet Bye and Bye. He had only one great fear and he discussed it with me.

"The onliest thing I'm a'scared of, Bill, is going blind like DeDe."

"But, look at DeDe, Sam," I would say. "He gets along alright even though he's blind and you would too. You have people to look out for you."

"I don't care, Bill. That's the thing I fear most. I'd rather be dead than blind."

When Polo Barnes called me to tell me of Sammy's passing, I asked if he suffered much at the end.

"No, Bill. It wasn't like that at all. He only lived for a few days after the stroke. The only thing was, he was blind for his last days. That's all."

I cried for Penn.

Not because of his death.

Because of his blindness.

Then I got a call about Handy. It's strange but I do not remember who phoned. The caller said, "Handy died last night. He sat up in the middle of the night and yelled, 'I'm dying,' and he was gone. Just like that."

I read about Punch in the newspaper. By that time I was out of the jazz loop so long, people didn't bother with me anymore. I was just as happy that they didn't.

But two more inexplicable incidents were still to happen to me. I am not a believer in mysticism, particularly the bizarre cultist types that seem to grasp otherwise intelligent people nowadays. But I have no explanations for these things with which I am about to close this narrative. They happened precisely as I will relate them to you and you judge for yourself.

It was now the mid-Seventies. I hadn't seen Jim Robinson since the night he came and yelled for "Ice Cream" at Earthquake McGoon's in 1969. The Preservation Hall Band frequently came through Connecticut but I could never bring myself to go see them. There were too many explanations due regarding my disappearance from the scene. One afternoon I received a surprise phone call from Allan Jaffe.

"Jim asked me to call and tell you that we are playing in Westport this evening. He has been asking about you and would like to see you. He's not well, Bill. If you ever want to see him again, come tonight." He told me where the concert was and the name of the motel in Stratford where they were staying.

I thought about the call and Jaffe's closing remark the rest of the day. I decided to go. I attended the concert but could not get backstage during the intermission. On stage, Jim appeared coherent and performed well for his age. As usual he worked up the crowd with his dancing and handkerchief waving. After the concert I drove to the motel. I bumped into some of the other musicians and exchanged greetings, They directed me to Jim's room. He was alone and packing his bag. The door was ajar and I stepped inside.

He looked up at me and said, "Hello, man. How y'all?" He was drawn and thin. Close up, I was shocked by his appearance. I was frankly disappointed that he had not greeted me more warmly after having Allan call me. I attributed it to his obvious bad health. We talked for several minutes. He asked if I enjoyed the concert. I told him that I had. Then we had this startling conversation:

"Say, man, there's a boy I been looking for here in Connecticut."

I said, "What's his name. Maybe I know him."

"His name's Bill. Bill Bissonnette. They calls him Big Bill after me."

My heart broke as I realized just how sick this man I loved so much really was.

"It's me, Jim. I'm Bill Bissonnette."

He came close to me and stared into my eyes for an eternity. Then, slowly, as the recognition came to him, his face lit up. "Bill man! I been looking for you, man!" He put his arms around me. "I missed you man. How y'all been?"

We spent the last few minutes before he had to leave talking about auld lang syne.

"You working much, Bill?" he asked.

I told him I hadn't played in years.

"What!? You not been playing? Why not, man? Listen here, Bill, I wants you blowing that horn of yours. You hear me talking?"

I said I would think about it. He asked if I still had the mouthpiece he had given me back when I was taking lessons from him. It was one of my treasured possessions. I have it still in a little glass case in my living room. Allan came into the room, greeted me and said it was time to go. I walked out with them, carrying Jim's trombone case as I had done so many times in New

Orleans when I walked with him to the kitty halls. And I still felt that pride in carrying it as I had then.

The last time I ever saw Jim Robinson, he was smiling at me through a dimly lit bus window. He waved gently goodbye as the bus pulled away into the blackness.

- - -

I had no further contact with the musicians of New Orleans until the mid-Eighties. Then I was being encouraged to play again and I decided to take my son, Douglas, to the World's Fair in New Orleans. It would give me the chance to see if any of the old-timers were still alive and kicking. I didn't call anyone to let them know I was coming because I didn't know who to call who might care one way or the other that I would be there. We flew down and checked into the Olivier House for a week. On our first evening there, we went over to Preservation Hall. The girl at the door didn't know me but Bill Russell, who was sitting beside her, noticed me with a surprised look. As I handed over our four bucks admission, Bill waved it off. I walked to the side door and peered into the past. Kid Sheik was standing in front of the band singing. Sing Miller was on piano. But, the first to recognize me was Louis Nelson who was sitting next to the door leading the audience in hand-clapping. He stopped in mid-clap and held out his hand. I took it as he yelled to Sheik, "Look who's here!"

Sheik turned his head and burst out laughing, that wonderful cackling laugh that rocks the room. "Hey, Bill! How ya been, man? Sing, Bill from Connecticut's here!" Sing turned around and almost fell off his chair when he saw me. At the break we had a happy reunion. I asked about several of my friends and was told mournfully by Sheik and Sing who had died. I asked after Thomas. He was alive and well and still came to the hall to lead his band although he didn't play much on the job anymore. He was scheduled for the following night.

I arrived early the next evening to be sure I would get to see Tom before the gig began. As I waited in the carriageway, Allan Jaffe walked out from the rear dwelling. He spotted me and came over.

"I heard you were in town. You know it's incredible, but for the last few weeks, all Tom has talked about is you. He hadn't mentioned you for a long time and then all of a sudden he started asking me every night he played whether you were coming in. He's been asking everybody whether they knew when you were arriving. And now, here you are. Did you let him know you were coming?"

"No. I didn't mention it to anyone. I haven't talked to Tom in over fifteen years. What you're telling me is very weird."

Just then a cab pulled up and Kid Thomas stepped out.

God, he was old, I thought. Frail beyond my comprehension. But he was still "The Kid". I walked over and he stopped short as he saw me.

"Where you been, man? I been expecting you weeks ago."

We spent every break together talking about those wonderful times we had. His mind was lucid. There was no hint of senility. His memory was better than mine. We talked about Connecticut and Canada and California. We had a great time, like us old folk are supposed to have when swapping war stories. I saw him one more night and the other musicians said he played more horn that evening than he had in years. I like to think it was because he knew I was listening.

He died a few months later. To me, that was the real end of the Jazz Crusade. The closing of the book. So that's what I will now do.

But, one last question: how did he know I was coming?

Bill Bissonnette
January, 1990

LaGrange, Ga., Thursday, October 30, 1969

SAMUEL PENN
Cerebral Hemmorage

Stricken Musician Dies Here

Samuel Hughes Penn, stricken during a concert here Monday night, died this morning in City-County Hospital.

Penn was the drummer for the Preservation Hall Jazz Band which performed at La-Grange High School Monday, sponsored by the Mutual Concert Association.

He suffered a cerebral hemmorage during the performance and was taken to the hospital.

His wife, Beatrice, and three of his seven children arrived in LaGrange from their home in New Orleans Wednesday to be with the stricken musician.

Penn was born in Morgan City, La. and his first drums were a tin tub, a cheese box and sticks made from chair rounds.

When he was in his early teens he sat in with every band that went to Morgan City. Moving to New Orleans at the age of 22, all the New Orleans musicians already knew him.

He worked with Jules Barnes in New Orleans, then joined Buddy Petit until 1931.

Sammy Penn Obituary
LaGrange, Georgia
30 October 1969

Epilogue

So, let's add it up. During the seven years I was recording jazz, I produced 30 recording sessions which, had they all been released, would have resulted in 48 albums. That is an average of one album every 6.5 weeks.

If you prefer to view it in terms of the individual artists, it comes down to 18 albums by Kid Thomas; 14 by Sammy Penn; 12 each for Jim Robinson and Capt. John Handy; 7 by Manny Paul and Sing Miller; 5 apiece for Punch Miller, Alvin Alcorn, Polo Barnes, and Alec Bigard; 3 each for George Lewis and Kid Sheik. At least three dozen other New Orleans musicians appeared on at least one.

Of the supporting cast: I played on 39 albums; Dick Griffith and Dick McCarthy were tied with 33 each; Bill Sinclair was on 22; Sammy Rimington came in with 20, and Jim Tutunjian was on 12. All the others had less than 10 each.

As you can see from the above statistics, Jazz Crusade had a "stable" of artists I used repeatedly. In the case of the TOP 10 JC artists, I recorded each of them more than any other record producer; in some instances more than all of the other record producers combined. It isn't difficult to figure out who were my favorites among the New Orleans musicians of the 1960's.

How did all of this frenzied activity come about? Was it by happy accident? At least one of the ex-Riders thought so. I bumped into him at a New Year's Eve party in the mid-Seventies.

"You know," he said, "you were the luckiest bastard I ever met. The whole jazz scene here in Connecticut began just after you came back from the Army and petered out again right after you got out of it and left for California. You happened to be here at just the right time. That's what I call lucky."

Nothing he said indicated that he saw any cause-and-effect relationship between the events. I haven't disclosed his name because, well, I wouldn't want you to say I accused so-and-so of being an absolute idiot.

Starting in the early Seventies, the character of the New Orleans jazz scene changed. In the Sixties, Preservation Hall was at the pinnacle of the movement. In the Seventies it WAS the movement and remains so today. The other kitty halls shut down and so did most of the record producers. There was one notable exception and one important addition. The exception was, of course, George Buck who bought up most of the small independents and thus assured that their legacies would not be lost. The addition was SMOKEY MARY records, produced by Frank Demond, an extraordinary protege' of Jim Robinson and a member of the Preservation Hall Jazz Band.

As the New Orleans jazzmen died off, there were younger men of high caliber and integrity who stepped in to fill the void: Barry Martyn, Frank Demond, Lars Edegran, Orange Kellin, Chris Burke, Wendell Brunious and Clive Wilson, to name a few who resided in New Orleans. The Hall Brothers continued with their excellent band featuring skilled musicians such as Charlie DeVore, Mike Pollad and, Butch Thompson who has gone on to greater and greater successes. And, soaring above them all, was the entrancing clarinet of Sammy Rimington, the man who is today the living symbol of New Orleans jazz just as his predecessor, George Lewis, was before him. Each of these men have earned the respect they enjoy today.

Of the Easy Riders, excepting Rimington, Mouldy Dick McCarthy retired from music when I left for California and has not played since, justifiably content with the mark he made with the Riders. Dick Griffith, having overcome both a bout with cancer and a near fatal car crash, still plays now and then with a local band. Vigorito, Kalet and Sinclair still have their locally successful dixie band which has played continuous weekly gigs for almost two decades in the same pub. They have never added a permanent trombone player to the band. Guess they learned their lesson. Pulver and Fargo moved out of Connecticut. I run into Bill Connell now and then. He has reached retirement age as a school teacher and still talks about getting serious about his music someday.

In 1985 George Buck conducted a new Jazzology Jazz Poll; the first in twenty years. With most of the black New Orleans musicians dead, the poll took on a new complexion. . . whiter. In accompanying remarks, George commented about the importance of recent recording in determining the results. Maybe. He didn't mention an interesting fact: six members of the original Easy Riders Jazz Band, not one of whom has made a recording in the intervening two decades, had either retained or improved their poll position. The only such group of jazzmen to do so. The Riders, as a band, dropped from 9th to 21st among Favorite Jazz Bands, but, without a single new album release over the entire period, still led many excellent current bands.

Those original Jazz Crusade albums are highly prized collector's items today. I watched as one of them was auctioned off for $175 in France. They tell me the highest price ever paid for one of them was for a copy of the Riders first album with Kid Thomas and Manny Paul. It sold for $360. When, then, Nina Rimington decided to move to America, she raised the plane fare for herself and her children by selling her Jazz Crusade record collection.

There is a discotheque in Lyon, France called B. C. Blues. For over a generation it has featured Jazz Crusade recordings almost exclusively. . . for dancing.

There has even been a mythology built up around Jazz Crusade. Lazy reviewers and critics have concocted their own versions of events, of which they have no direct knowledge, apparently to maintain their status as "experts." Not one of them ever asked for the facts. They preferred to make them up as they went along. Now, with this book the record has been set straight at last.

There is no intentional confabulation in this book. It is the true story of the events as they occurred. There are a few things I left out regarding personal feuds within the band, womanizing and, in at least one case, manizing, or small things that might be of embarrassment to individuals, because they are inconsequential to the sweep of the story. Essentially it is complete and accurate and will stand the tests of scrutiny and time. Jazz Crusade meandered along through Connecticut, Texas, New Orleans and finally emptied its silt into San Francisco Bay; I trust doing no harm to its ecology. I sailed along the whole way, the only one to buy the round trip ticket. Others got on and off at stops along the way.

In 1984, Orwell's year, I did what I swore I would never do. I pulled my dusty old trombone case out from under the bed and oiled the slide. I hope that doesn't mean another book twenty years from now.

As I have repeatedly said, and will say again and again, the ONLY things of importance in jazz are the recordings. The story behind their making will, I hope, be of interest to you; which is why I have told it. But it is the recordings that count. A hundred years from now, people, perhaps only a few, will still be listening to the Jazzology Poll Winners, Big Jim's Little Six and the December Band on some audio technology unknown to us today. Robinson will still be pumping brass. Kid Thomas will still be outraging listeners with his unorthodoxies. George Lewis will still haunt the souls of those who hear that deep, broad tone. Handy will still raise hackles about his place in, or out of, the style. The last banjo on planet Earth may well reside on display in some museum case between the glass harmonica and the lute, but somewhere jazz fans will still argue over who was its master: Lawrence Marrero or Creole George Guesnon. But, and listen because this is the most important of all, somewhere, in France, or on Mars, or in Japan, or maybe even in Bridgeport, Connecticut, a group of youngsters will be trying their damndest to copy every note they hear on those records and hoping that people will listen. They will have started their own Jazz Crusade.

Big Bill Bissonnette Cover
Mississippi Rag
March 1986

Automobile License Plate
Bill Bissonnette
State of Connecticut

Regrets, I Have A Few ...

I made many mistakes along the way of the JAZZ CRUSADE. That is to be expected when one is, how did George Guesnon put it?, oh yes, "young and stupid." The only regrets I have are for the recording sessions I might have done and didn't, or in changes I could have made to the ones I did. There are, of course, many New Orleans jazzmen I would have liked to record and had neither time nor money such as: Pete Bocage, Avery Howard, Albert Warner, Eddie Sommers, Joe Watkins, Dave Oxley (did anyone get him?), Paul Barbarin, Mile' Barnes, Wilbert Tillman and others. But the sessions I let slip through my fingers are the ones that haunt me:

** I should have added Israel Gorman to the Algiers Stompers session I did in New Orleans. He would have added significantly to the recording and he was THE man I miss recording more than any other.

**I should have recorded a session with Kid Thomas, Edmond Hall and Zutty Singleton with members of the Riders. It would have been so easy to do and I never did.

**I should have bootlegged a concert recording with Billie and DeDe Pierce with the Easy Riders. It was a great tour and should have been recorded, even if never released.

**I should have added Pops Foster and Alton Purnell to the California Kid Thomas recording session.

**I should have tried to arrange the recording session with Lu Watters and Albert Nicholas. I didn't know where Nicholas was at the time but it would have been an interesting session.

**I should have recorded Capt. John Handy and George Probert with a good, hot rhythm section.

Photo
Miscellany

1. Bill Bissonnette & Jim Cullum Jr. first band in San Antonio, Texas.

2. George Lewis and the Easy Riders Jazz Band at the Ambassador Restaurant in Hamden Connecticut. (Robert C. Bissonnette photo)

3. The Reception Brass Band meets the Easy Riders at New Orleans International airport. (Sue Griffith photo)

4. Dick Griffith

5. Mouldy Dick McCarthy

6. Jim "Tut" Tutunjian (Ed Lawless photo)

7. Big Bill Bissonnette (Ed Lawless photo)

8. Big Bill Bissonnette (drums)

9. Easy Riders Jazz Band - 1985: Big Bill Bissonnete (tb), Bob Shallue (pn), Jim Tutunjian (sbs), Bob Lasprogato (dm), Paul Boehmke (reeds).

10. Paul Boehmke, Big Bill Bissonnette - Lyon, France. (Michele Chalandon photo)

11. Big Bill Bissonnette, Paul Boehmke with Captain Flapscat - Lyon, France. (Christian Genin photo)

12. Marie Dandreiux, France's leading lady drummer and Big Bill Bissonnette.

13. Big Bill Bissonnette signing autographs - Ascona, Switzerland 1986.

14. Big Bill Bissonnette and the German Friends: Tom Schilp (dm), Hans Beck (tp), Adolph Klapproth (cl). (Fredrich Hachenberg photo)

15. Big Bill Bissonnette and Paul Boehmke at "Dr. Jazz", Dusseldorf, Germany. (Wolfgang Kubiak photo)

Bill Bissonnette, Jim Cullum Jr.: First Band

George Lewis & the Easy Riders Jazz Band

THE "RECEPTION" BRASS BAND

L-R: KID THOMAS VALENTINE, SAMMY PENN, ALECS BIGARD, PUNCH MILLER, WORTHIA "SHOBOY" THOMAS, PAUL "POLO" BARNES, (driver), BOOKER T GLASS, KID SHEIK COLA, BIG JIM ROBINSON, EMANUEL PAUL. (band assembled to welcome members of the EASY RIDERS JAZZ BAND to New Orleans. 6 May 1967 - New Orleans International Airport.)

The Reception Brass Band

Dick "Griff" Griffith

Mouldy Dick McCarthy

Jim "Tut" Tutunjian

Big Bill Bissonnette

Big Bill Bissonnette

Easy Riders Jazz Band 1985: Big Bill Bissonnette, Bob Shallue, Jim Tutunjian, Bob Lasprogato, Paul Boehmke

Paul Boehmke, Big Bill Bissonnette: Lyon, France 1985

Big Bill Bissonnette, Paul Boehmke with Captain Flapscat
Lyon, France 1985

Marie Dandrieux, Big Bill Bissonnette: France 1986

Big Bill Bissonnette: Ascona, Switzerland 1986

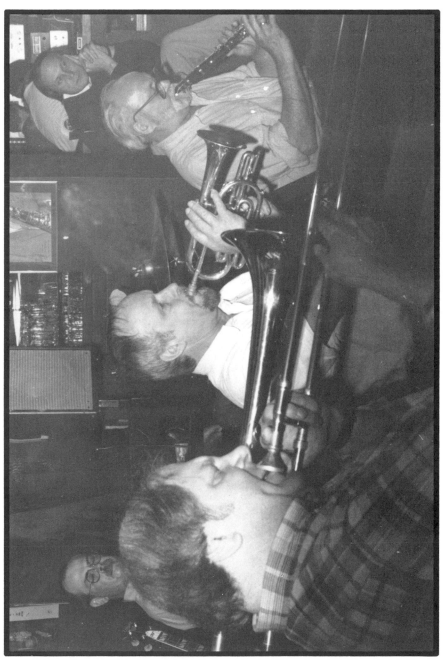

Big Bill Bissonnette and the "German Friends"
Tom Schilp (dm), Hans Beck (tp), Adolph Klapproth (cl)

Big Bill Bissonnette & Paul Boehmke
Lous Dassen's DR. JAZZ, Dusseldorf, Germany

DISCOGRAPHY

Listed chronologically by year, are the recording sessions I personally produced. These contain personnel and songs.

Also listed, just by title, are sessions released on JAZZ CRUSADE which were produced by others.

1962

NEW ORLEANS JAZZ - UPTOWN STYLE
THE EASY RIDERS JAZZ BAND

December 1962. Bridgeport, Ct. Bill Bissonnette (tb), Bob Fargo (tp), Bill Connell (cl), Noel Kalet [Kaletsky] (cl), Bill Sinclair (p) Earl Capron (bn), Dick McCarthy (sbs), Art Pulver (dm)

Sometime My Burden's So Hard To Bear, Ice Cream, When My Dreamboat Comes Home, I Shall Not Be Moved, Doctor Jazz, You Always Hurt The One You Love, It's A Long Way To Tipperary, Willie The Weeper, Chimes Blues, Joe Avery's Piece.

JAZZ CRUSADE JC-1001

1963

MY LIFE WILL BE SWEETER SOMEDAY
THE EASY RIDERS JAZZ BAND

May 1963. Bridgeport, Ct. Bill Bissonnette (tb), Bob Fargo (tp), Noel Kalet (cl), Bill Sinclair (p), Dick McCarthy (sbs), Dave Duquette (bn), Art Pulver (dm)

Make Me A Pallet On The Floor, Over In The Gloryland, Take My Hand Precious Lord, When You Wore A Tulip, Jazzin' Babies Blues, Walk Through The Streets Of The City, The Bucket's Got A Hole In It, Don't Go Way Nobody, The Bells Of St. Mary's, My Life Will Be Sweeter Someday.

JAZZ CRUSADE JC-1002

1963

CLASSIC DIXIELAND - THE GOOD TIME SIX
JAZZ CRUSADE JC-1003

TRADITIONAL JAZZ AROUND THE WORLD
JAZZ CRUSADE JC-1004

GEORGE LEWIS CLASSICS - SAMMY RIMINGTON
JAZZ CRUSADE JC-1005

THE GOTHIC JAZZ BAND
JAZZ CRUSADE JC-1006

1964

NEW ORLEANS RENAISSANCE - A MONO SAMPLER
JAZZ CRUSADE JC-2001

1963

KID THOMAS, EMANUEL PAUL

AND THE EASY RIDERS JAZZ BAND

May 20, 1964. WTIC-TV studio, Hartford, CT.

Kid Thomas Valentine (tp), Emanuel Paul (t-s), Bill Bissonnette (tb), Noel Kalet (cl), Fred Vigorito (tp), Dick Griffith (bn), Dick McCarthy (sbs), Bud Larson (p), Art Pulver (dm)

(w/Thomas) Victory Walk, Eh! Las Bas, I Can't Escape From You, Just A Closer Walk With Thee, (w/Vigorito) Old Rugged Cross, Bye And Bye, Sing On, Hindustan.

JAZZ CRUSADE JC-2002

not issued: In The Mood

KID SHEIK IN ENGLAND

JAZZ CRUSADE JC-2003; reissue G.H.B.-187

1964

THE INTERNATIONAL JAZZ BAND

July 23, 1964. Actors Colony Inn, Derby, Ct.

Kid Thomas Valentine (tp), Emanuel Paul (t-s), Bill Bissonnette (tb), Sammy Rimington (cl), Bill Sinclair (p), Dick Griffith (bn), Dick McCarthy (sbs), Barry Martyn (dm)

(vol. I) Introduction Blues, Put On Your Old Gray Bonnet,
Milk Cow Blues, Walking With The King, Marie, Pretend, Burgundy St. Blues, Panama Rag.

G.H.B.-20

(vol. II) Kid Thomas Boogie Woogie, Hindustan, Old Rugged
Cross, I'm Confessin', Muskat Ramble, When The Saints Go
Marching In, That's A'Plenty.

G.H.B.-21; (K.T. Boogie only: CTJC-1)

Unissued masters: I Can't Escape From You, Battle Hymn of
the Republic

1964

VICTORIA SPIVEY

AND THE EASY RIDERS JAZZ BAND

August 9, 1964. Palace Theater, Wallingford, Ct.
Victoria Spivey (v), Bill Bissonnette (tb), Fred Vigorito (tp),
Noel Kalet (cl), Bill Sinclair (p), Dick Griffith (bn), Dick Mc
Carthy (sbs), Art Pulver (dm)

(w/Spivey) Sister Kate, See See Rider, Careless Love, Mama's
Gone Goodbye, I Ain't Gonna Give Nobody None Of This
Jelly Roll

G.H.B.-17

(omit Spivey) not issued: Mama Inez, Rose Room, Get Out Of
Here.

1965

GEORGE LEWIS

AND THE EASY RIDERS JAZZ BAND

January 26, 1965. Ambassador Restaurant, Hamden, Ct.

George Lewis (cl), Bill Bissonnette (tb), Fred Vigorito (tp),

Noel Kalet (cl, p), Dick Griffith (bn), Dick Mc Carthy (sbs),

Art Pulver (dm)

Jambalaya, Saturday Night Function, I Shall Not Be Moved,

Creole Love Call, Just Because[v-Bissonnette], St. Louis Blues,

Corrine Corinna, Just A Little While To Stay Here, Should I,

Now Is The Hour

G.H.B.-29

St. Phillip St. Breakdown[Kalet-2nd cl], Pork Chops, A Shanty

In Old Shanty Town, Ice Cream, I'm Confessin', On A

Cocoanut Island, Walking With The King, Mood Indigo, Girl

Of My Dreams[v-Bissonnette], Lonesome Road

PEARL-PLP-2; reissue G.H.B.-39

GEORGE LEWIS & EASY RIDERS JAZZ BAND (cont.)

Bill Baily

CT.TRAD.JAZZ CLUB-CTJC-1

not issued: Burgundy St. Blues, Canal St. Blues, Tiger Rag,

Moose March, Bugle Call Rag, Redwing [masters destroyed]

1965

SLOW DRAG'S BUNCH

April 21, 1965. Preservation Hall, New Orleans, La.

Jim Robinson (tb), Albert Burbank (cl), Fred Vigorito (tp),

Don Ewell (p), George Guesnon (bn), Alcide Pavageau (sbs),

Bill Bissonnette (dm)

Move The Body Over, Struttin' With Some Barbeque, Little

Brown Jug, I Can't Escape From You, Brahm's Cradle Song,

Creole Song, Stack-O-Lee Blues, Climax Rag

JAZZ CRUSADE JC-2005

Alternate takes on all above.

G.H.B.-54

1965

THE JAZZOLOGY POLL WINNERS

April 22, 1965. Preservation Hall. New orleans, La. George
Lewis (cl), Kid Thomas Valentine (tp), Jim Robinson (tb), Don
Ewell (p), George Guesnon (bn), Alcide Pavageau (sbs), Josiah
Frazer (dm)

Sentimental Journey, Ciribiribin, Home Sweet Home, Lil Liza
Jane, All Of Me, Rose Room, Sheik Of Araby, When I Grow
Too Old To Dream, You Always Hurt The One You Love
        JAZZ CRUSADE JC-2004; reissue: G.H.B.-200
Alternate takes on all above except: All Of Me
and add: Golden Leaf Strut"
                G.H.B.-30

1965

KID THOMAS AND HIS ALGIERS STOMPERS

April 23, 1965. Preservation Hall, New Orleans, La.

Kid Thomas Valentine (tp), Louis Nelson (tb), Emanuel Paul (t-s), Octave Crosby (p), George Guesnon (bn), Joseph Butler (sbs), Sammy Penn (dm)

My Blue Heaven, In The Mood, Stardust, Clarinet Marmalade, Gettysburg March, Alexander's Ragtime Band, Summertime, Algiers Strut.

JAZZ CRUSADE JC-2006; reissue:G.H.B.-80

Alternates on all above except: My Blue Heaven

UNISSUED

THE EASY RIDERS JAZZ BAND

Summer, 1965. Moose Lodge Hall. Stamford, Ct.

Bill Bissonnette (tb), Fred Vigorito (tp), Sammy Rimington (cl), Bill Sinclair (p), Dick Griffith (bn), Dick McCarthy (sbs), Art Pulver (dm)

Four Or Five Times[omit Bissonnette], That Teasin' Rag[omit Vigorito], Bugle Boy March, I Walk The Line.

G.H.B.-17

Lead Me Saviour

CT. TRAD. JAZZ CLUB CTJC-1

Other material on same concert date

UNISSUED - MASTERS DESTROYED

1965

THE DECEMBER BAND

December 3, 1965. Moose Lodge Hall, Stamford, Ct.

Kid Thomas Valentine (tp), Jim Robinson (tb), Capt. John

Handy (a-s), Sammy Rimington (cl), Bill Sinclair (p), Dick

Griffith (bn), Dick McCarthy (sbs), Sammy Penn (dm)

(vol. I) Introduction Blues[intro Bissonnette], Lil Liza Jane, Ice

Cream, You Are My Sunshine, Someday Sweetheart, Bugle

Boy March.

JAZZ CRUSADE JC-2007; reissue: G.H.B.-197

(vol. II) High Society, Careless Love, Handy's Boogie, Uptown

Bumps, You Tell Me Your Dream, Just A Closer Walk With

Thee.

JAZZ CRUSADE JC-2008; reissue: G.H.B.-198

(continued next page)

(vol. III) Sleepy Time Gal, Oh Lady Be Good, Peg Of My Heart, Washington And Lee Swing, St. Louis Blues, Smile Darn You Smile.

CENTER CLP-2; reissue: BIOGRAPH CEN-2

When The Saints Go Marching In, Burgundy St. Blues

UNISSUED - MASTERS DESTROYED

DECEMBER BAND (cont.)

December 4, 1965. WTIC-TV studio. Hartford, Ct.

Same personnel: Television taping.

DECEMBER BAND (cont.)

December 6, 1965. West Haven Motor Inn, West Haven, Ct.

Same personnel

(vol. I) Introduction Blues[intro Bissonnette], Hindustan, Sister Kate, Who's Sorry Now, I Can't Escape From You, Washington And Lee Swing.

G.H.B.-41

DECEMBER BAND (cont.)

(vol. II) Chinatown My Chinatown, I'm Alone Because I Love You, Mack The Knife, Bill Baily, Someday Sweetheart, Ice Cream.

G.H.B.-42

(vol. III) Bourbon St. Parade, Moonlight And Roses, Come To The Mardi Gras, Ting-A-Ling, Cap's Blues, Tiger Rag, When The Saints Go Marching In.

G.H.B.-43

1965

THE EASY RIDERS JAZZ BAND

Aug. 10,1965 - January 1966 Various sessions

Bill Bissonnette (tb), Fred Vigorito (tp), Sammy Rimington (cl), Bill Sinclair (p), Dick Griffith (bn), Dick McCarthy (sbs), Art Pulver (dm)

Java, If I Ever Cease To Love, Ory's Creole Trombone, The Sheik Of Araby, Early Hours, Chimes Blues, Algier's Strut, St. James Infirmary, Just A Closer Walk With Thee, Ciribiribin, Tin Roof Blues, It's Tite Like That, Trouble In Mind, Gettysburg March, Sheik of Araby, Blues for Jimmy Yancy

UNISSUED

1966

THE EUREKA BRASS BAND

February 25, 1966. Glorietta Manor, Bridgeport, Ct.

Percy Humphrey (tp), Peter Bocage (tp), Milton Batiste (tp),

Willie Humphrey (cl), Emanuel Paul (t-s), Earl Humphrey (tb),

Oscar Henry (tb), William Grent Brown (sous), Chester Jones

(sdm), Booker T. Glass (bdm)

Jambalaya, Nearer My God To Thee, Oh Didn't He Ramble,

St. Louis Blues.

JAZZOLOGY JCE-35

1966

THE EASY RIDERS JAZZ BAND

February 25, 1966. Glorietta Manor, Bridgeport, Ct.
Bill Bissonnette (tb), Fred Vigorito (tp), Sammy Rimington
(cl), Bill Sinclair (p), Dick Griffith (bn), Dick McCarthy (sbs),
Art Pulver (dm), Georgia Louis (v)

Bugle Boy March, Dead Man Blues, Over The Waves, I'm
Alone Because I Love You, Summertime, It Feels So Good,
Tiger Rag, Climax Rag, After You've Gone, Lead Me Saviour,
Rose Room.

UNISSUED

1966

REDWING

March 13, 1966. Moose Lodge Hall. Stamford, Ct.
Kid Thomas Valentine (tp), Bill Bissonnette (tb), Sammy
Rimington (cl,t-s,a-s), Bill Sinclair (p), Dick Griffith (bn), Dick
McCarthy (sbs), Art Pulver (dm)

Redwing, Algiers Waltz, I'm Looking Over A Four Leaf
Clover, It Had To Be You, Exactly Like You, I'm Alone
Because I love You, Shake It And Break It, Everybody Loves
Somebody[omit Bissonnette], Walk Through The Streets Of
The City.

     JAZZ CRUSADE JC-2009; reissue: G.H.B.-189
Unissued masters: Panama Rag, When You're Smiling, Isle of
Capri.

ECHOES FROM NEW ORLEANS

CREOLE GEORGE GUESNON

JAZZ CRUSADE JC-2011

1966

VERY HANDY

May, 1966, Syncron Sound Studio, Wallingford, Ct.

Capt. John Handy (a-s), Bill Bissonnette (tb), Clive Wilson (tp), Sammy Rimington (cl-gu), Bill Sinclair (p), Dick Griffith (bn), Dick McCarthy (sbs), Art Pulver (dm)

Give Me Your Telephone Number, Walking By The River[guitar Rimington], On Moonlight Bay, Chicken (Ain't Nothin' But A Bird), Golden Leaf Strut, Mahogany Hall Stomp, Easy Riding, I'll Always Be In Love With You.

JAZZ CRUSADE JC-2013

Unissued masters: Running Wild, Get Out of Here, Rose Room, When I Grow Too Old to Dream

----

CREOLE GEORGE GUESNON'S SECRET SESSIONS

(Scheduled as JAZZ CRUSADE JC-2012: UNISSUED)

1966

ON TOUR

KID THOMAS, SAMMY PENN & EASY RIDERS

June 24, 1966. Essex Yacht Club Boat Shed, Essex, Ct.

Kid Thomas Valentine (tp), Bill Bissonnette (tb), Sammy

Rimington (cl,a-s), Bill Sinclair (p), Dick Griffith (bn), Dick

McCarthy (sbs), Sammy Penn (dm)

Basin St. Blues, Isle Of Capri.

June 25, 1966. Huntington Grange Hall, Huntington, Ct.

Darktown Strutters Ball, Ballin' The Jack, Mack The Knife,

Honeysuckle Rose, Tin Roof Blues, Panama Rag.

JAZZ CRUSADE JC-2014-CS

Unissued masters: Jada, When My Dreamboat Comes Home

1966

NEW ORLEANS RASCALS IN AMERICA

July 29, 1966. Holiday Inn, Meriden, Ct.

Ryoichi Kawai (cl), Keitaro Shiga (tp), Tsunetami Fukuda (tb),

Satoshi Adachi (p), Junichi Kawai (bn), Mitsuo Yano (dm)

[on Bugle Boy March only add: Jim Robinson (tb), Kid Sheik

Cola (tp), Bill Bissonnette (tb), Sammy Rimington (sx), Dick

Griffith (bn), Dick McCarthy (sbs)]

Yaaka Hula Hickey Dula, Sukura Sukura, Bourbon St. Parade,

Love Songs Of The Nile, Song On The Shore, Clarinet Mar-

malade, Baby Won't You Please Come Home, Bugle Boy

March.

(Scheduled as JC-1007: UNISSUED)

All other tracks of concert: MASTERS DESTROYED

1966

BIG JIM'S LITTLE SIX

July 31, 1966, Moose Lodge Hall, Stamford, Ct.

Jim Robinson (tb), George "Kid Sheik" Cola (tp), Sammy

Rimington (cl, a-s,Eb-cl), Dick Griffith (bn), Dick McCarthy

(sbs), Bill Bissonnette (dm)

(vol. I) South, Back Porch, Bye And Bye[v-Robinson], Bye Bye

Blackbird, In The Gutter, Song Of The Islands, Lord Lord

Lord, What A Friend We Have In Jesus, Dippermouth Blues.

JAZZ CRUSADE JC-2010-CS; reissue: G.H.B.-185

(vol. II) Dipsey Doodle, My Darling Nellie Grey, Whooping

Blues, Birth Of The Blues, Back Home Again In Indiana,

When You And I Were Young Maggie, Down By The River-

side[v Sheik], Angry, Hindustan

G.H.B.-76

(cont. next page)

BIG JIM'S LITTLE SIX

(vol. III) [Omit Sheik all tracks - released under title: 1944

REVISITED]

Beautiful Dreamer, San Jacinto Stomp, Moose Hall Blues,

When You Wore A Tulip, Nearer My God To Thee, Faraway

Blues, My Life Will Be Sweeter Someday, The Valley Of

Death, Royal Telephone(Telephone To Glory)

     JAZZ CRUSADE JC-2015-CS; G.H.B.-196

Unissued masters:(from July 29, 1966 concert) Marie, Old

Gray Bonnet.

1966

THE MOULDY FIVE

September, 1966. Wallingford, Ct.

Sammy Rimington (cl), Bill Sinclair (p), Dick Griffith (bn), Dick McCarthy (sbs), Bill Bissonnette (dm)

(vol. I) Tie Me To Your Apron Strings Again, Favorite Rag, You Were Meant For Me, I Want To Be Happy, Londonderry Air, In The Good Old Summertime, Felicity Rag, Move The Body Over.

G.H.B.-181

(vol.II) Lead Me Saviour, Chloe, The Second Line, Louisiana, Porter's Love Song, High Society, Darkness On The Delta, San.

G.H.B.-182

1966

LOVE SONGS OF THE NILE

KID THOMAS & THE EASY RIDERS

September, 1966. Wallingford, Ct.

Kid Thomas Valentine (tp), Bill Bissonnette (tb), Sammy Rimington (cl), Bill Sinclair (p), Dick Griffith (bn), Dick McCarthy (sbs), Art Pulver (dm)

Love Songs Of The Nile, Ceilito Lindo, Pagan Love Song, One Night, The World Is Waiting For The Sunrise, Tiger Rag, Bells Of St. Marys, Bugle Call Rag, Somewhere Over The Rainbow, I'll Be Glad When You're Dead You Rascal You.

JAZZ CRUSADE JC-2019; reissue: G.H.B.-183

Alternate master: Bugle Call Rag. Other alternates: DESTROYED.

1967

OH! LADY BE GOOD

February 26, 1967. Moose Lodge Hall, Stamford, Ct.

Punch Miller (tp), Albert Burbank (cl), Jimmy Archey (tb),

Dick Griffith (bn), Dick McCarthy (sbs), Sammy Penn (dm)

Sister Kate, Jambalaya, Shake That Thing, Mama Don't Allow,

Oh Lady Be Good, Shine, I Believe I Can Make It By Myself,

Happy Birthday Kenneth.

JAZZ CRUSADE JC-2016-CS

Unissued masters: Old Gray Bonnet, Rita's Blues, Shanty In

Old Shantytown, Sheik of Araby, That's My Home, Home

Sweet Home, San.

Unissued second session: (Same personnel except Bill Bisson-

nette replaces Jimmy Archey. Febr.25, 1967 concert) Down By

The Levee, The Sheik of Araby

(complete session to be re-released as GHB BCD-310)

1967

KID THOMAS AT MOOSE HALL

March 11, 1967. Moose Lodge Hall, Stamford, Ct.

Kid Thomas Valentine (tp), Bill Connell (cl), Dick Griffith (bn), Dick McCarthy (sbs), Bill Bissonnette (dm)

Careless Love, I Want To Be Happy, On A Cocoanut Island, Jambalaya, Old Rugged Cross, Old Gray Bonnet, St. Louis Blues, Till We Meet Again, When The Saints Go Marching In, Just A Closer Walk With Thee, Marie, St. James Infirmary.

JAZZ CRUSADE JC-2018-CS

Unissued masters: Washington and Lee Swing, Tom's Blues, Just A Little While To Stay Here.

(complete session to be re-released as GHB BCD-305)

1967

ALCORN, BARNES, BIGARD

April 3, 1967. Moose Lodge Hall, Stamford, Ct.

Alvin Alcorn (tp), Paul Barnes (cl,a-s), Bill Bissonnette (tb),

Dick Griffith (bn), Dick McCarthy (sbs), Alecs Bigard (dm)

Bourbon St. Parade, Blueberry Hill, Maryland My Maryland,

Down In Honky Tonk Town, Yearning, Beale St. Blues, War

Cloud, Mood Indigo, The Sheik Of Araby.

JAZZ CRUSADE JC-2017-CS

Unissued masters: Bogalusa Strut, Yearning #2.

1967

DANCE HALL DAYS

September 17, 1967. Moose Lodge Hall, Stamford, Ct.
Kid Thomas Valentine (tp), Emanuel Paul (t-s), Bill Connell
(cl)[vol.I only Dick Griffith (bn), Jim Tutunjian (sbs), Sammy
Penn (dm), Bill Bissonnette (tb)[vol.II only]

(vol. I) Rum And Coca Cola, Babyface, When You And I Were
Young Maggie, The Object Of My Affection, Pennies From
Heaven, I'm Forever Blowing Bubbles, I'll See You In My
Dreams

(vol. II) Washington And Lee Swing, Rose Of Old San Antone,
Lonesome Road, Corrine Corrina, Coquette, Linger Awhile,
You Always Hurt The One You Love.

UNISSUED

1969

KID THOMAS IN CALIFORNIA

February 17, 1969. Earthquake McGoon's, San Francisco, Ca.

Kid Thomas Valentine (tp), Capt. John Handy (a-s), Bill Bissonnette (tb), Cyril Bennett (p), Dick Griffith (bn), Jim Tutunjian (sbs), Sammy Penn (dm)

St. James Infirmary, At The Mardi Gras, Say Si Si, Joe Avery's Piece, Over the Waves, Rose Room, Just A Little While To Stay Here, See See Rider, Oh! Lady Be Good.(3 takes each)

March 10, 1969. South San Francisco, Ca.

Same personnel except add: Carol Leigh (v)

I Wonder Where My Easy Rider's Gone, Make Me A Pallet On The Floor.

UNISSUED:(to be released as GHB BCD-296)

1969

LIVE AT EARTHQUAKE MCGOON'S

July 19, 1969. San Francisco, Ca.

Alvin Alcorn (tp), Paul Barnes (cl, a-s), Bill Bissonnette (tb), James "Sing" Miller (p), Jim Tutunjian (sbs), Alec Bigard (dm)

I Left My Heart In San Francisco, Ting-A-Ling, Muskat Ramble, It Feels So Good, Forgive Me, That's A' Plenty, Clarinet Marmalade, Lil Liza Jane, It's A Sin To Tell A Lie, Bugle Boy March, Royal Garden Blues, Old Spinning Wheel, Just A Closer Walk With Thee, Washington & Lee Swing, Indian Love Call, Basin St. Blues, Linger Awhile, Red Sails In The Sunset, Swing Low Sweet Chariot, Who Threw The Whiskey In The Well, Bill Baily, Whole World In His Hands, Amen, Old Rocking Chair, Say Si Si.

UNISSUED: (to be released as GHB BCD-238/239)

1969

PUNCH AND HANDY'S CALIFORNIA CRUSADERS

August 9, 1969. McGoon's, San Francisco, Ca.

Punch Miller (tp), Capt. John Handy (a-s), Bill Bissonnette (tb), James "Sing" Miller (p), Jim Tutunjian (sbs), Sammy Penn (dm)

(vol. I) Joe Avery's Piece, My Poor Nellie Gray, Girl Of My Dreams[v Penn], Darktown Strutter's Ball, Somebody Stole My Gal[v Punch], My Bucket's Got A Hole In It[v Sing], Tuck Me To Sleep In My Old Kentucky Home[v Punch], Hindustan.

G.H.B.-191

(vol. II) Sister Kate, Exactly Like You[v Punch], I'm Alone Because I Love You[v Sing], Shake It And Break It, I Like It Like That[v Sing], Nagasaki[v Punch], You Can Depend On Me/That's My Home[v Punch], Milneburg Joys.

G.H.B.-192

(cont. next page)

PUNCH & HANDY CALIF.CRUSADERS (cont.)

(vol. III) Ice Cream, Jelly Jelly Jelly, Careless Love[v Penn],
Darktown Strutter's Ball #2[v Punch], Oh How I Miss You
Tonight[v Sing], Basin St. Blues, My Blue Heaven[v Sing],
Happy Birthday[v Sing], When The Saints Go Marching In[v
Punch/Sing/Penn], Now Is The Hour[v Sing]

G.H.B.-193

1985

BILL BISSONNETTE & THE

ORIGINAL EASY RIDERS JAZZ BAND

September 2, 1985. TNA Studio, Wallingford, Ct.

Bill Bissonnette (tb), Paul Boehmke (cl,t-s), Bob Shallue (p),

Jim Tutunjian (sbs), Bob Lasprogato (dm)

Perdido St. Blues, Bring It On Home To Grandma, The

Mooche, Deed I Do, Black Gal You Better Use Your Head,

Get Out Of Here, Sweet Mama, Short Dress Gal, Apex Blues,

Love Songs Of The Nile.

MEMORIES ME07 (French)

As above and add: Shreveport Stomp, Wall St. Wail

SPECIAL REQUEST CAS-03 (Cassette only)

Lead Me Saviour, The Second Line

UNISSUED

1986

RHYTHM IS OUR BUSINESS/

ROCKIN' N' RHYTHM

September 5, 1986. TNA Studio, Wallingford, Ct.

Bill Bissonnette (tb), Paul Boehmke (cl,t-s), Bill Sinclair (p),

Jim Tutunjian (sbs), Bob Lasprogato (dm)

(vol. I) Bugle Call Rag, Dallas Blues, That's A' Plenty, What

Am I Living For, Rhythm Is Our Business, Big Chief battle-Ax,

The Bells Of St. Marys, Tie Me To Your Apron Strings Again,

Beale St. Blues, Running Wild.

      SPECIAL REQUEST CAS-04 (Cassette Only)

(vol. II) Girl Of My Dreams, In The Upper Garden, On A

Cocoanut Island, Dead Man Blues, Chicago Rhythm, Rockin'

N' Rhythm, I'll Take The South, Black Cat Moan, Isabella,

Someday Sweetheart

      SPECIAL REQUEST CAS-05 (Cassette Only)

1985

LIVE IN LYON

November 21, 22, 24. Lyon, France.

Bill Bissonnette (tb), Paul Boehmke (cl), Philippe "Mozart" Harbonnier (pn), and SWEET MARY CAT: Christian "Kiki" Genin (ct), Catherine "Cat Cat" Gerdil (bn), Guillaume Gerdil (sbs), Marie "Zuttyface" Dandrieux (dm).

Bells of St. Marys

Bissonnette, Boehmke, Harbonnier, Hannes Anrig (tp), and CAPTAIN FLAPSCAT: Denis Staub (bn), Pierre Scharff (sbs), Guy Vial (dm).

Careless Love, Little While to Stay Here, Old Grey Bonnet

Bissonnette (dm), Boehmke, Genin, Harbonnier, Staub, Scharff, Denis Limonne (tb), J-Philippe "Pif" Roybier (cl/sx)

Say Si Si

Bissonnette, Boehmke, Captain Flapscat, Marc Molinier (bn), Sauveur Rodriguez (pn), Harbonnier (ct)

Tiger Rag

   JAZZOGIE JLP1 (94, rue du repos-69007, Lyon, France)

1989

BIG BILL, PAUL AND THEIR GERMAN FRIENDS

October 1989, Idar-Oberstein, Germany

Bill Bissonnette (tb), Paul Boehmke (cl/sx), Hans Beck (tp), Adolf Klapproth (cl), Manny Buhne (bn), Ralf Koschnicke (sous), Tom Schilp (dm)

Bugle Boy March, Mood Indigo/Creole Love Call, Old Rugged Cross, Careless Love, Just A Little While to Stay Here

omit Koschnicke & Buhne. Add Hans-Werner Grunewald (bn), Andreas Brinkmann (sbs)

When My Dreamboat Comes Home, Milk Cow Blues, Lonesome Road

Same except omit Grunewald & Brinkmann. Add Buhne & Koschnicke

Exactly Like You, Short Number, Tin Roof Blues, Marie, SPECIAL REQUEST CAS-06; CD-06

The Album Covers

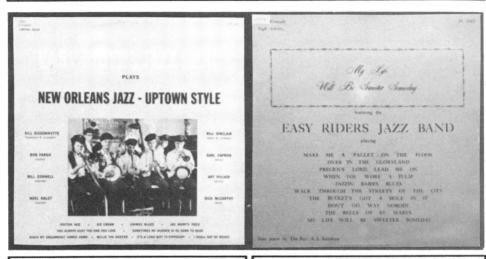

New Orleans Jazz-Uptown Style Easy Riders Jazz Band Jazz Crusade JC-1001	My Life Will Be Sweeter Someday Easy Riders Jazz Band Jazz Crusade JC-1002
Classic Dixieland Good Time Six Jazz Crusade JC-1003	Trad. Jazz Around The World Various Artists Jazz Crusade JC-1004

The Album Covers

George Lewis Classics Sammy Rimington Jazz Crusade JC-1005	The Gothic Jazz Band Jazz Crusade JC-1006
New Orleans Renaissance Various Artists Jazz Crusade JC-2001	Kid Thomas/Emanuel Paul & the Easy Riders Jazz Band Jazz Crusade JC-2002

The Album Covers

Kid Sheik In England	The Jazzology Poll Winners
Jazz Crusade JC-2003	Jazz Crusade JC-2004/GHB-200

Slow Drag's Bunch Slow Drag Pavageau Jazz Crusade JC-2005	The Algiers Stompers Kid Thomas Valentine Jazz Crusade JC-2006/GHB-80

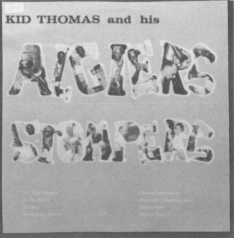

The Album Covers

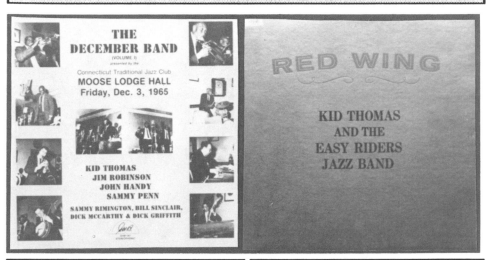

The December Band - Vol. I/II Jazz Crusade JC-2007/8 GHB-197/8	Redwing - Kid Thomas & the Easy Riders Jazz Band Jazz Crusade JC-2009
Big Jim's Little Six Jim Robinson/Kid Sheik Jazz Crusade JC-2010	Echoes From New Orleans Creole George Guesnon Jazz Crusade JC-2011

The Album Covers

Creole George
Guesnon's
Secret Sessions
(unissued)

Unissued	Very Handy - Capt. John Handy
(Creole George's Secret Sessions)	& the Easy Riders Jazz Band
Jazz Crusade JC-2012	Jazz Crusade JC-2013

On Tour	1944 Revisited
Kid Thomas/Sammy Penn	Jim Robinson
Jazz Crusade JC-2014	Jazz Crusade JC-2015

The   Album   Covers

Oh! Lady Be Good Punch Miller/Jimmy Archey Jazz Crusade JC-2016	Alcorn, Barnes, Bigard Jazz Crusade JC-2017
At Moose Hall Kid Thomas Valentine Jazz Crusade JC-2018	Love Songs Of The Nile Kid Thomas & the Easy Riders Jazz Crusade JC-2019

The Album Covers

Victoria Spivey & the Easy Riders Jazz Band GHB-17	The International Jazz Band I/II Kid Thomas/Manny Paul GHB-20/1
George Lewis & the Easy Riders Jazz Band GHB-29	Don Ewell In New Orleans the Jazzology Poll Winners (alt.) GHB-30

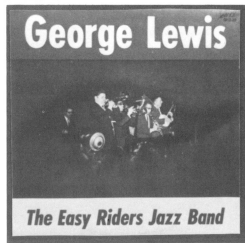

The Album Covers

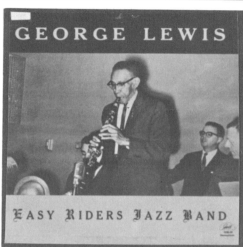

George Lewis and the Easy Riders Jazz Band - Vol. II GHB-39	All Aboard - Vol. I Capt. John Handy GHB-41
All Aboard - Vol. II Capt. John Handy GHB-42	All Aboard - Vol. III Capt. John Handy GHB-43

The Album Covers

Drag's Half Fast Jazz Band Slow Drag Pavageau GHB-54	New Orleans Stompers Kid Sheik/Jim Robinson GHB-76
The Mouldy Five - Vol. I/II Sammy Rimington GHB-181/2	Love Songs Of The Nile Kid Thomas & the Easy Riders GHB-183

The Album Covers

Big Jim's Little Six Jim Robinson GHB-185	Kid Sheik In England GHB-187
Redwing - Kid Thomas & the Easy Riders Jazz Band GHB-189	California Crusaders - I/II/III Punch Miller/Capt. John Handy GHB-191/2/3

The Album Covers

1944 Revisited **Jim Robinson** **GHB-196**	**The Brass Bands** **Eureka Brass Band** **Jazzology JCE-35**
Jazz at the Ct. Trad. Jazz Club **Various Artists** **CTJC-1**	**George Lewis** **& the Easy Riders Jazz Band** **Pearl PLP-2**

The Album Covers

| Sleepy Time Gal
The December Band (Vol.III)
Center CLP-3 | Jim Robinson's Band
The December Band (Vol.III)
Biograph CEN-2 |

| Live In Lyon
Bill Bissonnette/Paul Boehmke
Jazzogie JLP1 | Bill Bissonnette & the Original
Easy Riders Jazz Band
Memories ME07 |

The Album Covers

Big Bill Bissonnette
selects the BEST of the

Jazz Crusade

George Lewis, Big Jim Robinson, Kid Thomas,
Capt. John Handy, Victoria Spivey, Punch Miller,
Sammy Penn, Louis Nelson, Alvin Alcorn,
Polo Barnes, Kid Sheik, Sammy Penn,
Albert Burbank, Slow Drag Pavageau, Cie Frazier,
Creole George Guesnon, Alec Bigard, Sing Miller,
Manny Paul, Don Ewell, Sammy Rimington,
Carol Leigh, Dick Griffith, Mouldy Dick McCarthy
and many others playing with:
The Jazzology Poll Winners, The Algiers Stompers,
the Easy Riders Jazz Band, The Mouldy Five,
The International Jazz Band, Big Jim's Little Six,
New Orleans Rascals, The December Band

RHYTHM IS OUR BUSINESS

Big Bill Bissonnette and his
EASY RIDERS JAZZ BAND

Best Of The Jazz Crusade
Vol. I/II - Various Artists
Special Request CD-01/2

The German Friends
Bill Bissonnette/Paul Boehmke
Special Request CAS-06/CD-06

Rhythm Is Our Business - I/II/III
The Orig. Easy Riders Jazz Band
Special Request CAS-03/4/5,
CD-03

Big Bill Bissonnette / Paul Boehmke
The German Friends

Tom Schilp, Hans Beck, Adolph Klapproth, Manny Buhne,
Hans-Werner Grunewald, Ralf Koschnicke, Andreas Brinkman

EUR   USA

D

for information on
Special Request
albums, cassettes, CDs
& books contact:
Special Request
585 Pond Street
Bridgeport, CT 06606

Phone: (203) 372-0597
Fax: (203) 371-4330

Index

Index

Index

Index

Index

Index

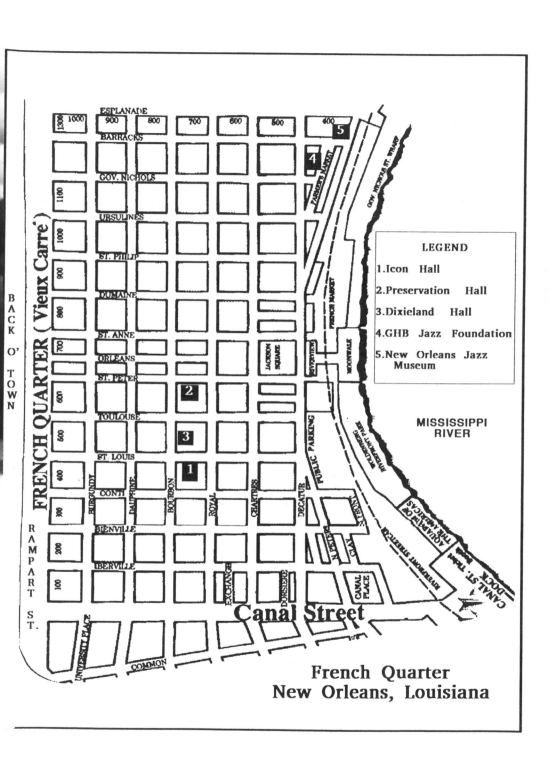

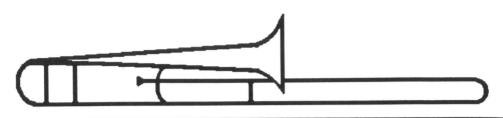

Big Bill Bissonnette
European Tours

```
85 Nov Lyon, France (3)
       Fourques, France

86 Apr Dendermonde, Belgium (2)
       Macon, France (2)

86 Jun Dendermonde, Belgium
       Ninove, Belgium
       Paris, France
       Macon, France
       Nimes, France
       Ascona, Switzerland

87 May Ninove, Belgium
       Dendermonde, Belgium
       Dusseldorf, Germany
       Bad Nauheim, Germany
       Bad Homburg, Germany
       Undenheim, Germany
       Biefeld, Germany
       Minden, Germany
       Marburg, Germany (2)
       Hannover, Germany
       Hamburg, Germany (7)

91 Oct Prague, Czechoslovakia (2)
   Nov Bratislava, Czechoslovakia (2)
       Dusseldorf, Germany (2)
       Idar-Oberstein (2)
       Darmstadt (3)
```

Big Bill Bissonnette

Big Bill Bissonnette selects the BEST of the JAZZ CRUSADE

1. BOURBON ST. PARADE - Alcorn, Barnes, Bigard
   Alvin Alcorn (tp), Paul "Polo" Barnes (cl), Big Bill Bissonnette (tb), Dick Griffith (bn), Mouldy Dick McCarthy (sbs), Alec Bigard (dm)
2. SISTER KATE - Victoria Spivey and the Easy Riders Jazz Band
   Victoria Spivey (v), Big Bill Bissonnette (tb), Fred Vigorito (ct), Noel Kalet (cl), Dick Griffith (bn), Bill Sinclair (pn), Mouldy Dick McCarthy (sbs), Art Pulver (dm)
3. KID THOMAS BOOGIE WOOGIE - The International Jazz Band
   Kid Thomas Valentine (tp), Emanuel Paul (sx), Big Bill Bissonnette (tp), Sammy Rimington (cl), Bill Sinclair (pn), Mouldy Dick McCarthy (sbs), Barry Martyn (dm)
4. STRUTTIN' WITH SOME BARBEQUE - Slow Drag's Bunch
   Big Jim Robinson (tb), Albert Burbank (cl), Fred Vigorito (ct), Don Ewell (pn), Creole George Guesnon (bn), Alcide "Slow Drag" Pavageau (sbs), Big Bill Bissonnette (dm)
5. REDWING - Kid Thomas and the Easy Riders Jazz Band
   Kid Thomas Valentine (tp), Big Bill Bissonnette (tb), Sammy Rimington (sx), Dick Griffith (bn), Bill Sinclair (pn), Mouldy Dick McCarthy (sbs), Art Pulver (dm)
6. LIL LIZA JANE - The Jazzology Poll Winners
   Kid Thomas Valentine (tp), George Lewis (cl), Big Jim Robinson (tb), Don Ewell (pn), Creole George Guesnon (bn), Alcide "Slow Drag" Pavageau (sbs), Cie Frazier (dm)
* 7. OLD GRAY BONNET - Big Jim's Little Six In Concert
   Big Jim Robinson (tb), George "Kid Sheik" Cola (tp), Sammy Rimington (cl), Dick Griffith (bn), Mouldy Dick McCarthy (sbs), Big Bill Bissonnette (dm)
8. UPTOWN BUMPS - The December Band
   Kid Thomas Valentine (tp), Big Jim Robinson (tb), Capt. John Handy (sx), Sammy Rimington (cl), Bill Sinclair (pn), Dick Griffith (bn), Mouldy Dick McCarthy (sbs), Sammy Penn (dm)
9. MY BLUE HEAVEN - Kid Thomas and his Algiers Stompers
   Kid Thomas Valentine (tp), Louis Nelson (tb), Emanuel Paul (sx), Octave Crosby (pn), Creole George Guesnon (bn), Joe "Kid Twat" Butler (sbs), Sammy Penn (dm)
10. YOU RASCAL YOU - Kid Thomas and the Easy Riders Jazz Band
   Kid Thomas Valentine (tp), Big Bill Bissonnette (tb), Sammy Rimington (cl), Dick Griffith (bn), Bill Sinclair (pn), Mouldy Dick McCarthy (sbs), Art Pulver (dm)
*11. BUGLE BOY MARCH - New Orleans Rascals, Mouldy Five, Jim Robinson, Kid Sheik
   Big Jim Robinson, Big Bill Bissonnette, Tsunetami Fukuda (tbs), Kid Sheik Cola, Keitaro Shiga (tps), Sammy Rimington (sx), Ryoichi Kawai (cl), Satoshi Adachi (pn), Dick Griffith, Junichi Kawai (bns), Mouldy Dick McCarthy (sbs), Mitsuo Yano (dm)
*12. SAY SI SI - Kid Thomas In California
   Kid Thomas Valentine (tp), Capt. John Handy (sx), Big Bill Bissonnette (tb), Dick Griffith (bn), Cyril Bennett (pn), Jim "Tut" Tutunjian (sbs), Sammy Penn (dm)
*13. MAKE ME A PALLET - Carol Leigh, Kid Thomas, Capt. John Handy, Sammy Penn
   Carol Leigh (v), Kid Thomas Valentine (tp), Capt. John Handy (sx), Big Bill Bissonnette (tb), Dick Griffith (bn), Cyril Bennett (pn), Jim "Tut" Tutunjian (sbs), Sammy Penn (dm)
*14. IT FEELS SO GOOD - Alcorn, Barnes, Miller, Bigard
   Alvin Alcorn (tp), Paul "Polo" Barnes (sx), Big Bill Bissonnette (tb), Sing Miller (pn), Jim "Tut" Tutunjian (sbs), Alec Bigard (dm)
*15. DOWN BY THE LEVEE - Punch Miller, Albert Burbank
   Punch Miller (tp/v), Albert Burbank (cl), Big Bill Bissonnette (tb), Dick Griffith (bn), Mouldy Dick McCarthy (sbs), Sammy Penn (dm)

* Previously Unissued   Time: 72:28